ROSE BRU

Theatre

ew this

rred on it

ELECTRIC SHADOWS

AN INTRODUCTION TO VIDEO AND PROJECTION ON STAGE

Nick Moran

ENTERTAINMENT TECHNOLOGY PRESS

Application & Techniques Series

For my Mum Veronica and in fond memory of Andy Collier

Front cover image : "It Must Be Madness" a musical review staged in the Embassy Studio at Central School in 2008. Written and directed by Vikki Coote, lighting by Nick Moran, set, video and projection by Nick Moran and Cate Blanchard.
Photo: Patrick Baldwin

ELECTRIC SHADOWS

AN INTRODUCTION TO VIDEO AND PROJECTION ON STAGE

Nick Moran

etpress

Entertainment Technology Press

Electric Shadows

An Introduction to Video and Projection on stage

First edition published December 2013
by Entertainment Technology Press Ltd
The Studio, High Green, Great Shelford, Cambridge CB22 5EG
Internet: www.etnow.com

ISBN 978 1 904031 73 4

A title within the
Entertainment Technology Press Application & Techniques Series
Series editor: John Offord

CODE / ESh2-04/14

CONTENTS

1 WHY USE VIDEO ON STAGE?

Video – in all its forms – is all around us. It may have begun on our home TVs, but we now see video on our phones, game consoles, tablets and PCs, and on advertising billboards and even on the sides of buses. So it's probably natural that many people making theatre, at all levels, want to use video on stage too. Theatre has always played with technology. Way back in Roman times, the Coliseum had sophisticated stage machines to introduce wild animals into the arena and to do much more. It's not surprising then that many present day theatre makers want to use video on stage for all kinds of reasons. Until relatively recently however it has been too expensive to even think about, but no longer. This book aims to help first-time users, and perhaps disillusioned second- or third-time users, to successfully make creative use of video stage.

With big budgets and sponsorship, large scale concert touring has been using video cameras and projection on stage for some time now. At first, video cameras and screens were used for advertising and image magnification – that is projecting the image of the key performers at many times life size to help audiences in arenas and sports stadiums see their heroes close up. As time went on, creative 'video designers' have found other ways of making use of the video image and the projection screens. They give the audience new and interesting views of the action and offer multiple perspectives at the same time. They introduce pre-programmed visual material, mix it up, and create visual spectacle on a huge scale.

Some experimental theatre companies have been playing with projection and live cameras on stage for quite a while too. Dance Theatre in particular has played with lighting performers with the light from video projectors, and found interesting ways to make that light respond to the movement of the dancer. Projectors don't have to only be pointed at screens!

The big budget concert design, and all the experimenting and playing at smaller scale, has influenced more mainstream theatre makers. And now it's your turn! Today smaller theatre companies and even reasonably well resourced school or amateur theatre makers can achieve things that only a few years ago would have cost tens or even hundreds of thousands of pounds or dollars. But to use any technology successfully on stage takes time, technical knowledge, aesthetic understanding – and an ambition to make it work.

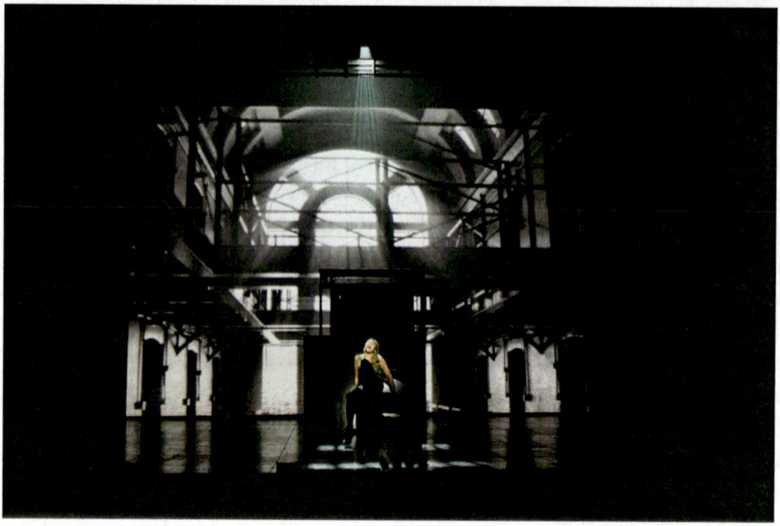

From the 2007 London production of Bad Girls the Musical, with projection designed by Mic Pool.

All of the background "prison" set, including the big window, and the arched roof, is a projection – as you can see more clearly from the photograph of the stage below, where the projectors are displaying a test image on the large screen that forms the back of the stage set.

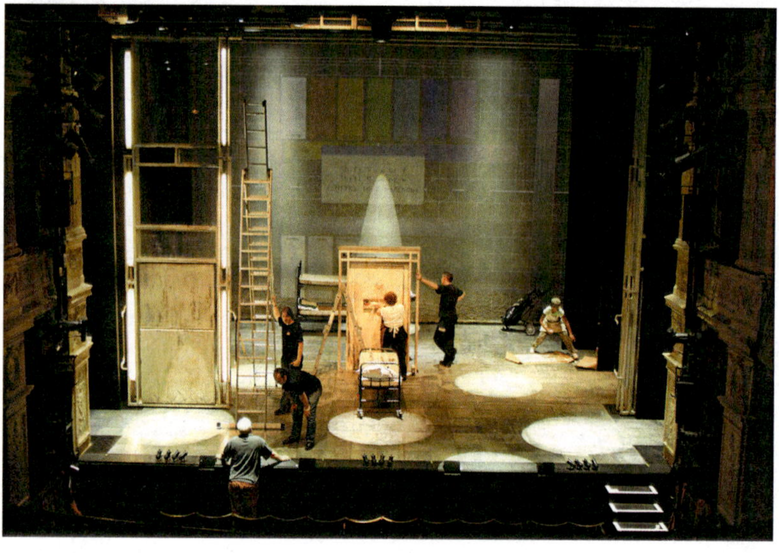

If a Picture Paints a Thousand Words – The Poetry of the Image

It is often said that today we live in a visual culture. After centuries with the printed word as king, digital imaging has made high quality pictures more available to more people than ever before. Like the cathedral builders of long ago, who filled their great windows with dramatic images to tell stories, once again we are communicating in pictures.

While the poetry of words is not dead – indeed in many places it too is more alive and shared than ever – the poetry of the image is once again a force in the world. It's different from the poetry of the Mediaeval stained glass images or the images in religious renaissance paintings. Back then (almost) everyone who would see the paintings or windows had a common cultural background – they all knew how to interpret the main components and the surrounding detail. Most of us now live in a world with more diverse cultural reference points than could be imagined by any previous generation. We don't just have a few windows of images either. From advertising billboards and road signs to the icons on our mobile phones, and much more besides, we get more information from images than ever before.

Not all image is poetry, just as all words are not poetry. Just as with words though, when a single image or a string of images go beyond simple communication and affect us more deeply, I think we can usefully start to talk about the poetry of images. Part of the point of the poetry of the image is that it *can* say more to us than words at times. And we don't all have to understand the same written language to understand some visual poetry. In a multilingual world, pictures *can* speak coherently to more people than words.

Just as with written poetry, visual poetry has a huge range of expressive styles, from high gloss fashion and advertising images to comic and serious cartoons and graphic novels: crude, rude and violent, beautiful and peaceful, sentimental and glamourised, raw and visceral, naturalistic or photo-realist, sketchy and outline or abstract to name just a few.

Bad Poetry?

On stage, sometimes the poetry of the image does upstage everything else, and then people are disappointed, perhaps even upset. Sometimes, the poetry is absent and the images add nothing to the production. And sometimes the image just can't be seen, the technology has failed, or something else has gone wrong. Video on stage can be a nightmare!

This book aims to help you avoid any of these pitfalls, or at least to be able to recover from the worst of them.

There is not very much here about the detail of how to make specific bits of technical kit work. This is because digital equipment gets out of date fast, and whatever equipment I write about today is likely to be out of date by the time you read this! The best place to find an up-to-date equipment manual is the web site of the equipment or software manufacturer or re-seller. Some of you will be using quite old equipment too. Don't despair – even if the original manufacturer has gone out of business (or just taken the manual for your bit of kit off their web site) there are plenty of web forums ready to offer help and advice too.

Software changes fast too, so you won't find much detail here about how to use any of the software packages mentioned. The best place to find up-to-date tips and tricks to make your software and hardware really 'sing' is often an internet forum or a YouTube channel. If you are near a computer now, try a YouTube search for tutorials on After Effects or Photo Shop and you'll see what I mean. (After Effects is one of the most commonly used programs for professional video design).

What is Video Design?

Video design on stage can mean a number of different things, and the role of the video designer is not the same for every production. If you take on the role of video designer it usually means deciding which images, referred to in this book as 'content', get displayed where, and when. It will usually include taking responsibility for creating some or all of the content, and may also require you to design something to display the images on – a 'screen' or 'screens'. It may require you to design the video system, specifying all the equipment and cables that link it.

The content might be present throughout the performance, for only a small part of it, or anything in between. The screen might be the whole wrap-round background, a small section of the set, or even part of a performer's body. The video design might be a "nice to have" but not essential, or might be something the whole production depends upon. The content might be abstract, fantastical, realistic or impressionistic – or any other imaginable visual style, and the screens might be flat, or consist of multiple surfaces, or be invisible to the audience, creating 3D images. What ever video design is for a particular production will depend on the design decisions of the creative team (the director/producer, set, costume, lighting, sound and video designers and others) and practical considerations too.

To create a full video and projection design requires a diverse range of artistic and technical skills, including:

- a deep knowledge of the text of the piece and…
- a sympathetic understanding of the director's vision of it, and…
- an advanced visual vocabulary to draw on for inspiration and discussion, and…
- the visual imagination, compositional, and technical skills of a good photographer or film maker to create the content, and…
- the aesthetic sensibility of a stage designer to ensure the images work with other elements of the design – set, costume, light, sound etc. and…
- some of the skills of a lighting designer, to guide the focus of attention of the audience, and to judge the cueing of the content – the timing of when and how it appears on stage, and…
- the technical knowledge to select the right equipment, get it into the right places, and make it work, and…
- the technical knowledge and an aesthetic understanding of the piece to program the equipment in (and prior to) the technical rehearsal, and to ensure it does what it should, reliably for every performance, and…
- the sensitivity and skill to adapt the design through rehearsals, as the piece subtly changes, and…

Well, quite possibly a lot more, but that's enough to be going on with.

On many (probably most) projects, all these understandings and knowledge are shared by several people. Exactly what the video designer does is not the same for every show. Sometimes the person most responsible for the design of the video being projected onto stage is not even called the video designer.

In professional theatre, job titles in the area of video design include projection designer, animator, video engineer, camera operator, system designer, video operator, compositor, video programmer and on the largest projects, project manager.

Some projects have people who specialise in finding, editing, animating and otherwise manipulating still and moving images and making them ready for projection. Some projects have specialists responsible for selecting, mounting, and maintaining the projectors and ancillary equipment. Some projects require high-speed computer networks to feed the insatiable desire for data of the big high definition projection systems with multiple input and output channels. Some projects will use a specialist team just to shoot the video footage

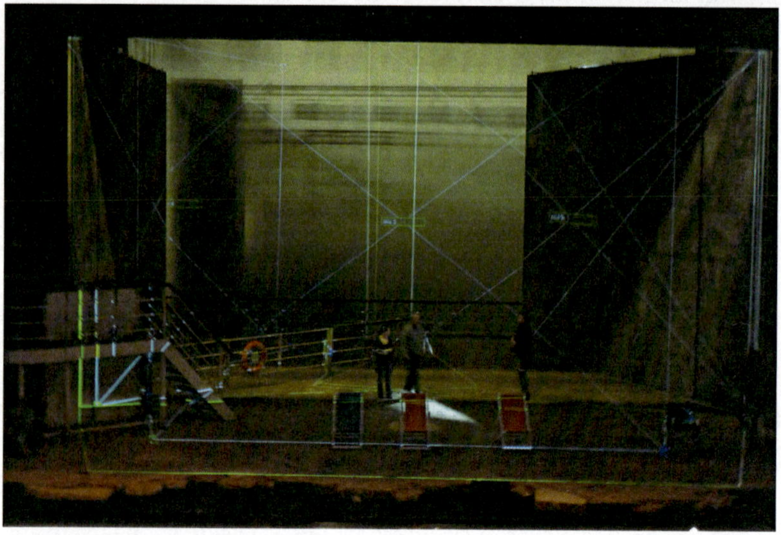

Death of Klinghoffer

The transformation of a set through video projection. These two pictures were taken during rehearsals for ENO's production of the opera Death of Klinghoffer in 2012. Multiple high definition projectors covered the whole stage, set walls and floor. Above is the line-up, below is something close to the final stage picture. Video designer Finn Ross had a team that included a projector system specialist, an animator and a programmer.

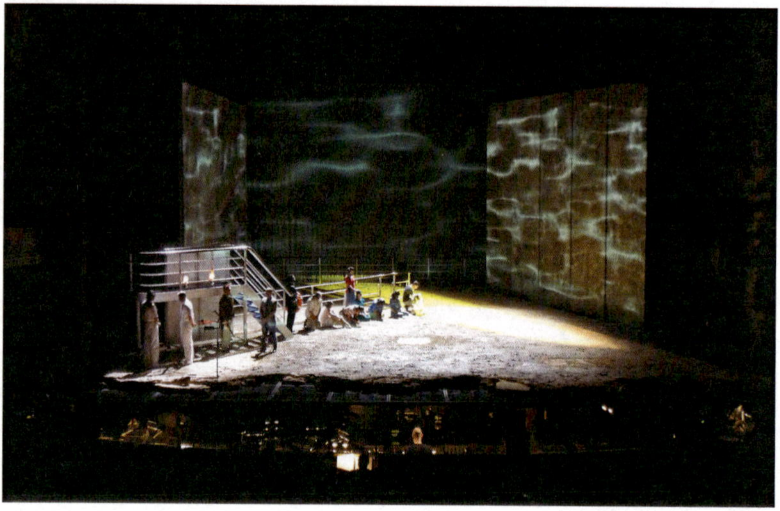

required for the show, while others will incorporate the output of video cameras shooting the show as it happens (usually called live camera). And some projects will have one person, finding and preparing the images, specifying and rigging the projection system, programming the video cues, and operating the show every night. Projects with large specialist teams probably (hopefully) don't need this book! I hope that if you are the one person doing everything you will find something helpful here.

A Few Definitions

Video design, like many specialist areas of theatre practice, has its own specialist language, some of which I've already used. As a relatively young discipline, the language is still evolving. Not everybody uses the same words for things or the same words in the same way. So in this book I will aim to stick to the following definitions:

Video Content: the video images that appear on the screen(s). It can be still pictures or video clips, animations, blocks of colour, abstract patterns, live camera (see below) or anything else that can be projected on the projection screens or displayed on the display screens. (In some designs, the 'projection screens' may be used for other things – such as shadow play, or may be lit by the fixtures in the lighting rig. While this may well be the idea of the video designer, it is not strictly speaking video content.)

Screen: anything that ends up having images projected onto it, or that shows images. So if we have one or more projectors, this could be a cinema style screen, made of high-tech material and stretched on a flown frame, through to a sheet held in the right place by the performers, or the pale T-shirt of a dancer. But it might also be any kind of computer display screen or television, from the latest large format modular LED panels through to a modified domestic TV. When it is necessary to distinguish between these two, I will refer to the first type as projection screens and the second type as display screens.

Video System: the collection of equipment and specialist cables required to get the content onto the screen or screens. Usually this will include a device for storing content, a device for accessing and playing content on cue, a cable system that carries the video information to the projector(s) or display screen(s), and those projector(s) and/or display screen(s). It might also involve specialist rigging equipment for projectors (or display screens).

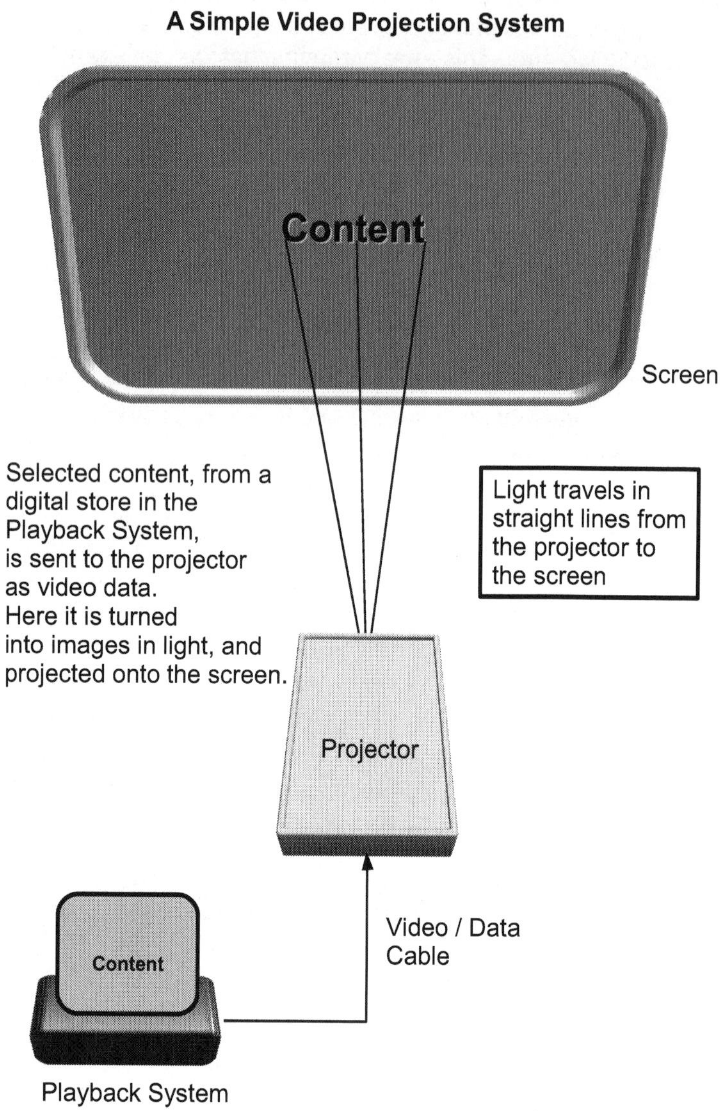
A Simple Video Projection System
Content
Screen
Selected content, from a digital store in the Playback System, is sent to the projector as video data. Here it is turned into images in light, and projected onto the screen.
Light travels in straight lines from the projector to the screen
Projector
Video / Data Cable
Content
Playback System

Figure 1

Front Projection means the projector is on the same side of the screen as the audience (and usually the actors). In most set-ups this will mean the projector or projectors are 'out front', in the same part of the theatre as the audience. This usually means that we want to make sure they don't make too much noise, from fans and such like, and distract the audience attention (or we might put the projector(s) in a sound-proof box at the back of the auditorium). One disadvantage of front projection is that performers standing close to the screen often cast shadows onto the screen, disrupting the projected image. They can also finish up with some of the image being projected onto their face and body, which can be distracting.

Rear Projection, also called back projection, means the projectors are the other side of the screen from the audience (and usually the performers). In most set-ups this means the projector(s) are upstage – at the back of the stage. Rear projection has the advantage of allowing the performers to walk right up to the screen without casting a shadow onto it, or getting any of the image on themselves – but is can be costly, in terms of both space and materials. There needs to be a fair amount of space behind the screen to allow the projector's beam to spread sufficiently to fill the screen. This is not always easy to achieve. It also means the screen more or less has to be made of specialist material, stretched on a specialist frame with no cross bracing. (Anything between the projector and the screen will cause a shadow on the screen. This includes cross-braces and other structures that are normally used to keep a largeish frame rigid.)

Pixels are what digital images are made of. When an image is created or stored digitally, it is separated into tiny discrete dots or pixels. Each pixel has a number of digital values attached to it – numbers that represent for example, where it is in the image (1014 rows down, 785 columns across – that kind of thing), what colour

Digital systems use the binary system to store all information. If the system uses 8-bit storage, there are 256 different values possible. If the intensity of each pixel is recorded as an 8-bit value, a pixel with no intensity would have an intensity value of 0, while a pixel with maximum intensity would have a value of 255 (that is 256 numbers bigger than 0). Most image storage systems use 16- bit, 24-bit or even 32-bit technology, which give a much larger range of values, and potentially much greater accuracy when capturing or reproducing an image. For example a 16-bit display enables 65,536 different colours, while a 24-bit display enables up to 16.8 million colours. However high bit values can lead to very large digital files. This is one reason why photographs taken with a high quality digital camera take up far more space on your hard drive than those taken with a low resolution web-cam (for example).

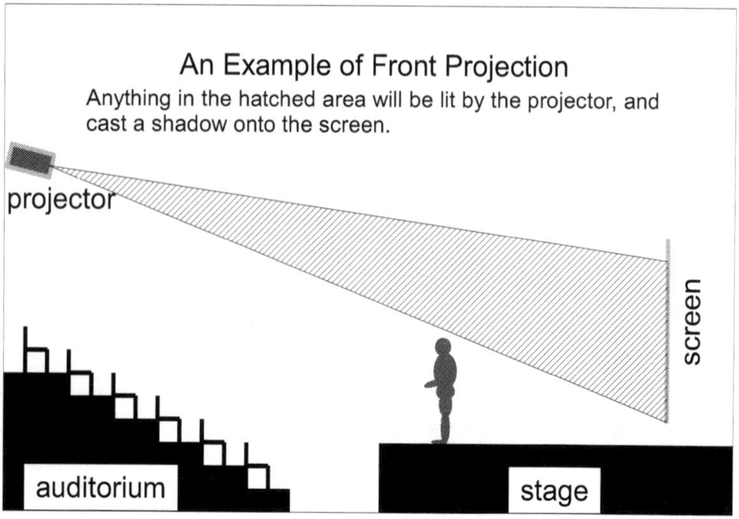

Front projection usually means the projector is in the auditorium
Often it means the performers cannot get close to the screen.

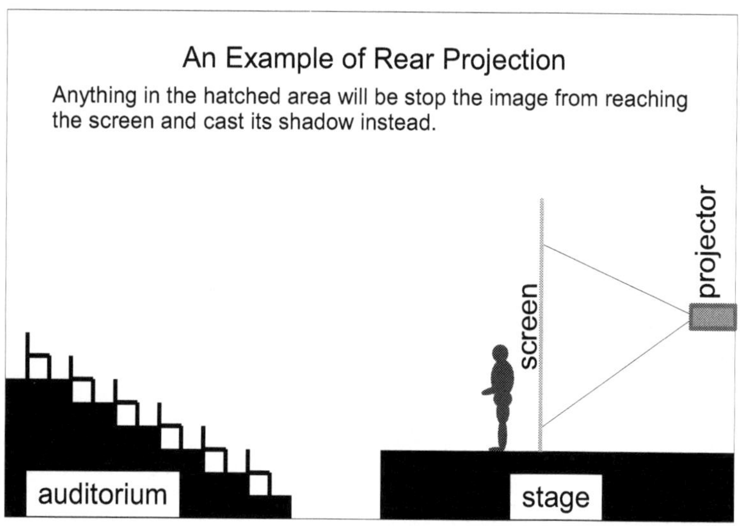

Rear projection usually means the projector is on stage.
This can significantly decrease the area of the stage available for action.
It can mean that the performers can work very close to the screen.

Figure 2

the image is at that point and how much intensity is required at that point to project the image. For a projected image, when a pixel is 100% on then that part of the image is 'white'. If the pixel is totally off then that part of the image is 'black' and ideally no light is present at the screen. The number of digital values associated with each pixel, and the maximum size permitted for each of these digital values, does a lot to determine the quality of the image. Basically higher numbers = better quality.

Resolution is related to the sharpness and clarity of the image. In the digital world, this usually refers to the number of pixels present in the image. Basically, the higher the resolution, the more pixels, the clearer or sharper the image. There are some industry standard resolutions for digital projectors and digital display screens that we will come across later.

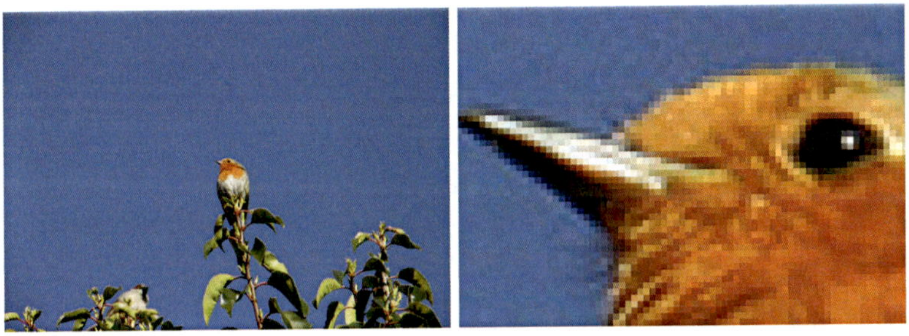

Robin Standard Resolution and a zoomed up section showing what decreasing the resolution does, and how the image is made up of pixels.

Projection field is all the available pixels a projector can display. For any given distance between projector and screen, the projection field is the largest image that can be projected. For a number of reasons it is not normally possible to use the whole of the projection field for content.

Live Camera: The images from any camera being used live as well as the camera itself. It is quite common to want to use live images, in stage video design, perhaps from backstage or perhaps magnifying detail or even live from another location (illustrated overleaf).

Short Throw, Long Throw is the distance between the projector and the screen. A long-throw means the projector and screen are a long way apart, while a short-throw means they are close to each other. In the drawing of simple front and rear projection systems above, the projection system in the front projection set up has a long-throw whilst in the rear projection set-up has a short-throw. Projection systems designed for a

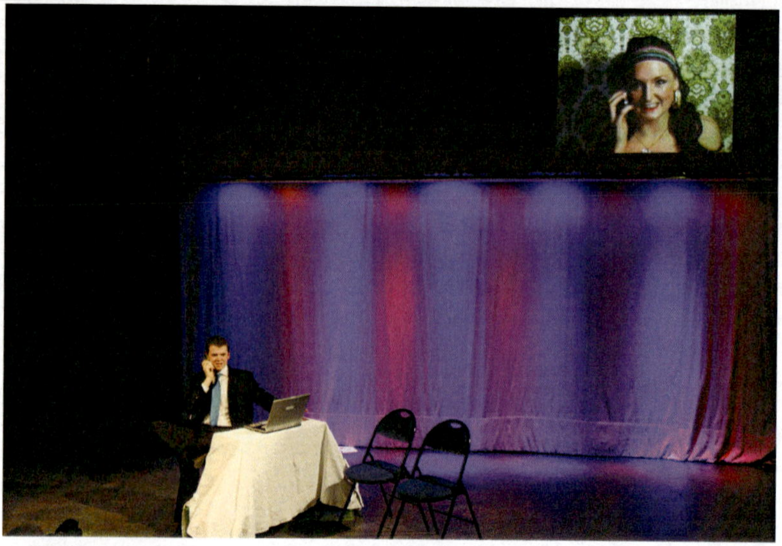

It Must Be Madness, a studio musical for Central School in 2008

The boy and girl are making a phone call. The image of the girl is from a Live Camera back stage, projected into part of the back wall of the stage set. (Just out of shot is the microphone used to pick up her voice, which then comes through the stage sound system, slightly distorted, to complete the illusion of the phone call)

short throw usually have a wide angle lens, while long-throw projection systems have narrow angle lenses, sometimes referred to a long-throw lens. There is more on this in the next chapter.

Production Design: I'm going to use this term to describe the entirety of the look, feel and sound of the production. It will be the result of the creative efforts not only of all the designers (set, costume, light, sound and video) but also of director, choreographer, performers, writers, musicians and often many others. The success of most video design depends on how well it is integrated into the whole production design – the whole world of the production including the set, costumes, lighting, sound-world, blocking and choreography, performance style, etc.

Video Design: The term usually refers to both the video content, and the system required to play back the content on stage, including the projectors, screens, computers and other devices, and all the interconnections.

> *Others have used "mise-en-scène" or "scenography" instead of production design, but these words have troubled meanings in English. Scenography in particular is often interpreted in Europe and elsewhere as "set design", marginalising other design elements and the work of the director, choreographer, performers and even the writer, in the responsibility for the ordering of everything that helps to convey meaning to the audience. The term production design is also not without its problems, and has a particular meaning in cinema and film for example, but I hope it is less open to misinterpretation than either of the other terms.*

Video Designer is the person who is primarily responsible for the creation of the video design – including creating the video content, designing the projection or display screen set-up, and all the video system that gets the video content on stage and in front of the audience.

Video Cue: These words are used for both the point in the show when a particular piece of content is displayed (or starts running, or changes) and that particular piece of content. So the footage of water projected onto the walls of the *Death of Klinghoffer* set pictured towards the beginning of this chapter, might be designated 'video cue 101' (the scene shown is near the end of the opera). A particular point in the music would then be designated 'video cue-point 101', and that would be where the water footage fades up or appears in some other way.

It is very useful to have a good understanding of the idea of cues, cue-points and cueing, in order to overcome some of the practical difficulties of making video an integral part of a production.

Especially when video imagery is a significant part of the overall design, the video designer will need to collaborate closely with the director and other creative team members to ensure that the overall look and feel of the production works. The video designer will need to have some input into aspects of the production design including the size, shape, position and other properties of the screens and the location of the projector(s). As well as these more obvious considerations, as we shall see, the video design will also be affected by such things as where the performers move and stand (known as 'performer blocking') and, often crucially, the lighting design. Because of this, and because it is difficult to over-estimate the amount of time it takes to produce high quality video content, successful video design requires the video designer to play an active part in the creation of the production from as early a stage as possible.

On a large scale project, the video designer might only come up with the concept, leaving one team to create the content, one to design and maintain the system, and another team to program and run the show. This is rare however – and as the video designer, you will often have to do all this!

Other theatre makers, even those with extensive experience, will often not realise the extent or complexity of the role of video designer. Whenever you take on this role (or give it to someone else), it is important to be clear about exactly what the expectations and responsibilities are. Ask: "Will there be someone else making the content? Designing, hiring and putting together the system? Programming the cues during the technical rehearsal? Or is that all me?"

A little bit of History

Using projections to help tell stories is not really a new thing. There is evidence that our cave dwelling ancestors made use of projected shadows thousands of years ago, using the light of their fire to make images on the wall of their caves. We know that in Renaissance Europe (during the 15th and 16th centuries) people shone light through painted glass to animate their play-stages and pageants. Much later, in the 19th century travelling story-tellers used magic lanterns – early slide projectors using painted glass slides – to entertain audiences in public halls. In Victorian theatre the so called Pepper's Ghost trick became a popular novelty. With it, the theatre makers were able to project 'ghosts' and other effects onto the stage using a "screen" of plate glass.

Towards the end of the nineteenth century, with the inventions that enabled photography and then cinema, still more became possible. By the middle of the 20th century, powerful projectors were available in opera houses and many other large theatres. Beautiful images from hand-painted glass slides could replace painted scenery, and 'movie' clips could be projected too. In the second half of the 20th, many large theatres in the UK and elsewhere also showed commercial movies, and so had large and powerful cine-projectors permanently installed (often alongside the followspots, high up

The origins of the illusion usually called Pepper's Ghost predates the Victorian John Pepper (who popularised the trick on stage) by at least 200 years. The illusion uses a sheet of plate glass to reflect a "ghost" image from an off stage space onto the stage. This ghost image can appear to pass through solid objects on the stage. Today it is still used, often with video projection. The musical Ghost used the trick in this way to allow an actor playing the part of the ghost to pass through an apparently solid door. It's is hard to pull off the trick effectively without considerable resources and planning.

at the back of the auditorium). Both serious and light-hearted theatre productions could incorporate movie clips. One common use of this was in British pantomime, projecting a moving street background behind a stage chase, helping to give the impression of large scale movement on stage.

The projection equipment used for this was expensive and more or less immovable, and producing 35mm film was expensive. Productions often used 'stock' film, hired from specialist libraries, to avoid the high cost of producing their own images. In spite of these obstacles, some theatre makers continued to experiment successfully with projected images as part of stage design.

In Europe, from 1925 onwards, the German born theatre maker, Erwin Piscator used still and moving images as an important part of the staging for his Epic Theatre work with Bertolt Brecht and others, while throughout the 1960s and 1970s Josef Svoboba made many innovative experimental productions with his company Laterna Magika based in Prague.

With the development of affordable analogue video equipment in the 1980s, experimental performance artists such as The Wooster Group in the US and Forced Entertainment in the UK made extensive use of video technology. Also based in the UK Forkbeard Fantasy made great use of film and later video too. Other groups making use of video at this time include the Bill T. Jones/Arnie Zane Dance Company who sometimes used video monitors on stage, and Robert LaPage's company Ex Machina, who made extensive use of both video and high quality large format slide projection.

But it is the digital revolution, powered by affordable computer-driven technology, that has made possible much more widespread use of projected images on stage. Modern video projectors can be quiet and bright (though getting both in the same machine can still stretch even the most generous budget), and creating content – the images to be projected – no longer requires the patient skill of a painter or the expense involved in shooting moving pictures on film. Still and moving images suitable for projecting on stage can now be created using relativity inexpensive cameras and computer software.

In this book I will be concentrating on digital video projection. Many of the physical principles are the same for older projection technologies – things like the relationship between the type of lens in the projector and the size and brightness of the image on stage for example. However, when we come to discuss content my focus will be on making digital images, as this is by far the most common way of working in Europe and North America at the moment.

Re-Orientations, produced by Border Crossings

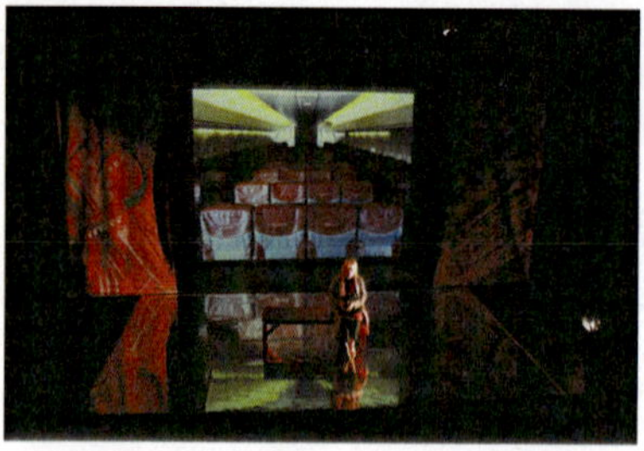

Scenic projection helps set the scene for a segment of the play set on an aircraft

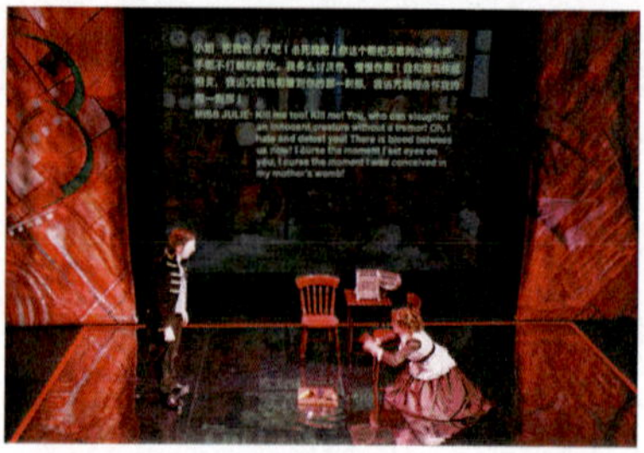

Simultaneous translation or surtitles were used at various points during this multilingual production.

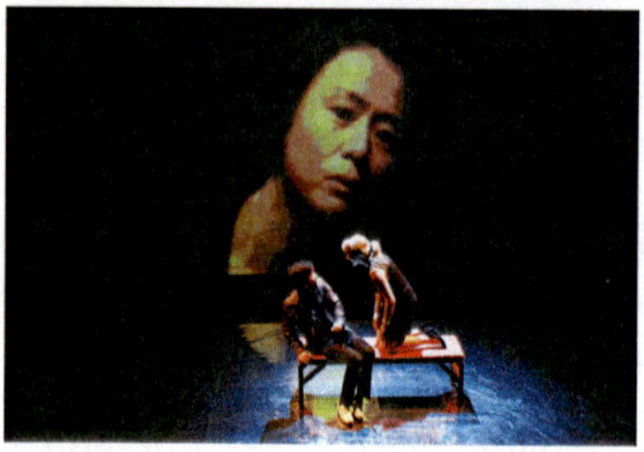

Live camera, in this case from off stage, heightens a sense that the off-stage character (on screen) is a voyeur of the on stage scene (as are the audience of course).

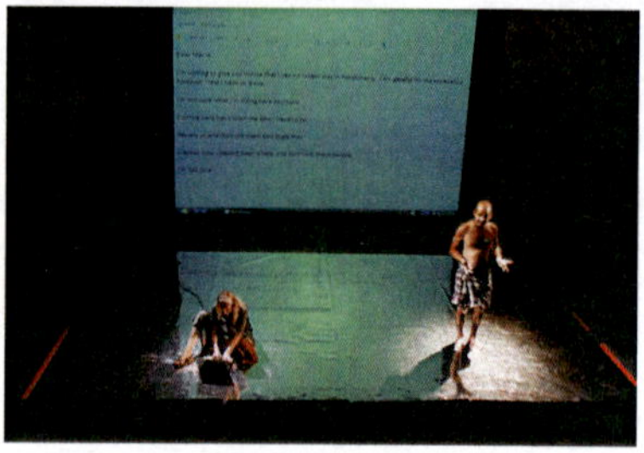

Live feed from an onstage lap-top computer enables the audience to see the character compose an e-mail.

Re-Orientations, produced by Border Crossings, *was a low-budget show with high aspirations for the ways it wanted to used video on stage. The video had to perform many different functions for the production. Everything was accomplished with a the minimum of kit, and an Apple Mac Mini.*

Projection as an Element of a Production Design

Projecting images onto the stage is part of the production design, and needs to be thought about with the same level of attention to detail as all the other key elements of the production.

There are few hard-and-fast rules for production design, and probably any that do exist can be broken in some contexts. However a good guiding principle is: "Nothing should get on stage without a good reason".

Here's a version of an old joke: "When is a door not just a door?" "When it's on stage".

Performers don't generally *need* a door to get on or off stage. They can enter from behind a curtain or exit into a dark space. Live performance contains a kind of make-believe element that can take us back to the "let's pretend" world of childhood games. Let's pretend that this stage that we know for sure is no bigger than 12m wide (because we drove all round the theatre looking for somewhere to park before we arrived) surrounded by black curtains, is actually a vast battle field, or one room of a grand mansion, or three rooms separated by great distances – in space and / or time, or many different places over the course of the evening's show. Audiences are not only able but also willing to play the game with us – if we give them a little help.

Audience members look for meaning in the things we place on stage. Everything we put on the stage is a potential source of extra meaning for the audience. Every object should help the audience to find out what the show is all about. The choice of the style and colour of the door, its size and shape, and even the hinges and door handles all have the potential to tell the audience more about the world they are watching on stage – about what's going on, who the characters are, what sort of place they inhabit, and how the audience should react to what they are seeing, hearing, even smelling and feeling.

When we watch a show on stage, we bring all our experience – of other

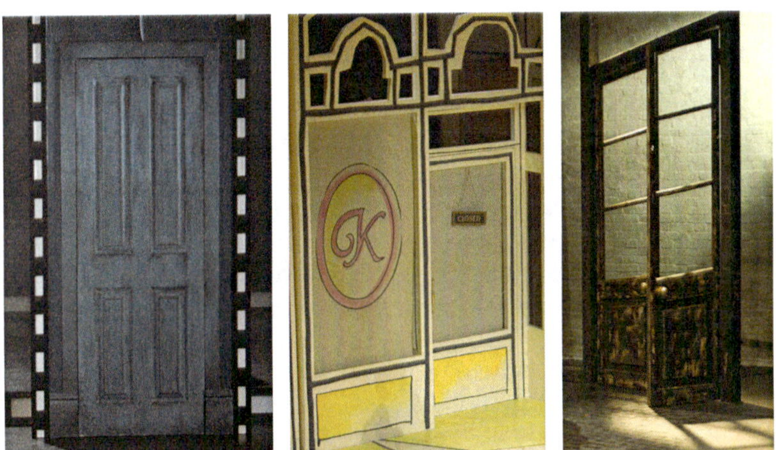

Image of 3 doors with the caption "what kind of people live behind each of these doors? Every detail of the design of each of these doors is capable of telling the audience something about the imaginary space on stage, and the characters who live there.

shows and the rest of our lives – with us. We use this experience to help us find meaning in the objects on stage – consciously and subconsciously. To return to the door: if it is a house front door, clean and brightly painted with a house number and a letter box, immediately we know we are outside on a street – in front of a smart house that someone looks after. If a different door – still with a house number and a letter box – but this time broken, dirty, and with cracked glass panels, splashed with dried up egg yolk and egg-shell or daubed with graffiti, the audience will start to draw quite different conclusions, about the area we are in, and the people, or characters, who live behind and in front of that door.

Theatre makers ask the audience to pay a special kind of attention to the objects on stage. Stage designers usually want the audiences to 'read' into those objects things that will help them understand something about the piece. For example, the first door with its hand drawn comic-book look will help the audience understand the piece is a comedy before any line is spoken. The second door with its distorted perspective hints that the world on stage is distorted in some way too. The third door painted to look neglected and edged with a pattern hinting at film stock tells the audience the room attached to it is run-down whilst reminding the audience of the many cinematic references in the piece. (The doors are from stage designs for *On The Razzle*, *Tales From The Vienna Woods* and *City of Angels* respectively.)

As a video designer I hope that the audience will give a special kind of attention to the images I've chosen to show on stage too. To help make sure this happens, good video designers should always be asking "Why is this image here? What does it do for the piece?" "How is it likely to help the audience understand the story or get more out of the piece?"

Just as every object placed on stage needs a reason to be there, so every image, what it is, and where and when it is projected or displayed, also needs to have a reason to be on stage. The video designer needs to be sure that the meaning that most of the audience get from the video design works with the rest of the production design. She or he will also want to aim for content that does not unintentionally upstage the actors, or distract the audience from the agreed focus of the production.

Most actors, dancers and singers don't respond well when they feel the audience is distracted from their performance (sometimes referred to as being up-staged). This can happen if the choice of what, where, when and how images are projected onto stage is not carefully considered. For example, if the design includes the projection of images behind the actors, the actors may well feel uncomfortable because they know something is changing behind them, but they can't see what it is. For many actors, if there is one thing worse than another actor steeling the attention of the audience, it is a projected image doing that. It is worth considering too that many actors feel much more comfortable performing in front of real objects, and may need help if the production design substitutes these real objects for projected images.

What Makes a Video Design?

We can think of a video design as being made up of four distinct elements:

1. **A Projector:** a device that produces a still or moving image in light. It is important to remember that the projector produces an image made of light, and that light obeys certain physical rules that we can't change. It travels in straight lines for example. We'll be coming back to this later. The projector itself has three important elements – the light source (usually a specialised bulb), something that generates the image, and the lens. Most projectors bright enough for use on stage have available a range of lenses, from wide angle (usually for short throws) through zoom lenses to special narrow angle lenses for long throws. Choosing the right lens for your projector is an important part of most video designs.
2. **A Screen:** something for the light to hit *and* reflect from so the audience can see the images. Another property of light is that it is invisible until it hits something and is reflected – so to see our projected image we will need something for the light to hit. (If light were not invisible, space would not be dark. The light from the sun passes through empty space, and we don't see it till it hits something – say the moon or another planet – and is reflected towards us. When we can see beams of light, we are looking at the light reflected from dust particles or smoke.) As already mentioned, your screen need not be a conventional cinema screen, but as a video designer you will usually need to give a good deal of consideration to exactly what your screen is (or screens are) to get the results you want. More on this in Chapter 3.
3. **Content:** images to project. Here too you will need to pay attention to the properties of light, the ways in which human vision works, and some legal niceties such as copyright. There is more on copyright in the appendix, and more on making content in Chapter 4.
4. **Playback Device(s):** machine(s) to store and playback content on cue. For smaller systems the playback device could be a DVD player, or a single lap-top computer. For large and complex systems, dedicated media servers are common, often controlled from a moving light console. These are expensive machines. However, ambitious results can frequently be achieved without this level of capital investment and complexity. More on all of this in Chapter 5.

Together these elements make up our video system. Each element will have an impact on what you can (and cannot) achieve in the video design.

One of the most important considerations in any projection set-up is the amount of light you can get out of the projector. Generally, the more usable light that comes out of the projector, the fewer other problems you are going to encounter. Matching the brightness of the projector and its lens to the size of the venue, the size and other properties of the proposed screen, the type of content to be projected, and the available budget, is an important step on the way to designing an effective video system.

More on Screens

While there may be times when the appropriate design solution to what the screen should be is a cinema style screen, very often this will not be the case. Images can be projected onto almost any surface. The properties of the surface will determine how the audience sees the image projected onto it. The surface need not be white, flat and rectangular like a cinema screen – in fact it can be fun to surprise the audience by projecting images onto something they would never of thought of as a screen. We will be looking at these issues in more detail in chapter 2.

Of course, to get video images onto stage we can also use TV screens, computer video monitors, or LED arrays – what I have called display screens. LED arrays are used extensively at the moment by set designers for concerts and TV light entertainment and music shows. Many of the technical and aesthetic considerations that apply to projected images on stage also apply to display screens.

From a technical point of view, the only thing that is different in set-ups that don't use a projector is simply that – no projector. The screen is the TV set, video monitor or LED array – and we still need to produce some content to show on the screen(s) and we still need to find a way to connect the playback device(s) to the display screen(s).

Generally the brighter the projector the more you will have to pay to buy or hire it. Also bright projectors generate heat and need to be cooled - usually by internal fans - which can be noisy. On a more positive note, it seems that at the moment at least, with every year you get more light for your projection money - though of course if you decide you must have High Definition, the price is going to go up too.

From an aesthetic point of view, a display screen, such as a television set, remains a television set even when it is switched off. This is not always the case with a something we use as a projection screen. If we project images onto a wall, a floor, or even a performer's body, before we project, and once we stop projecting, the surfaces are seen as just a wall, a floor or a body. Making unexpected use of surfaces and objects as projection screens can be exciting and powerful when incorporated into a production design. On the other hand, TV sets and video monitors on stage are pieces of contemporary (or vintage) technology as well as a surface showing an image. When the images are turned off, the object remains – be it a computer display screen, a domestic television or an LED array.

The Lure of the Screen

Projected images, and especially projected moving images, seem to have a strong appeal to our eyes – often drawing our attention away from the live actors. This phenomenon – called the "lure of the screen" by UK based theatre maker Katie Mitchell – can result in most of the audience focusing their attention on the projected images rather than the actors. Of course theatre makers can use this to their advantage too – distracting the audience from a clumsy set-change with some attractive moving images for example. As a video designer though you will need to be aware of the potential power of the moving image to draw attention. Even five or six generations after becoming commonplace through much or the world, projected moving images still seem to have some sort of magical appeal to the human imagination. Integrating projected images into the world of the production, balancing the lure of the screen with all the other elements of the production design – can be the hardest part of achieving a successful video design.

Look back to the production photographs of *Re-Orientations* earlier in this chapter. The static scenic projection of the aircraft interior fades into the background of the audience consciousness once it has done its job of establishing where we are. Something quite different happens in the scene with the very large face observing the stage action in the live camera example. This face draws audience attention strongly, probably because it is moving rather than static, but certainly because it is recognisable as a human face – and our brains are hard-wired from infancy to pay attention to human faces. The eye-line of the projected oversized human face tracks the action on stage, and this helps the audience re-focus their attention back onto the stage. Without that, it is likely that most of the audience would not see any details of the live action on stage, instead focusing solely on the large projected face. This is one example of the lure of the screen.

Why use Projected Images on Stage?

So, we return to the reason for using video on stage, for incorporating video projection or display screens into a live performance design. The following are just a few reasons why you might chose to use video projection on stage.

For a particular effect. This might be: displaying adverts or a sponsor's logo during the interval; showing a video sequence that provides context for a play with a complex 'back-story' (the sort of thing that many TV serials do to enable new audiences to catch up with previous episodes); to establish a particular time, place, season, or emotional state (maybe the large-scale projection of a sea-scape over the whole stage as the audience walk); to tell a particular part of the story in a particular way (as in the RSC production of *Matilda*, where a video projection of shadow puppetry supports part of the little girl's story) or simple to animate a song-sheet for a pantomime.

Often these specific uses of projection are very effective and the systems can be optimised to perform really well. Sometimes it can be hard to resist the temptation of doing other things with the projection once its there, perhaps less well thought through and consequently less effectively.

Because our fast-paced piece has lots of locations. Many plays and other types of theatre require multiple locations with rapid changes between them. It can be a good design choice to evoke or indicate these locations through projected images. Ways of doing this range from a simple projection of the name or the place or the time somewhere where the audience will be able to read that information, through photo-realistic background projection such as that used to depict the jail in *Bad Girls* in the production shot at the beginning of this chapter. Between these two extremes, there are a good many other style choices available to the video designer:

Because we don't have any scene painters and/or space to fly painted cloths. OK but here is a warning! Many production designs are unsuccessful simple because someone has underestimated the work involved in "just making the video do a few backcloths". If you are thinking of using video as an alternative to painted scenery, don't be fooled into thinking this is necessarily a simpler or cheaper way of working. It's also worth remembering that just as it takes a skilled scenic artist and designer to make a flat canvas look three dimensional, it takes a skilled photographer and video designer to do the same with video.

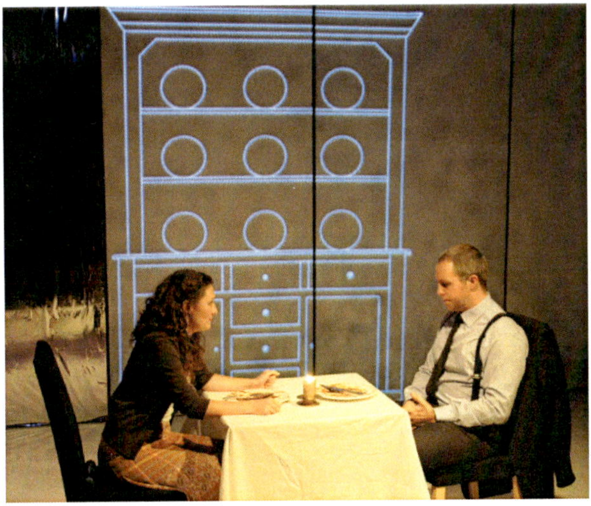

Simple cartoon or line drawings evoke rather than attempt to fully reproduce the setting of a scene. *Video designer Adam Young used projected outline drawings to help place scenes in this low-budget student production of Oliver's Army.*

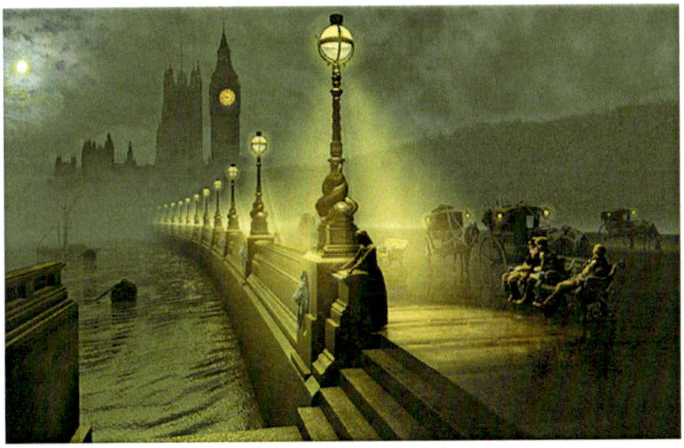

Hyper-reality – 3D digital animation *(virtual worlds, made with the same technology used to make video game environments).*

An example of a digital created Victorian London scene beside the Thames, created for a big-budget production of Peter Pan, using the software programme Cinema 4D by UK based set designer Bill Dudley. With enough computer power, an image like this can be animated so that the waves on the river, and even the people on the benches, move during the scene. Photo: Bill Dudley.

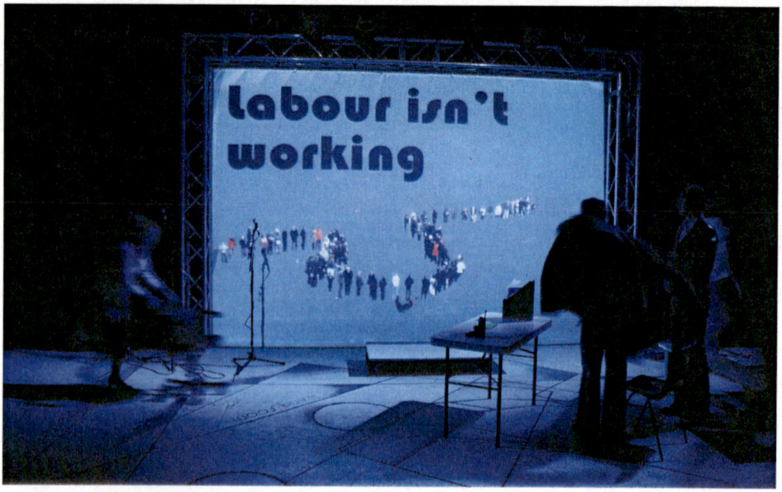

Taking a particularly iconic image to set time and place.

Video designer Chris Hilficker used a well known poster from the UK general election campaign of 1979 to set up both the time period and political context during a scene change in Keeping the Faith.

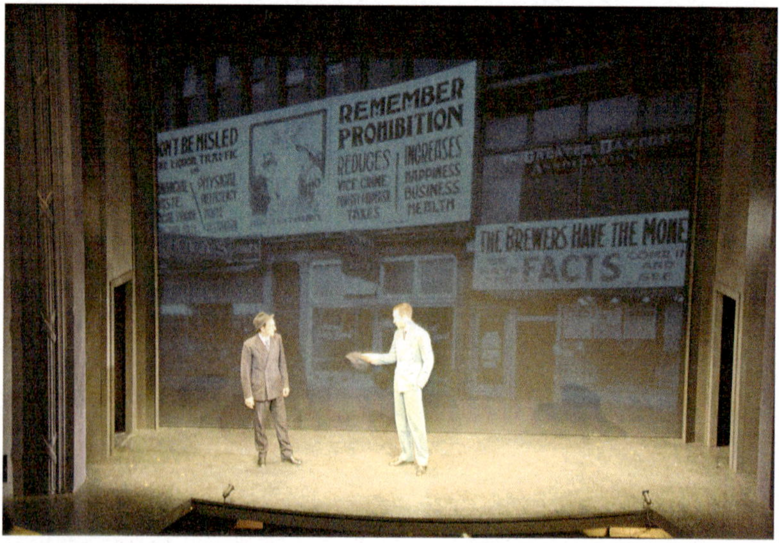

Guy's and Dolls in the Embassy Theatre at Central School 2011.

This is not a great picture (opposite page), but it does illustrate several of the difficulties encountered when using front projected content to replace what would have traditionally been scenic painting. The picture shows what is knows as a "front-cloth scene" – a full stage width "cloth" is flown in to allow the stage set behind (up-stage) to be changed (re-set). Meanwhile a small scene takes place in front (down stage) of the "front-cloth". In this production design, several different locations for the front-cloth scenes were evoked using a different projected still image for each location. Each front-cloth scene used the same flown cloth as the screen.
The Actors are standing in the beams of the projectors - you can see the shadows of the actors masking some of the content at the bottom of the front-cloth. To get enough light onto the actors to wash out the projection on their faces means the effective brightness of the projected content is not great. This neatly illustrates the main problem with using projection to replace scenic art for this kind of scene.
(The video design used two projectors mounted either side of the auditorium centre line – see the off-axis illustration at the end of chapter 2. This means even though there are performer shadows on the screen from one projector, the other projector's content is still present. This is a good way to reduce the side effects of this kind of set-up.)

To show the audience what is going on inside a character's head. This might be 'thought bubbles' or maybe a 'conscience' talking to the character. It is a technique very often found in TV cartoons such as The Simpsons – and can prove useful for adding a bit of humour.

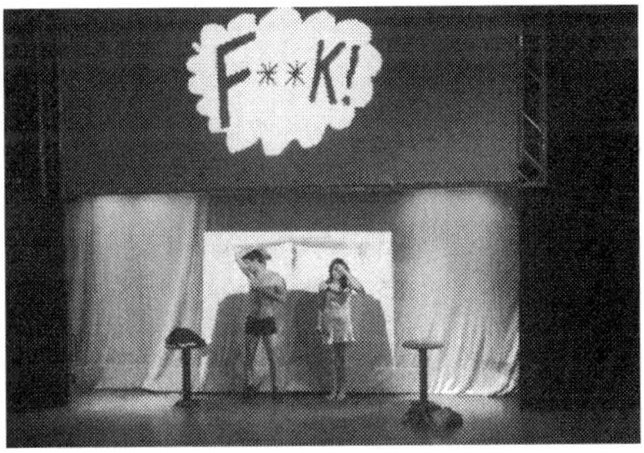

Can you guess what is going on inside the female character's head here?

To show characters in off-stage locations. This can be a bit like the thought-bubble mentioned above taken a bit further. Video projection can be used to show the other end of a phone-call being made by an on-stage character or literally to show a character appearing on TV in front of the live performers.

To show the audience details they would otherwise not see, either because the audience is too far away, or as a device for showing action off-stage. To do this may require one or more live cameras, possibly operated by performers, or by remote control. Alternatively the action may have been prerecorded and played back. For the production of *Re-Orientations*, mentioned later in the book, we hooked a lap-top up

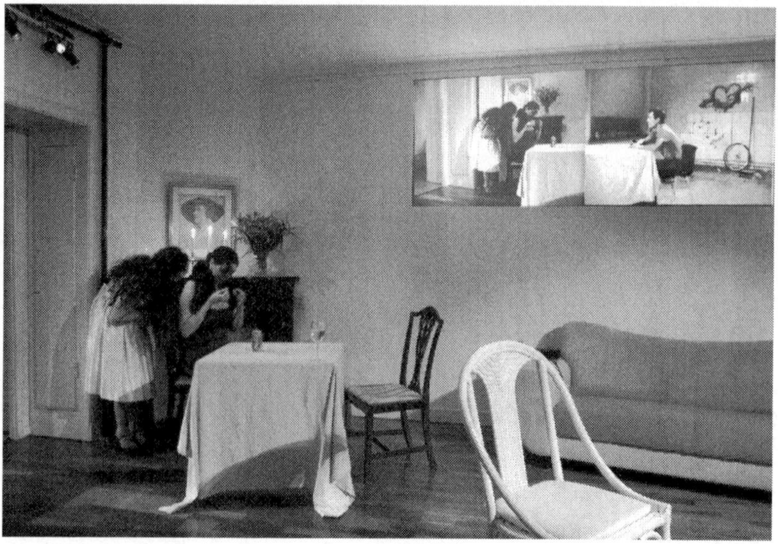

Station House Opera's Life From Paradise (2004)

Like much of the company's work, this production took part in several places at once, linked by internet video. In each space, the stage set includes a screen where video from the other sites – or from this site – can be shown. The performers interact not only with others in their own space, but also with people in the other spaces. There are many examples of telematic performance on the internet.

to the projector to allow the audience to see a character writing a difficult e-mail.

To play with the idea of what it means to be 'in front of an audience'. Companies such as Station House Opera in the UK use the technologies of video conferencing to link multiple performance sites and audience sites, creating work that combines present and projected performers. There are many technical challenges to this kind of work – sometimes called 'telematic performance' – and it remains a specialist area largely beyond the scope of this book. Telematic work is hard to represent coherently in photographs, but if you are interested, take a look at the website of companies such as Station House Opera.

Because it adds another dimension to the audience experience. This might be through giving documentary context to a production – showing news footage or press cuttings or simple text containing background information, to help the audience gain a better understanding of the piece.

But it might equally be projecting abstract or metaphorical images over the performance primarily to add to the visual spectacle of the piece.

To underline what the performers are saying or doing on stage. We might think of this as a kind of visual re-enforcement, similar to sound re-enforcement. It might be similar to showing detail to the audience, mentioned above, but it might also be literal re-enforcement of the performer's movement or spoken or sung words – images of calm to accompany calming speech or actions, or images of storms to make visual words spoken or sung about bad weather.

To counterpoint the actions of words of the performers, to provide contrast. For example, we might have calming words spoken while a projected storm rages all around, or images of lakes and fertile fields surrounding a performer portraying thirst and starvation. Just as counterpoint in music often provides additional aural depth and beauty, so these uses of projected video can provide visual depth and beauty on stage.

It's worth remarking here that some reviewers and commentators have accused productions that use video to add extra visual dimensions, or to highlight or counterpoint, of visually overloading their audiences and undermining the text. These productions are also sometimes accused of confusing their audience. This may be true, but it may also be underestimating the ability of contemporary audiences to respond to many different types of information at the same time.

In our daily lives, we are often surrounded by multiple visual and audio stimuli, and seem (for the most part) to cope quite well, sorting out what is important and what isn't. Think of a person driving a familiar car, in moderate traffic, on a familiar route. This person will probably find it no problem to listen to the radio and hold a conversation – at the same time as reading the road and operating the controls of the car. Lots of incoming information – multiple channels of visual, audio and kinaesthetic information – all being processed, and being responded to simultaneously. Another example might be a group of sports fans watching simultaneous matches on multiple screens in a busy bar, while at the same time talking to each other, relating to others in the bar, and perhaps engaging

Kinaesthetic information can be thought of as the body's physical feedback system. For example it helps us to be aware of where each part of our body is in space without having to look. In the context of driving a car, one example of the use of kinaesthetic information would be helping the driver balance the force of her foot to the resistance of a foot pedal, to produce the appropriate amount of acceleration or braking.

with remote friends and the presenters of the TV programmes through mobile social media networks too.

This kind of engagement with a number of different sources of information at once is sometimes called 'multi-channel'. It demonstrates that there are situations when people can acknowledge and respond to many different visual and audio stimuli simultaneously.

It is probably a mistake to think that this is a particularly modern thing for humans. Think about the multiple channels of information – including sounds, smells, sights and touch – that our ancestors had to process successfully to hunt and kill animals much larger and faster than themselves. Our ancestors used all this information to perform one very specific and important task, and perhaps this gives us something to think about when creating a production design. If we make the audience care enough about their task – say working out what is happening on the stage – they can "cope with" or "make use of" all the multiple channels of information on offer.

Also worth mentioning is the increasing sophistication with which many people read screen images. Perhaps the skills that humans previously required for hunting big game with only stone weapons, have begun to morph into the skills required to rapidly gather and interpret information from screens. This might be made manifest in the ability to watch and engage with two football games at once, or to successfully complete multiple levels of computer games.

It is not uncommon now to find popular music videos that tell different stories with the visual channel to the one told by the words and tune of the music. This 'layering' of meaning is sometimes referred to as a post-modern effect, and it is of a feature of some contemporary video designs for the stage. (The term post-modern has been used as both insult and praise.)

All of this – the ability to engage with several channels of information, and the sophisticated way many people read visual imagery – could be used as a justification for multiple layers of visual image on stage. But remember that music videos, and even live TV, can be paused and rewound, meaning that missed fragments of conversations can be repeated on request. Social media too leaves its own trace that can be returned to later if you think you might have missed something. None of this is usually possible with live performance. To go back to our car driver, paying close attention to a conversation and the radio becomes much harder when traffic conditions are bad, the car is unfamiliar, or the driver is trying to navigate an unfamiliar route. Certainly it can be exciting to present the audience with a multi-layered, multi-channel experience, in the theatre or the concert venue, but as a video designer you may want to be careful when and how we use visual layering on the live stage.

Some audiences, for example for contemporary dance, some kinds of physical theatre, and some kinds of live concert, may have a more developed 'eye' for multi-channel performance. Many regular attendees at these and other performances are used to seeing and enjoying multiple images and multiple screens as part of the experience of live performance. Just as regular opera goes have no trouble hearing each line in a well-sung Mozart quartet, these audiences read and make sense of multiple layers of visual information (or just relax and let it wash over them). Other audiences may have a quite different reaction however. The difficulty for a video designer may be to know just who is likely to be in the audience for the shows they design.

Meanwhile, here are some other reasons you might want to think about using video as part of a stage design:

To be the main source of illumination through sections (or perhaps all) of the piece. This can be a really powerful way of working, offering opportunities for exciting collaborations and daring experiments. It is at present a quite new way of working (though a few theatre makers have a long history of making interesting work in this way).

Very often, the idea is to find a projector (or set of projectors) and to use the whole stage area as 'the screen'. Content is then created that illuminates the required area(s) of the stage in the required way. To do this successfully will require some knowledge of stage lighting design, as well as the technical and aesthetic skills of video design.

On stage, darkness is often at least as important as light, and one of the barriers to successful designs of this kind in the past has been that lack of true black in the projected image. (Most budget priced projectors still output a noticeable greyish light, even when the images is 'black', and this can become distracting for the audience.) However projectors with a much lower level 'black' are now available, and this can only help anyone wanting to experiment with this kind of design.

Design ideas might include making the area occupied by the performer(s) brighter than the rest of the stage, or a different colour, or a particular part of a much larger image.

One of the key decisions that will need to be made early in the design process is, will the projected image be prerecorded or interactively respond to the performer(s). Full interactivity – making the content respond automatically to the movements of the performer for example

– usually involves some advanced technology such as infra-red video cameras and very fast processing. This usually requires specialist knowledge beyond the scope of this book. Limited interactivity can however be achieved in less high-tech ways however, as we shall see.

Working with pre-recorded or pre-programmed content can be too much of a constraint for some performers and directors, though it's worth remembering that most dancers are comfortable working with pre-recorded music, and working with pre-recorded video may not be that different.

Working with only one projector can involve the rapid manipulation of a great deal of video data in order to make the content do some of the things expected of a traditional theatre lighting rig. This, and the need to make (or at least modify) content in the performance space, often constrains projects, and results in a less than happy outcome. Any experimentation in live performance design takes time, and high-tech

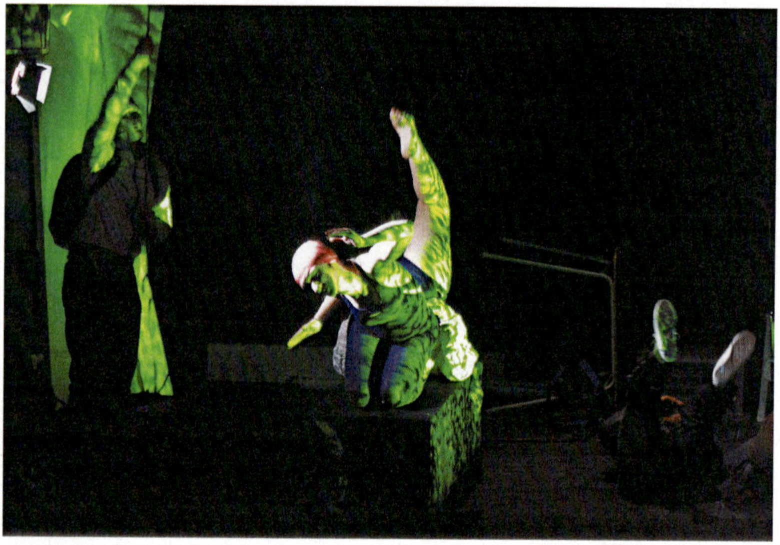

The Edge, A devised piece staged at The New Diorama in 2011

The performer in the centre of this shot is "drowning" in a green sea of projected light. The content was created from a video of water ripples in a shallow tray. This was then colourised and slowed down in the video processing software After Effects. The projector was positioned to provide cross-light for this action. The end result was the product of a considerable amount of experimentation.

experimentation often takes yet more time – so if you do set off down this path, make sure you have plenty of time (and patience).

Because it is mentioned in the script – though even in this case it still doesn't mean that video is the best solution for your particular production, or that if you do use video, you necessarily need to do exactly what the original production did.

The design for *Border Crossings' Orientations Trilogy* – three plays devised by the company over several years – was conceived from the beginning with a prominent projection screen and live camera. Although the dramatic function of some of the video content could be achieved by other means, significant portions of all three plays depend on the interplay between the live performers and recorded or live camera. It would significantly change the audience experience and the range of meaning it is possible to take from the plays if the video was left out.

To show the audience something that won't fit on our stage / get through our doors / we can't afford. What we are talking about here is 'illusion'. Theatre has specialised in illusion almost since its birth – and video can be used to create interesting and spectacular stage illusions, but it may not be the best way to solve every problem of this type.

For example, say a play calls for an elephant. With no projection, you could have the actors point off stage and play the sounds of an elephant. This requires the audience to pretend that they believe that there is an elephant in the wings. Even though most of them will probably know that there isn't one, they will usually willingly suspend their disbelief for you, and go with the idea.

If you decide to use projection to 'show' your audience an elephant, you may decide to project the image of an elephant onto a wall of the stage set or you could have the actors look through a stage window at a projection of an elephant apparently outside their window. This image will most likely be seen by the audience as projections and not as a real elephant. However it may be just the right thing for your production.

If you decide that your elephant has to appear as real as possible on stage, you could try to project a three dimensional moving elephant on stage using Pepper's Ghost techniques previously mentioned. This will present to the audience the appearance of a real elephant. Setting aside for the moment the very real technical difficulties involved in realising such a large three dimensional effect on stage, even if your audience don't know how the trick is achieved, they will probably be aware that an elephant is not actually present, no matter how well the illusion is executed. In many circumstances, the best you can hope for is that your audience is impressed with the trick. The video designer, director, and others, will need to decide if this is the right thing for the production…

In other circumstances, it is perfectly possible to create believable illusions on stage with the help of video, and to play with the audience's perceptions too. The biggest illusions in large theatres need big budgets and teams of skilled people, and are beyond the scope of this book. However some really effective illusions can be achieved in a smaller space with much less in terms of equipment – as I hope you will see later.

Many productions play with the idea that the audience 'make up' in their own heads, the missing part of what is presented as the production design. For example, even the most realistic/naturalistic box set has (at least) one missing wall and often no ceiling – but as audience we accept it as a representation of a room. Sometimes video can lead designers down a path of presenting too much in a literal way, leaving the audience nothing to make-up.

Because the director (or the producer, or the main artist) wants it. Possibly not the best place to start with any video design project. So, the first thing to do is to get to a better stating place: try and find out is why this person wants to use video, and what they expect it to do for the piece. (It is just possible that they want video on the project primarily to boost their own reputation – thought that will usually be harder to find out, and takes us again into areas beyond the scope of this book!)

Once you have established why video is considered to be so important for the project (and it won't necessarily be an easy task) the next thing to do is to research how you (as video designer) are going to achieve the desired aim.

What Projection Can't Do (and what this book can't show you)

Video is not the solution to every staging or presentation problem! For example...

- You can't climb up a purely projected set of steps,
- or walk through a projected door
- or climb out of a window projected onto a solid wall,
- or enter through a trap-door projected onto a solid floor,
- or pick up a projected cup and saucer.

Apologies to anyone who thinks this is completely obvious – but you may be surprised by the number of people who think it is perfectly possible to do all these things and more. Projection is light. It does not fundamentally change the nature of the surfaces it hits. If there is no hole in the surface you project an image onto, then projecting a window frame and open window onto it will not create a real hole anyone can climb through! (And while we are at the projected window, making it look as if there is light coming through the window from outside can also be a problem.)

Of course there are tricks to be done, real steps to be concealed, trick flats to be constructed and real trap-doors to be hidden in an apparently solid stage. These effects can be great fun to design and build, but they can also cause extreme frustration for all concerned in the effort to get it right!

To be effective, tricks such as these are likely to require the skill of many different theatre and performance experts – from set constructors and painters to members of the lighting and stage-management teams, the director and choreographer, and the performers, perhaps even a consulting magician – and of course a good video designer. So if you are going to try it, make sure you have lots of good people round.

Holograms

Many effects dubbed hologram are (at the moment at least) a version of the Pepper's Ghost illusion. As I write, it is a big budget illusion. As the cost of high quality bright and quiet video projectors comes down, and advances are made in the materials needed to reflect an image into the stage environment, this illusion will come within the reach of productions with more ordinary budgets. However, while a well executed Pepper's Ghost can look very real:

- using this illusion puts significant constraints on both lighting and set design,
- the projected image can't hold solid objects, (so you can't put a real teapot down on a projected table),
- and the performers working along side the 'ghost' image can't always see it (although this can be overcome).

This old/new technology can be very appealing, and it has been used to great effect in live theatre productions, in dance, and on the concert stage – and at MTV awards ceremonies (look it up on YouTube). But it has limitations, and it can be very expensive. Creating the effect at a scale for a live show is beyond the scope of this book, and requires specialist advice.

People have been telling me the true holographic projection is just round the corner for over 25 years. Who knows, as you read this it just might be, but as I write this (in 2013) there are some pretty large technical and safety hurdles to overcome before we can get true holograms on stage.

Fully Interactive 3D Environments

I've played with my Wii and a projector, and now I want to create a fully interactive 3D environment!

While it is increasingly possible to make low or mid-budget video systems for the stage with some degree of interactivity, a fully interactive system is beyond the scope of this introductory book. As my late grandmother used to say: "If you want to get there, you don't want to start from here." In other words, you will need a great deal of engineering and video knowledge – and a theme-park sized budget – to even begin contemplating something like this, but good luck, and let me know when I can come and try it out!

Now let's get back to what we *can* do with video!

2 BRIGHTNESS

Intensity and Brightness

Many production designs based on video projection run into trouble because the image does not look bright enough. There are a lot of factors that affect the perceived brightness of projected images on stage, so its hardly surprising that it proves difficult to get it right all the time. In this chapter we are going to look at the part played by the choice of screen and projector, and the physical relationship between them. We will also touch on some important aspects of human vision. In later chapters we will look at other factors including how the screen is integrated into the rest of the set and the nature of the content.

Our eyes are not like a camera, and don't register absolute intensity in the same way that say, a light meter does. A light meter measures how much light is present at a particular point. For the same quantity of light, the reading on the light meter will always be the same. Human vision is quite different when it comes to assessing brightness. It is not unusual for us to see the same intensity as bright in some circumstances and dim in others. For example, a screen image may appear quite bright in a theatre, even with the house lights set ready for the audience to walk in. Outside in the daylight however, the same screen image with the same measurable intensity, will not look bright at all. The average intensity level outside during the day varies a lot, but is likely to be at least 10 to 50 times higher than the average intensity in a theatre auditorium.

For the rest of this book, when I mention **intensity** I'll be referring to the level of light as measured by a light-meter, or a camera, or any device that does not have a brain attached. When I write about **brightness** of our projected content for the audience members, I'll be referring to the subjective perceptions of an average viewer or audience member. To discuss brightness we will need to take into account such things as what else is going on in the observer's field of view (which will include the stage lighting at that moment), and what the observer was just looking at (which will include the previous stage lighting state) and several other factors, such as **image contrast**.

More on Intensity vs Brightness: Scientists describe light in terms of a flow of photons – the fundamental particles of light. They refer to a beam of light as a flux of photons. For any given flux of photons, that is given number of photons per second hitting (for example) the sensor of a light meter, the meter will give the same reading. Human vision on the other hand registers the intensity of a small section of the field of view relative to the average intensity of the whole field. Our perception of brightness is also affected by the average intensity immediately prior to the present scene (see the longer section Brightness Contrast and the Human Eye and the Adaptation Level). This means that absolute intensity is less important than relative intensity: relative in space (other areas of the visual field) and time (previous average and extreme intensities).You can find out a lot more about the way our visual system works from scientific sites on the internet. For example I found some particularly interesting lecture notes using the search terms "*light intensity perception*".

Screens, and Aspect Ratio

The beam of a projector is generally rectangular. If the projector was made for Standard Definition video, this rectangle will be 4 units wide by 3 units high. This means that if the beam is 4 metres wide, it will be 3 metres high. If the full size image is 6 metres wide at the screen, it will be 4.5m high. (6 times 3 divided by 4) The ratio of the width to the height is called the aspect ratio. For a standard definition projector, the aspect ratio can be written in several ways: 4:3 or 4x3 or 4 to 3 or 4 by 3.

Generally the first number in any aspect ratio is the horizontal dimension, the width, and the second is the vertical, the height. Most projection assumes a 'landscape' format – that is with the longest dimension in the horizontal plane. If we wanted to indicate that our screen or content is in 'portrait' format, tall and narrow rather than wide and short, we might use the aspect ratio 3:4. I will need

It is possible to set up most professional video projectors to display in several aspect ratios. Sometimes this happens automatically, depending on the system. All projectors have a native aspect ratio (and native resolution too but we'll come to that later). This is defined by the size and shape of the internal LCD or DPP chip on which the image is produced. It is sometimes worth finding out what this is, as it will help you to calculate the effective screen size for different lenses with greater accuracy - as we will see later.

to come back to aspect ratio in more detail in Chapter 4 when we discuss content.

Screen and Content Shape, and Projector Aspect Ratio

Just because the full projector image is 4:3 does not mean that all our content – or our screen – have to have the same aspect ratio. You can design your screen or screens to have any aspect ratio you wish, and of course design your content to match. You don't even have to stick to a regular rectangle. This chapter is about brightness however – and if we are not using all of the available beam of the projector, which we will call the projection field, we are also not using all the available brightness.

Even when the effective screen is not 4:3 or the content does not fill all the available projection field, you will usually need to know what shape and size the 4:3 projection area will be on stage. This will help you make sure you have as much of the projector's available brightness, and as many pixels as possible, in your design. (More pixels = higher resolution, smoother curves, etc., but also more light). See Fig 1 Aspect Ratio overleaf.

Even if your screen, and your content, don't completely match the projection field, the 4x3 area for a standard definition video projector, that area is what the projector projects. Parts of the projection field that don't have your image in, are filled with projector 'black'. Any measure of the total light output of the projector will include that part of the projection field that you are not using. Unfortunately, there is no way to gather the light that your images are not using and re-direct it into the parts of the projection area that you are using. If your screen is significantly smaller than the projection field you are 'wasting' light, and wasting potential brightness.

The other thing to consider here is that – for all but the top of the range video projectors, 'projector black' is not actually no light. Most projectors 'leak' a dull grey light, even when sent a totally black image. This can lead to a distracting grey rectangle being seen on stage in darker scenes. There are ways round this, but they need to be carefully thought through and planned.

Video projectors have a native resolution. A common mid-priced device such as an XGA – type projector, has a resolution of 1024 x 768 pixels (which works out as 4:3). If you are not using all the available projection area, you are not using all the pixels. The fewer pixels you have available to make up your projected images, the less likely they are to look good. This means that in most circumstances, we need to try to ensure that our content and stage screen use as much as possible of the total available field of the projector.

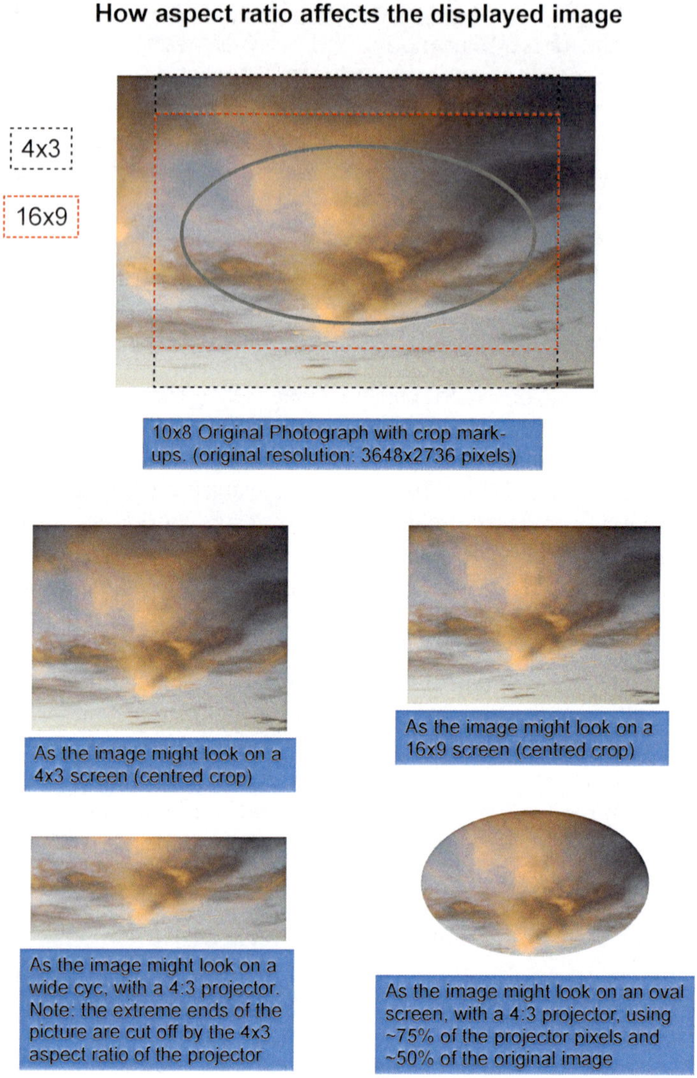

Figure 1: Aspect Ratio.

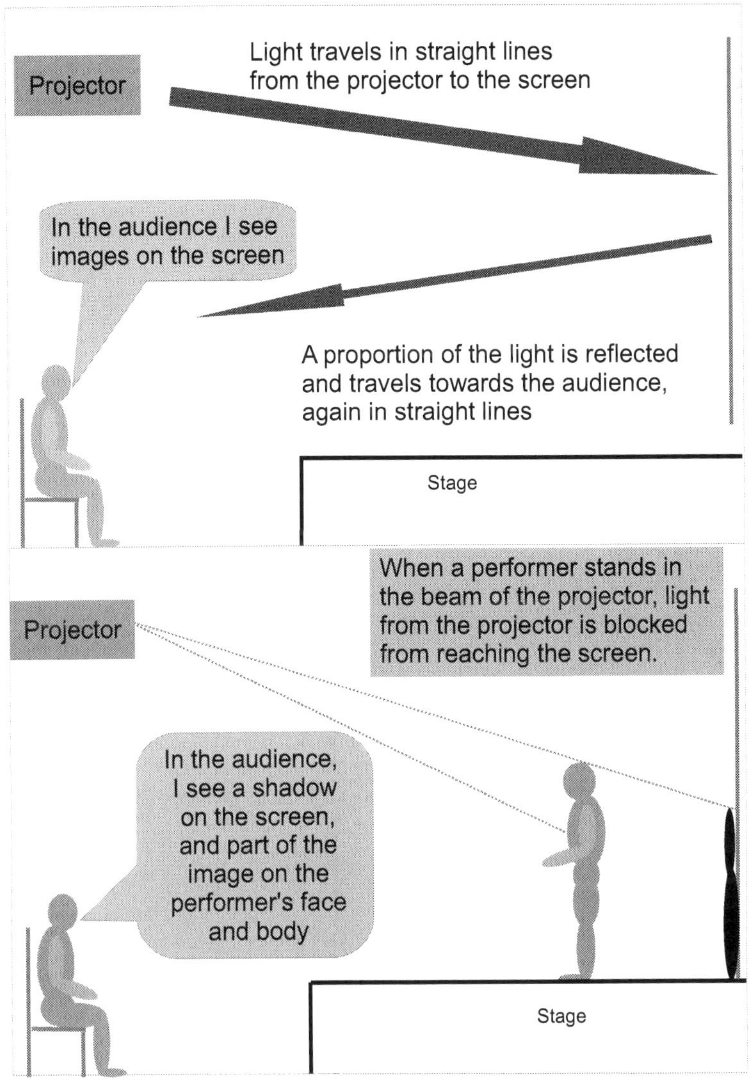

Figure 2: Light reflects from the screen.

Brightness, Contrast and the Human Eye - an Introduction

Human visual perception is a complex thing, involving our eyes and many areas of the brain, linked in ways scientists are only now beginning to fully understand. This visual system allows us to see in a huge range of lighting conditions - from starlight to bright sun. In physics terms, that is an intensity range of around 1014 or 1 with 14 zeros after it.

However we can't see in starlight and bright sun at the same time, or even see well when moving between much less extreme differences in brightness. For example when you go from a dark interior into the bright out-doors it is quite normal to be dazzled for a short time. Likewise moving into a dark room from a sun-lit exterior can leave us feeling almost blind before our eyes adjust to their new surroundings. This process of adjustment to the average intensity of light around us called brightness adaptation. It involves more than just the opening or closing of the iris in each eye - it effectively needs a re-calibration of parts of the eye-brain system. Full brightness adaptation can take some time, and happens in phases. The first phase can take less than a second, then there is usually a slightly longer period of adaptation before good vision returns - between ten seconds and a several minutes depending on how extreme the change in intensity has been, and whether it was from bright to dark or dark to bright. It can take 45 minutes to attain peak vision in starlight for example.

The average brightness in our visual field is called the adaptation level. In many ways, this is similar to the average light level that a camera metering system would detect to expose a photograph, though the eye can usually detect detail in a wider range of light intensity either side of the average level than a camera can.

At any given moment, human vision can work with a difference in brightness, a contrast ratio, of around 1 to 1000. In camera terms that's very good. As of 2012, a good quality digital camera is capable of capturing a picture with a contrast ratio of around 45 to 1 (with a single exposure).

Because of the particular way the visual system works, our 1000 to 1 contrast ratio means that at best we can see detail in two objects at the same time, only as long as the one is not more than 30 times brighter or darker than the other. By comparison, a good quality digital camera (video or still) will struggle to see detail in two objects at the same time if one is as little as 6 times brighter or darker than the other.

Roughly speaking, at best we stop being able to see detail in areas that are 10 to 15 times brighter or darker than our current adaptation level. Areas that are more than 10 to 15 times brighter than the adaptation level are seen only as white, with no detail present. Similarly, areas more than 10 to 15 times darker than the adaptation level are seen as black, again with no detail.

It so happens that human vision is more sensitive to contrast than to absolute intensity, and most sensitive to abrupt changes in contrast. It also happens that our visual perception is governed much more by our lived experience than most people are probably aware – we often see things the way we have learned from experience that they are rather than as a camera does. These twin factors mean the eye can be 'tricked' into seeing things as we expect them to be rather than as they are. It also means that in the right circumstances, we see 'white' in images much less than 15 times brighter than the adaptation level – which can be good news for video designers, as we shall soon see.

Projectors: Light, Brightness, Angles and Shadows

Projection can be thought of as making a highly controlled beam of light shine onto a reflective surface so that images can be seen by the audience. In a simple video system, the images, which might be still photographs, digital drawings, animations or video clips, are selected in turn from the the playback system, and sent to the projector as data. The projector then turns the data back into a picture in light, and projects the images onto the screen. When the light hits the screen surface (or anything even partly reflective in its path to the screen for that matter) the audience see the images reflected on the surface.

Light and the Laws of Physics

The light that makes up the images we see on the screen obeys the laws of physics. For example:

- in air, light travels in straight lines, and ...
- light carries on travelling in straight lines until it hits something,
- spreading out all the time in ways governed by something called the 'inverse square law', and ...
- when light hits any surface, some of it is absorbed and some of it is reflected.

Unless the surface is a perfect mirror, the reflected light goes in many directions (scatters).

How much is absorbed and how much reflected depends on the material (its colour and other surface properties).

Every-Day physics vs 'proper science': OK, those amongst you with a scientific background will know that this is not a complete description, but let's not cloud the issue with talk of curved space-time or other phenomena. From the point of view of a theatre maker, light does travel in straight lines through air, and reflection from any matt surface involves scattering.

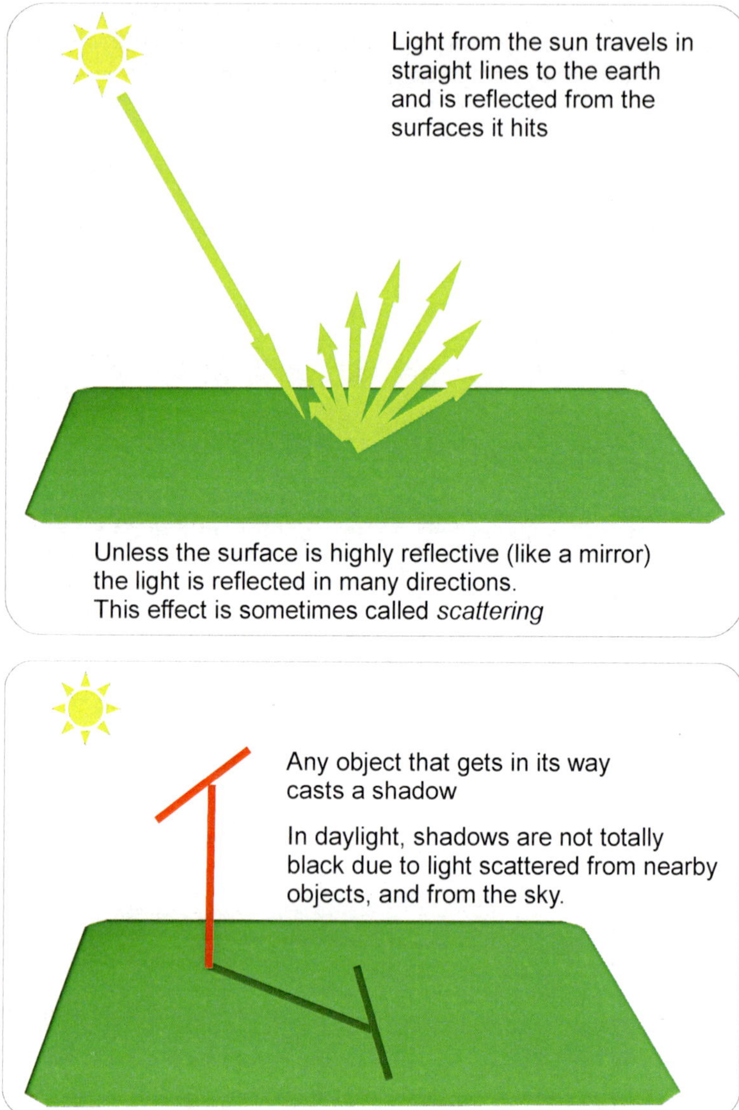

Figure 3: Light and shadows

- Any solid object in the path of a beam of light, reflects and absorbs the light that hits it, and ...
- stops it going any further in the original direction, causing a **shadow**.

It's worth remembering that any video image is itself a source of light, and that the light from a screen will often have a noticeable effect on the way the audience sees objects, surfaces and performers on stage.

Our visual systems do a great deal of processing of the actually quite limited information gathered by our eyes. For example, we can't tell if an object is emitting or reflecting light in isolation. We work out what is going on by using our experience; for example by seeing the source shining onto the reflective object or by observing shadows. Mostly we do this without consciously thinking about it. The brain interprets the information it receives from our eyes and compares new images to previous experience in many different ways. We subconsciously use our visual experience of the world to come up with the most likely interpretation of the visual information.

The subconscious interpretation of information such as where and how shadows are falling, relative intensity and geometry, helps us work out what the three dimensional world looks like with our primarily two dimensional sight. This processing can lead to a tendency to 'see' the world as it is most likely to be, based on our previous experience, rather than as it actually is. This fact is what lies behind many optical illusions – we see what we expect to see, even when things are quite different.

Intensity of a Projector

The intensity of a projector is a measure of the amount of light available to hit the screen. The intensity of the image is a measure of how much light is reflected from the screen (or emitted from the screen if it is a TV, computer monitor or LED screen). We want to know how much light from our content will reach the audience. This will depend on how much light is available from the projector (the intensity of the projector), how much of that light is projected (which will depend on the nature of the content) and how much of the light projected is reflected (or emitted) from the screen (the intensity of the screen). So all these factors are important to the video designer. As previously discussed, the audience's perception of the brightness of the image will depend on lots of other things too, but lets start with intensity.

Scientist and engineers are interested in something called the luminous flux of a light source, such as a candle, a light-bulb, or a projector. This is the total amount of light emitted by that object. In the

The units lumens and lux take into account several other factors that I have not mentioned here, such as the frequency response of the average human eye. There is also an alternative measurement system based on the luminous flux of an ideal candle. If you want to go further into the subject, it is easy to look up the details on the internet, using the search terms such as "lumen unit" and "candela intensity light" for the alternative system.

SI (or metric) system, luminous flux is measured in lumens. As practitioners, we are usually more interested in intensity than luminous flux. Intensity is the amount of light emitted from or falling on a particular surface area. Intensity is measured in lux. An intensity of one lux is defined as one lumen per square metre.

Most digital projectors are rated in lumens, which is a measure of the maximum total light output in ideal conditions. This means everything in the projector working perfectly, all the optical surfaces (mostly the lenses) clean, and each pixel fully 'on' – a totally white image.

At the time of writing, many mid-priced projectors have a rated output of around 5000 ANSI lumens. This is the total light output, and it will be spread across the whole area of our screen. The area of a rectangular screen is the width times the height. Say our screen is 4m wide by 3m high, which makes the projection area 12 square metres (4 multiplied by 3). So our 5000 lumens will be spread across 12 square metres, meaning we should be able to get a maximum of around 400 lumens per square metre, also referred to as 400 lux. Now 400 lux is close to the minimum intensity you would want to have available – though as we shall see there are plenty of other factors that effect the perceived brightness of projected images on stage. If we half the width of the projection area, to 2 metres wide, that will give us a height of 1.5 metres, so the projection area is 3 square metres (2 multiplied by 1.5). The brightness per square

A standardised procedure for testing projectors has been established by the American National Standards Institute, or ANSI. It involves averaging together several measurements taken across the whole of a projected image. Projectors that have been tested according to this procedure can use the term "ANSI Lumens". This distinguishes them from projectors tested by other methods. ANSI lumen measurements are usually considered to be more accurate, and provide a more useful guide for users, than other measurement techniques.
A 5000 ANSI lumen projector is sometimes referred to as "a 5k" - which can be confusing if you come from a lighting background where "a 5k" is a 5000 Watt lantern, one of the biggest units on a theatre stage. The average 5000 lumen projector uses between 500 and 600 Watts of electrical power. (The "k" is short for "kilo" - the term used for thousand in the metric system, hence 1 kilometre, or 1km is 1000 metres, or 1000m).

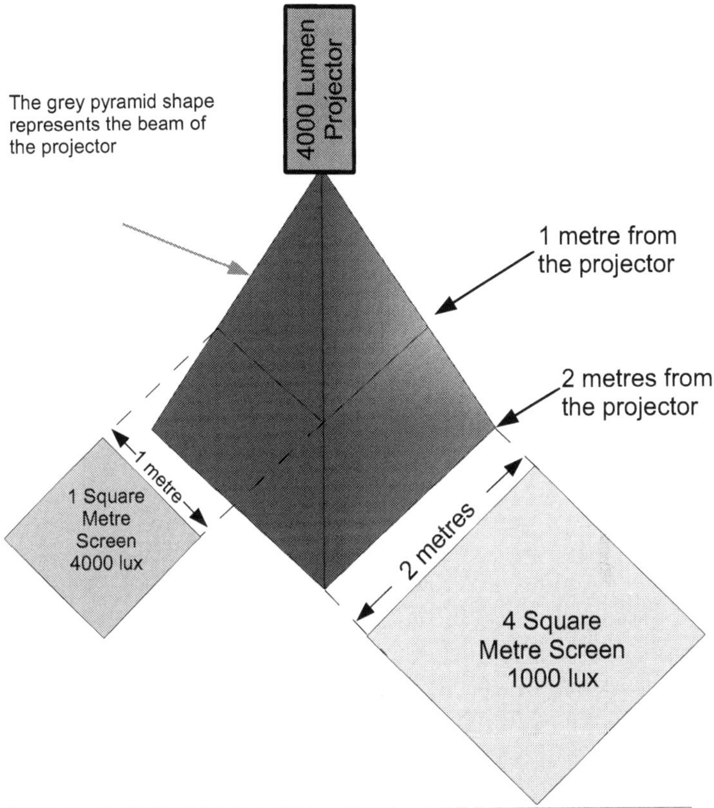

This slightly unusual, 4000 lumen projector, projects a square beam. With a screen 1 metre from the projector, the effective screen area Is 1 metre square and the maximum brightness available is 4000 lux (4000 lumens spread over $1m^2$).
With the screen 2 metres from the projector the effective screen area is 4 square metres (2m x 2m) and the maximum brightness available is 1000 lux (4000 lumens spread over $4m^2$).
An image on the $1m^2$ screen will be 4 times brighter than the same image projected onto the $4m^2$ screen.
Increase the distance between projector and screen by a factor of 2 (double), the intensity <u>drops</u> by a factor of 4! ($2^2=4$)

Figure 4: Inverse Square Law

metre is now around 1600 lux. When we halve the width and height of the screen, the image becomes four times brighter.

To reduce the width of the projection area by half (without changing the projector or its lens), we need to half the distance between the projector and the screen – so if the projector was 6 metres from the screen to begin with, it is now just 3 metres away. So if you halve the distance between the projector and the screen the image ends up half as wide but 4 times brighter. This is a manifestation of the inverse square law referred to earlier in the chapter.

Of course the opposite is also true. If we decide to double the width of the screen, without changing the projector, the intensity will be only one quarter of what it was. Figure 4 attempts to explain the main implications of this phenomenon for projection design.

Projector Lenses

Given a nice flat wall to project onto, and no obstacles between projector and wall, there are two factors that will decide how big the projected image is. The first – as already discussed – is the distance between the projector and the white wall. The further away the projector is the bigger (and less bright) the image will be. This is called the throw. The second factor is the lens.

Video projectors all require a lens to focus the projected image on the screen. The choice of lens defines the spread of the beam, and so the size of the image at the screen. The first difficulty in choosing lenses however is that there are several different ways of referring to the way that a lens spreads and focuses the beam. The second difficulty is linked to the way projectors are most often used in stage design – which is generally not the same as in a home cinema or classroom set-up as we shall see. The third difficulty comes when we use lenses other than the standard ones that come with the projector, when you may find that you need to know the size of the chip in the projector. (Choosing a non-standard lens may mean you lose some remote control features such as remote focus and zoom too.) All of this just needs to be worked through, in a calm logical way – and if you can do some trial set-ups to test out your calculations, so much the better.

I have already mentioned long throw and short throw lenses, in the context of front and rear projection. So called long-throw lenses produce a narrower beam angle from the projector, and a smaller image for any given throw. Short throw lenses produce a wider beam angle, and a larger image for the same throw. (Beam angle is a measure of the spread of a

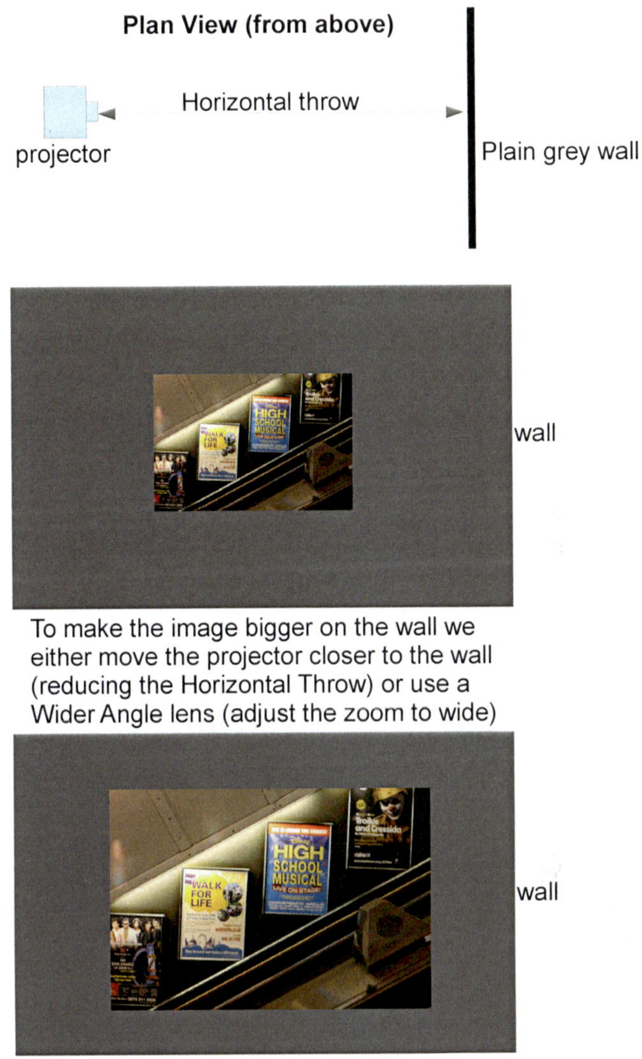

Figure 5: changing the size of the image

beam, for a projector or a theatre lantern.) (See also figure 2 in chapter 1)

Lenses in general are defined by their focal length. However, projector lenses are often called by the ratio of Horizontal Throw to width of Projection Field. This is handy if you know what width you want your content to be – you can use the ratio to find out roughly what throw you will need, that is how far away the projector will need to be.

For example, a fixed, short throw lens might be specified as 0.8:1. This would mean that at an image width of around 1m would require a throw of 0.8m. The first figure in the ratio is the horizontal distance between screen and projector required to give a 1 unit wide image – in the projector's native aspect ratio. A different lens might be called 2.8:1. This would mean a 1m wide image would need a throw of 2.8m, and a 3m wide image, a throw of 8.4m (2.8x3=8.4)

This calculation is also based on the projector being in line with the centre of the screen, both horizontally and vertically, and the content being in the projector's native aspect ratio – usually 4:3 for standard definition video projectors. All three of these conditions need to be true for the lens ratio calculation to work successfully.

Many of the projector manufactures provide calculators on their websites to help their customers choose the right lens for a given throw and desired image size. In stage design however, the physical

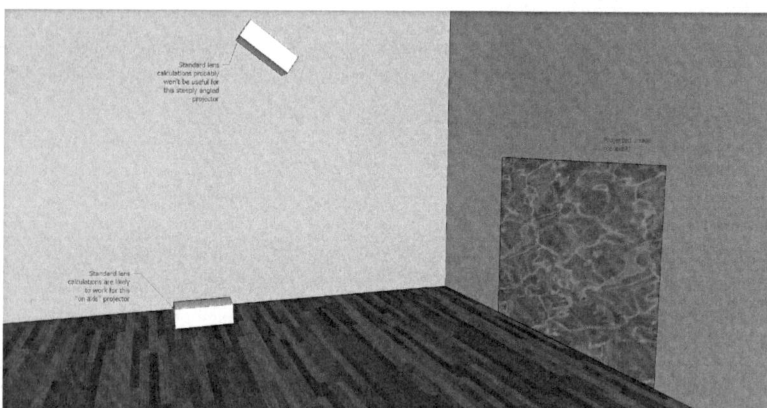

Most standard projector lens calculations assume the projector is "on axis", like the lower projector shown here. Much of the time in theatre, the projector(s) will not be "on axis" – more like the upper projector here – and the standard lens and image size calculations and tables will not be very useful.

set up and the aspect ratio of the content are often quite different from those assumed by propitiatory calculators, which makes using them problematic. If the projector is not directly in line with the screen, and/ or the content does not use the whole projection field then for any given throw, the image width is likely to be smaller than that calculated using either the manufacturers' tables or this simple formula.

Lenses wider than around 0.8:1 are rare. (For "rare" you might also read "expensive".) If you can find one, it may well distort your image. Lenses much narrower than 7:1 are rare too. Here though the problem is less to do with distortion and more to do with light throughput. Affordable long throw lenses tend to have a relatively high f-number. If you are familiar with SLR cameras, you will already know that the higher the f-number the less light is able to pass through the lens. The less light that gets through the lens, the less arrives at the screen, and the less brightness is available for your image.

With all this in mind, when planning your projector and screen set up, its best to find out what lenses are available for your chosen projector sooner rather than later.

Working with a Fixed Throw

If distance between projector and screen (the throw) is fixed, as it often is in theatre designs, you will need to do a bit more arithmetic. Here is one approach you can take if you have a fixed distance between projector and screen – say where the projector is already mounted in a fixed position in the auditorium, and the part of the set we want to project onto is fixed on stage.

Measure the horizontal throw, from lens of the projector to the centre of the screen. Then measure the width of the screen (or better still your best guess at the total projection field, allowing for distortions such as key stoning, and cropping.) These two numbers will give you the ratio you require to choose a lens.

Use the formula: Throw divided by Width of Projection Field = first number in the name of the lens you need.

Ideally you would visit the venue where your design is to be staged and accurately measure the distance between the lens of the projector and the centre of the screen – the throw – but more often than not this is not possible. You may be able to get hold of a scaled plan of the venue, or even better an accurate 3D digital model. Without actually visiting the venue and seeing exactly where your projector will be hung – and checking it will fit where you want it and there are no obstructions between it and the screen – it's difficult to be sure about measurements taken from a plan or a model.

Most of the time you will have to take your best guess at the throw measurement, and your best guess at how wide you want the image to be on stage. Make sure both measurements are in the same units – if the throw is measured in metres, then the width must be measured in metres too or the formula won't work. Enter the throw measurement into a calculator and divide that by the width measurement, and you should get a number for the name of the lens you need. (You will only be interested in the first 1 or 2 digits of your answer.) If the answer is between 0.8 and say 7 then your design is probably achievable. If it's outside that range you may need to think again...

Remember that the more guessing you do to get the figures for your calculations, the less likely they are to be correct, and the more likely you are to be surprised when you come to try out your set-up. It's a good idea to try and find out details of what has been achieved before in that venue, and what equipment was used (projector power and lens specification and screen size and position). This can help you decide if your design is practical.

Zoom Lenses, and Finding the Beam Angle

Most lenses made for video projectors have some flexibility built in – they are usually zoom lenses, with a range of focal length. They too are usually called by the ratio of throw to content width. So a zoom lens designed primarily for short throw work might be called a 1.1 to 1.5:1 (usually written as 1.1-1.5 : 1). A zoom lens designed for long throw work might be called 4.6 to 6.0:1 (usually written as 4.6-6.0 : 1).

Manufacturers can be – shall we say – optimistic when it comes to their product specifications. It's not a good idea to plan to use any zoom lens at its extreme setting. In fact, because of the uncertainty that arises from using projectors 'off axis', which is quite common in video design for theatre, it is not a good idea to assume anything when designing a projector/screen configuration. If at all possible, make an experimental set-up to test your assumptions, and the manufacturer's promises.

Many readers who come from a lighting design background, and perhaps others too, will be quite familiar with calculating the size of the beam of a theatre lantern using the throw and the beam angle. Even if you are not familiar with this way of working, there are some useful calculators that work with beam angle (on the internet and elsewhere). So, how do you work out the beam angle of a projector lens if all you know is the name? The first method relies on making an accurate scale drawing.

Method 1: Scale Drawing by hand or CAD

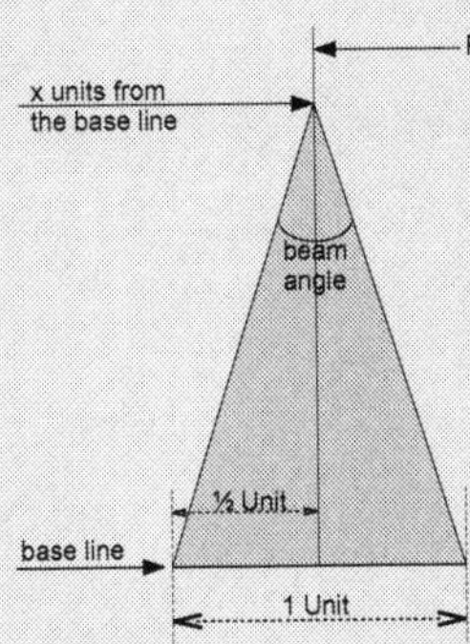

1. Draw a horizontal "base" line 1 unit long (at scale)
2. from the centre of this line, draw a perpendicular line
3. measure off "x" units (at scale) along this line, where "x" is the first number of the lens name
4. draw the triangle (shaded blue here)
5. measure the angle at the top of the triangle - that is the beam angle

The drawing shown is for a 3:1 lens

Method 2: Using Inverse Tangent function

Should you wish, you can calculate the beam angle directly using the ratio in the lens name. You will need to know the size from corner to opposite corner of the projection field, since this calculation is based on a regular cone of light rather than the rectangle produced by a projector. We will call this measurement the full image diagonal.

In most cases a perpendicular line from the centre of the screen to the projector lens will form the adjacent side of a right angle triangle. Half the screen diagonal will form the opposite side of this triangle, and half the beam angle will be the inverse tangent of the ratio (half full Image Diagonal / Throw), and the whole beam angle will be Tan-1 of full Image Diagonal / Throw.

This ratio can be approximated from the lens name. If the lens name is Z:1, then since Z is also the throw required for a 1 unit wide full screen image, the beam angle is the Tan-1 of 1/Z. For a projector with a 4:3 aspect ratio, the screen diagonal is 5 (that's just the way the geometry works out). So for these projectors, the ratio of the full image width to the full screen diagonal is 4:5. So to get from full image width to full image diagonal we need to multiply by 5/4 (or 1.25)

For a 4:3 aspect ratio:

Beam Angle for a Z:1 lens is Tan-1 of 1.25 x [1/Z]

Beam Angle for a 0.8:1 lens is Tan-1 of 1.25 x [1/0.8] which is around 57 degrees

Beam Angle for a 1.0:1 lens is Tan-1 of 1.25 x [1/1.0] which is around 51 degrees

Beam Angle for a 4.0:1 lens is Tan-1 of 1.25 x [1/4.0] which is around 17 degrees

Once you know the beam angle (or angles) of the available lens or lenses, you can do some more drawings or calculations to find out the likely outcome of possible set-ups.

Knowing the beam angles of the lens you have available can be especially useful if you have a 3D digital model of your stage design (say in Sketch-Up, AutoCAD or Vector Works). These programs will allow you to create and check the beam of your projector in 3D virtual space.

Keystone Correction

If you turn back to Figure 2 in this chapter, you will see an example of one of the biggest recurrent problems encountered when using front projected video on stage. In some areas of the stage, the performers get in the way of the projection. This has two consequences:

1. A shadow of the performer appears on the screen. This can be distracting for the audience, and can destroy any illusion of the reality of the images that the production design is trying to create.
2. The projected image appears on the body and costume of the performer. This too can be distracting for the audience and for other performers too. (It has been known to lead to unintended comedy too – for example when a performer was delivering lines about his clean white shirt which at that moment showed part of an image of graffiti on a wall.)

If you want to avoid both these things then the performers have to stay out of what might be called no-go areas near the screen. In figure 2 it looks like most of the stage is a no go area! There are several ways of addressing these problems, and getting back more of the stage for the performers. One way is to raise the screen, so that the lowest part of it is above the performer's heads. Another is to use rear-projection instead of front projection – but as we have seen this solution is likely to eat up stage space too.

By far the most common solution is to raise the projector above the level of the top of the screen, as shown in Figure 7.

This option however brings its own set of problems, and the first the distortion of the projected image. A simple video projector is designed to project an undistorted image onto a screen that is at a right-angle to the beam of the projector, with the projector lined up to the centre of the screen – horizontally and vertically. Most are able to correct the image to compensate for other set-ups. There are two types of correction called 'lens shift' and 'keystone correction'. Both are accessed through the projector's set-up menu. This built-in correction is usually designed to compensate for set-ups where the projector is in line with the top or bottom of the screen rather than the centre (horizontal lens shift) or the screen is not at a right-angle to the projector beam (keystone). Playing with these internal settings on the projector will often enable you to correct the distortion of the image that results from raising the projector above the top of the screen. However, in many instances, the internal adjustments will not be enough, and you will need to predistort you content.

The second problem is a knock-on effect of applying keystone

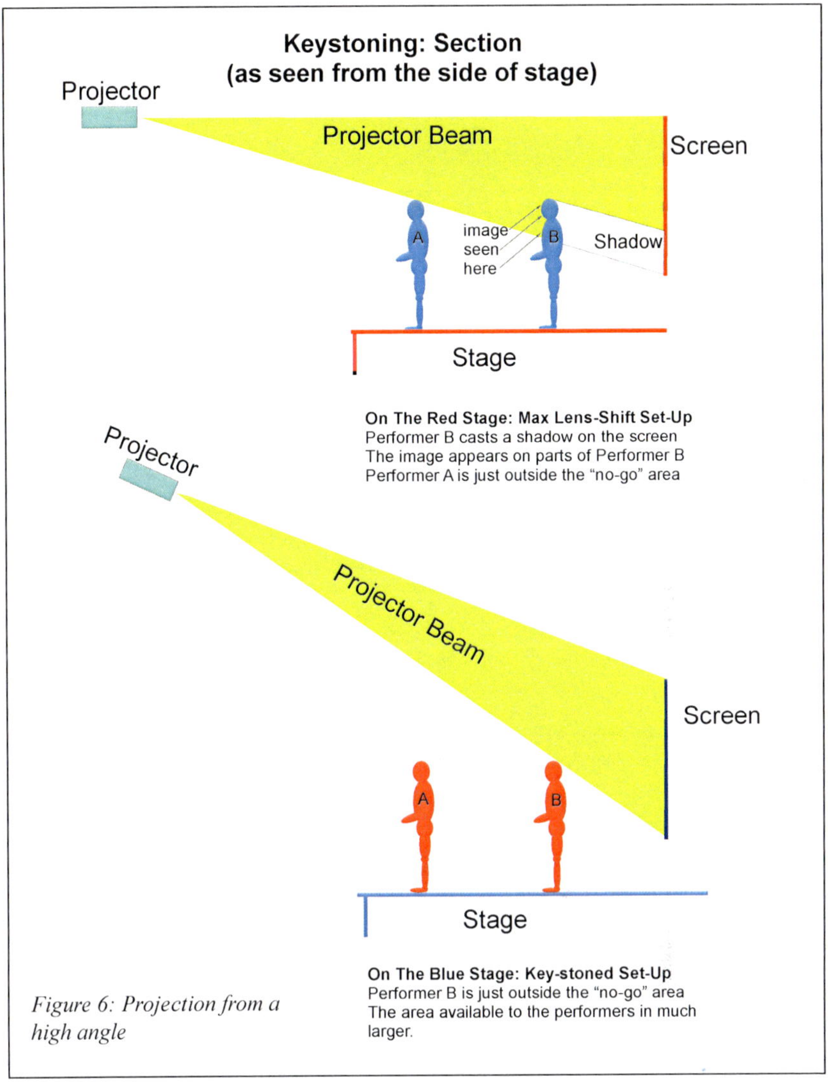

Figure 6: Projection from a high angle

correction. To correct for the distortion of the projected image effectively means we are distorting the image to make it look undistorted on the screen. If the projector is mounted higher than the top screen, the bottom of the image will need to be compressed and/or the top stretched out. This means there will be fewer pixels per centimetre of image at the bottom than at the top. This means that the bottom of the image will

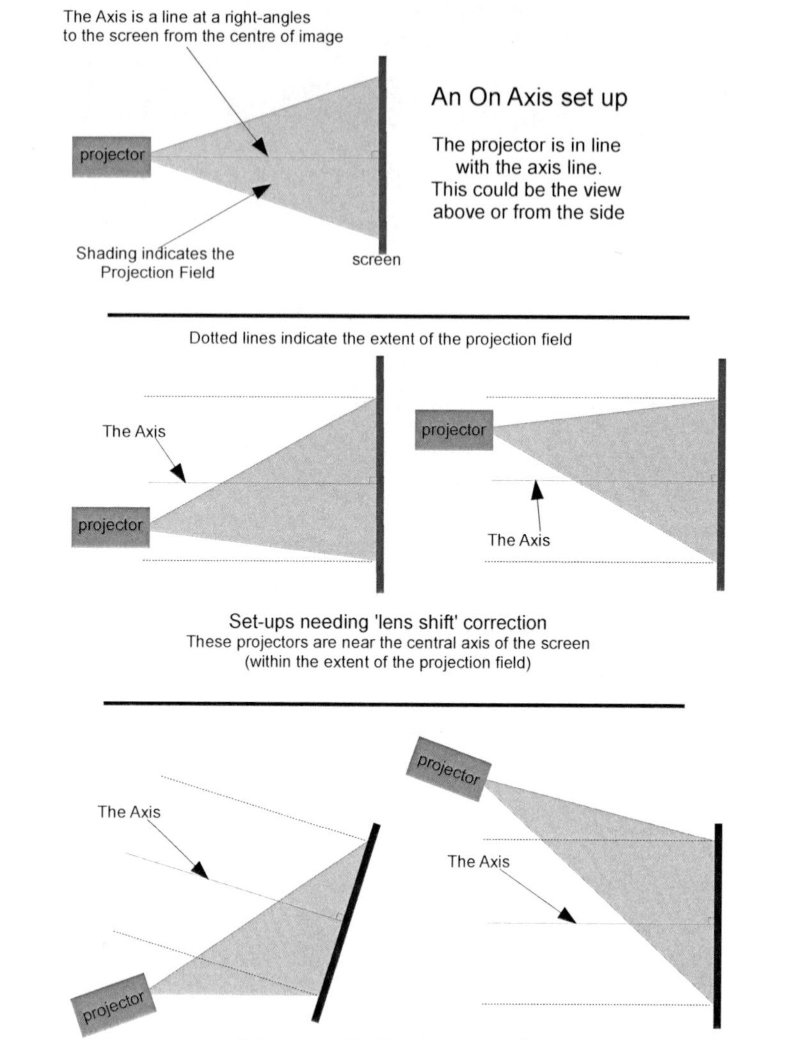

Figure 7a: Lens shift and keystone correction

have less resolution than the top, so for example curves may appear less smooth at the bottom than at the top of the screen. It may also mean that the bottom of the image has noticeably less brightness than the top.

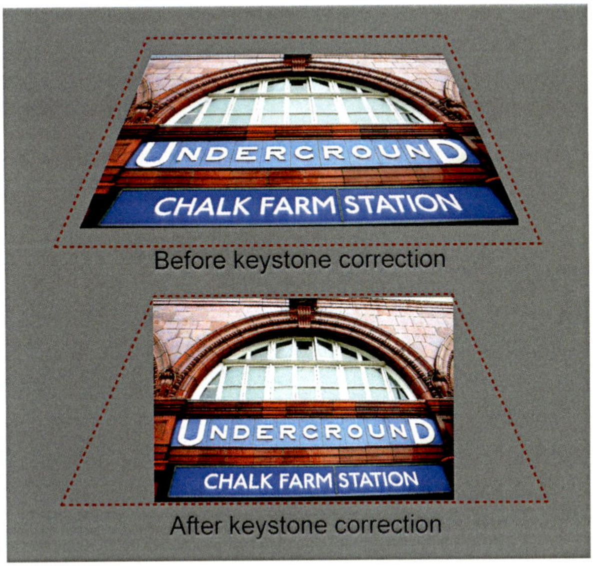

Mounting the projector higher than the screen (to reduce the "no-go" area on stage) causes the images to become distorted on the screen

With keystone correction applied to the content, the images are again seen undistorted. Some degradation of the image may be an Inevitable side effect of applying a lot of keystone correction

The full extent of the projection field is indicated by the red dotted lines. All the screen has to be within the full projection field

It is likely that some residual light from the projector will be visible at times from the "unused" part of the projection field

Figure 7b:
Keystone correction with an image

So, if we decide to raise the projector to reduce the no-go area of the stage, then we will need to do something to correct the resulting distortion of the projected image. But we will also be working outside the configurations allowed for in any manufacturer's guidance, or web-based lens calculator. This introduces an element of uncertainty regarding the size, shape and brightness of the eventual images on stage. The more distortion – the more uncertainty.

One way to reduce the uncertainty is to use accurate scale drawings – in plan and section – of the set-up you are proposing. With an accurate section you can often create something like the drawing here showing idealised and actual screens. With something like this you can return to the world of information from manufacturers' websites with more confidence that the data there will be relevant to your set-up.

Section drawing of a standard projector / screen set-up for a stage design

Viewing this drawing with the centre line of the projection beam horizontal will show the way most projector makers expect their equipment to be used. Many projection designs for the stage however use a set-up more like that shown when the drawing is viewed with this text horizontal and the "actual screen" vertical.

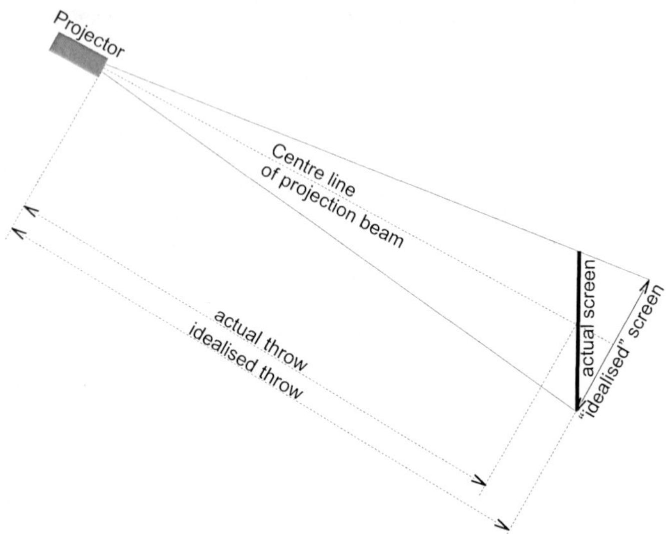

The idealised screen is perpendicular to the centre line of the projection beam – in both the horizontal and vertical planes (the drawing above shows only the vertical plane)

To make manufacturers' beam spread or image size calculations useful in a set-up where the projector is mounted well above the top of the screen, you will normally need to use the idealised throw and screen measurements.
To find the idealised measurements usually requires an accurate section drawing of the projector and screen set-up.
It is often the responsibility of the projection designer to find all the necessary information and to produce these drawings.

Figure 8: Idealised and actual screens

Better still, if you have enough accurate measurements and the relevant software, you may be able to create and use a three dimensional digital model of your venue in which to try out ideas – different configurations of projector and screens, different lens sizes, etc.

In the end though, even the best paper plans or digital models can trick or deceive us, and the only true test is often … to try it out. If at all possible, get your projector(s) and screen(s) into the venue, and give it a go well ahead of the final production rehearsals, and make sure you – and all the other members of the team – are happy with what can (and what cannot) be achieved. Trying out the set-up well ahead of time can help you make changes before it is too late too.

Priorities

Time spent doing drawings and lens calculations can be really important – but a video designer has a lot of other things to do and it can be tempting to "sort it out when we get to the venue". If the final size of the projected image is really important to the production design, then all the time spent working out the throw and which lens to use will not be wasted. The final size of the image usually matters most when the live performers interact directly with the video image – especially if the images are naturalistic. It is usually possible to scale the images up or down on the screen, using software, so if your calculations are a bit off it may not matter too much. Each situation, each design, will present you as video designer with a different set of priorities, but you will always have to do some work to make sure your chosen equipment will do the job you need it to, and help you solve the design problems. A big part of that work will be finding out which is the right lens for your set-up.

Life for a video designer working in live performance is rarely simple. Partly because many of your collaborators will have a limited understanding of your issues, it's easy to find things have changed without your knowledge. "Oh the screen had to move by half a metre. It's not a problem is it?" Or: "We had to hang some lanterns where you planned to hang your projector, but it should be OK because you have zoom lenses", are just two issues I have encountered. It's a good idea to under estimate everything. For example, if your design calculations say you will get a total image size that is just big enough, and big enough is important, change something so that you can be sure it will definitely be big enough.

Screens and Image Brightness and Contrast

If you look at almost any website selling home cinema equipment you will most likely find lots of claims made for the improved contrast ratio and the "gain" of their screens. I'll be looking at screens in terms of ways in which we can integrate them into a stage design in the next chapter, but here I'm going to take a look at how different screen materials work to make the content more or less visible to the audience. We are interested in both intensity, which is related to the amount of light reflected from the screen, and in contrast, which is related to the difference between brightest and darkest areas of the projected image. Contrast is at least as important as overall brightness when it comes to how well the content can be seen on stage.

Screen gain is a measure of how much light is reflected from any given screen or screen material. It is a comparative measure that helps designers assess whether a particular screen material will be brighter or darker than a perfectly flat, matt white screen. This perfect white screen is considered to have a gain of 1. Any screen that reflects less light than this perfect white screen has a gain less than 1 and anything that reflects more has a gain of more than one. Web sites selling home cinema screens use gain as a measure of how bright the image on their screen will be. They will also mention the viewing angle. This is a measure of

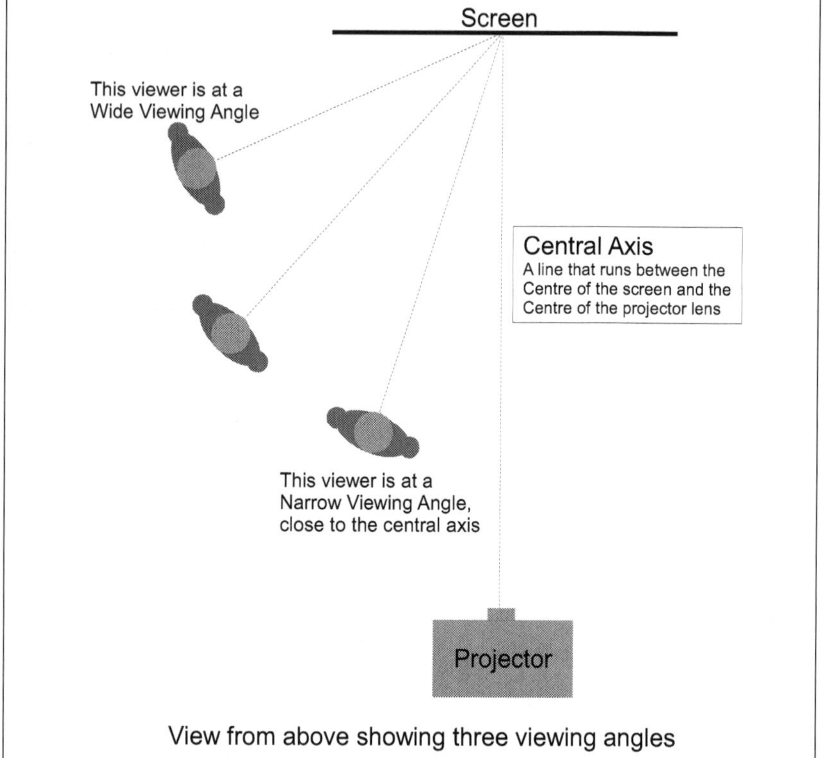

Figure 9: Viewing Angle

how far from the central axis of the screen the image can be seen clearly. The drawback of a high-gain screen is that very often the viewing angle decreases.

> *Remember that while Home Cinema buffs will be using specialist materials and a designated screen, very often, on stage, we will be wanting to make use of the materials of the set to project onto and be our 'screen'. In an attempt to try to avoid confusion, I'll use the term 'cinema screen' to describe something with a regular shape and a frame, and made of a specialist material. For any other surface that we design for our projected content to be displayed on, I'll use just the word 'screen'.*

A cinema screen with a gain of 1.0 reflects the same amount of light as a perfectly flat, perfectly matt white surface. It probably also has a wide viewing angle, meaning that the image can be clearly seen from more or less anywhere that you can see the front of the screen from. The higher the gain of a cinema screen, the brighter the image. However this additional brightness often comes at the price of narrowing the viewing angle – which may mean that the image cannot be seen clearly from all the seats in a wide theatre space, or one with the audience on three sides of a stage.

Screen Colour – white, black or grey?

If we have a white screen on stage, more of the brightness of the projected image will be reflected back for the audience to see – the projected image will be brighter. Also, a white screen will probably not distort colours in the content. *But* other light from the stage will also be reflected from the white screen – particularly the stage lighting.

Anyone who has worked with a white stage set will know how hard it is to get a good black-out. Even with all the theatre lights out, a white set is often still clearly visible to the audience. This is because any stray light is reflected by the white set. A white screen reflects lots of the light from the projector, but it also reflects lots of light from everywhere else – particularly stage light scattered from the floor and other walls of the set, and from the performers and their costumes. All this additional light reflected by the white screen 'dilutes' the light reflected from the projector – that is the image light – so the image does not look as clear, or as strong.

With a white screen, any black or dark sections of the projected image are likely to look grey instead of black. This is partly because protectors don't actually project black, they just project no light to sections of the image that are black. This means that any light that is around to be reflected from the screen will fill the areas of our image we had designed to be black. So for a white screen on a brightly lit stage the black areas of any projected image will not be black. If there is a lot of strongly coloured light around on stage, and objects for that coloured light to scatter off, this will affect how some of the colours in the content are seen, giving a coloured tint to some areas of the image, for example.

So on white screens:

- white parts of the image are bright,
- colourful parts of the image are likely to retain their hue,
- but we will probably struggle to make the black parts of the content read as black.
- A white screen will reflect a lot of the light from the projector,
- and quite probably a lot of other "scattered" light too, so...
- the image can be 'diluted' by this additional reflected light
- and our images can easily appear 'washed out'
- and possibly take on some of the colour of any strongly coloured stage lighting.

We will probably also have problems making the screen disappear too. White elements of any set are often still visible even in a black out – because they reflect any light that is about – even working lights off stage and the emergency exit lights in the auditorium. In some situations that might not be a problem. In others it will be possible to design a simple work-around. But in some situations having such a visible screen on stage all the time will not be an acceptable solution.

If we have a black screen, say we project onto unpleated black stage drapes, our screen will reflect very little scattered stage light, and any black areas of the content will most likely read as black. However a black stage drape probably reflects less than 10% of the light that a white screen would, so our image is going to be – at best, only 10% as bright as the same image projected onto a white screen. In home cinema terms that a gain of 0.1.

Sometimes though, black screen may still turn out to be a good design solution. In many situations black screens will work better than white ones – because while absolute intensity is important, and is not the same thing as perceived intensity. If the content is bright, high-contrast, with lots of white, a black screen could be a better solution. Certainly a black screen is going to be less affected by scattered stage light than a white one. Also any image projected onto a black screen will have less effect on the illumination of the rest of the stage.

Black drapes or curtains however, are unlikely to provide the best solution for any content that depends on subtle variation in colour or contrast for its effectiveness, such as images of gently moving water. Black drape will tend to decrease the perceived contrast in the projected images, partly because the overall intensity has been reduced and we see contrast better at higher rather than lower intensity. You may have noticed that it becomes harder to read a normal book with black printing on white pages under dim lighting? It is harder still to read (for example) black text on a blue background in dim lighting. Understanding these and other features of our visual system becomes more important when you are designing content – but they need to be considered when deciding on the screen material too.

Black drape is not the only black screen however. There are several specialist manufacturers making black screen material for front and rear projection. These specialist materials generally need to be framed into something approaching a cinema screen, but the frame need not be so regular in shape, and the material can be used in many different ways. These materials – while not reflecting as much light as a white screen, can have a gain of as much as 0.5. They also have the advantage of drawing less attention when not being used as a projection surface, because they reflect little scattered light, which can be very useful. Like all specialist materials, custom made black screens can be expensive, especially if you need your screen to be big. This often requires two or more strips of screen material to be joined together to make the large screen area, and this in turn usually requires specialist techniques.

So on black screens:

- the black parts of the image are likely to be properly black,
- but overall the image will not be as bright, in absolute terms.
- High contrast images are likely to read well,
- but lower contrast images are likely to be less successful – maybe disappointing.
- Colours are likely to read reasonably well,
- and less affected by strong colours in the stage lighting.
- The image will have less effect on the rest of the stage lighting.
- Black screens can be useful for high contrast images and large format text,
- are less likely to be affected by the stage lighting,
- and can be made unobtrusive when not in use.

So what about grey screens?

- Compared to a white screen, a grey screen reflects less light form the projector, but also less light from other sources.
- So an image on a grey screen will be less bright than the same image on a white screen, but brighter than an image on a black screen.
- Since a grey screen reflects less of the ambient light from sources other than the projector, the black areas of the image are more likely to remain black, and the image is likely to be clearer.
- A grey screen can give you better contrast than a black screen, though probably not as good as a white screen. However, if there is a lot of ambient light around, a grey screen may be better than a white one, because the black areas of the image will remain darker.
- Black areas of the image will usually appear darker on a grey screen than on a white screen, and white areas of the image will be less likely to be tinted by coloured light from other sources on stage.
- When not in use as a projection screen, a grey screen will 'disappear' better than a white screen – though probably not as well as a black screen.

So in many circumstances, a grey screen will provide a better solution for the production design. It is likely to result in higher contrast images with truer colours than a white screen. It will almost always give better and brighter, higher contrast images than a black screen, and will almost always be less obtrusive when not in use than a white screen.

One thing we didn't mention when discussing white screens was the tendency of the image to dominate the illumination of the space, especially if the screen is large compared to the size of the rest of the set. Bright images projected onto, or emitted from, a large white screen turn the screen into a significant source of soft light on stage. (Soft light is a term used to describe light that does not give defined shadows – in contrast to a hard light that gives crisp, well defined shadows. On a bright sunny day, direct sunlight is a hard light, while the light on an overcast day is soft.) Grey, and even black screens can also become a significant source of soft light, though since they reflect less light that a white screen this is likely to be less of an issue than is sometimes the case with white screens.

Incidental soft light from a video image – projected or emitted – can be an important part of creating the atmosphere on stage – or it can become a real problem. This is another reason to work closely with your lighting designer when creating a video design.

Coloured Screens

Often, the surface used to project images onto will not be a cinema-style screen. As already mentioned, a video design may use the floor or walls of the set as a screen, or even the costume or body of a performer. These screens may have a colour and texture – so how will this alter the way the audience sees the images? The only way to find out for sure is to experiment, but some general guidelines follow.

Rough matt surfaces usually absorb more light than smoother surfaces, leaving less of the light from the projected image to be reflected, resulting in less brightness for the audience. However if the surface is too shiny like a mirror, what ends up being reflected is the projector lamp and not the image at all. Generally an image projected onto a coloured bed-sheet will be brighter than the same image projected onto the same coloured blanket, because a bed-sheet is smoother than a blanket.

The colour of highly colourful screens will tend to be seen in projected images. Areas of the image that are white or nearly white will change colour to the screen colour, unless they are significantly brighter than the general level of brightness – the adaptation level. This means that if you want white in the projected image to be seen as white on stage, you will need a relatively powerful projector or a very dark stage.

Areas of the projected image that are black or nearly black will appear as the colour of the screen – unless there is very little other light around. This means that if you want dark areas of your image to appear black on stage, a powerful projector will help, but what will help more is a dark stage.

Textured surfaces will usually impart texture to the images projected on them. If there is a deep texture this may reduce or even completely obscure fine detail in the image. If the texture is very rough it may distort the images beyond recognition – which may be a bad thing, or may produce an interesting and useful effect.

Surfaces with a lot of pattern – that vary widely in colour or texture across the area used as a screen – will result in images that vary widely in brightness, texture or clarity. Again, while this is usually not desirable, there may be occasions when the effect is useful to the overall production design.

How bright is bright enough?

No absolute answers here I'm afraid. It depends on many different factors. Just as a guide, in an office or classroom you might expect to find an average light level of around 500 lux, while the theatre house lights might produce something like 150 lux in the auditorium.

Generally life becomes very hard for the video designer if she or he can't achieve at least 250 to 300 lux at the screen. If the show is going to be very brightly lit, double this might still not be enough! Naturally there are exception to this rule. If the performance space is small (say less than 100 audience seats), the lighting designer is able to keep scatter from the stage lighting away from the screen, and where other factors are in your favour, 150 lux might be enough. This may seem like a huge range, and it is. But then one of the great things about live performance is the huge range of presentational styles, and scale of productions.

Earlier in this chapter I stated that if something was 10 to 15 times brighter than the average brightness of our field of vision (the adaptation level) it would read as white, and if its 10 to 15 times darker, as black. So in an ideal world, we would be looking to obtain a maximum brightness of the image on the screen around 10 to 15 times brighter than the average brightness on stage. If the average brightness on stage is around 300 to 400 lux (not uncommon for a brightly lit show in a 1000 seat theatre) this means we would be asking for at least 3000 lux at the screen – assuming our screen has a gain of at least 1. Lets say the screen is reasonably large, around 6m (20 feet) wide, which might give us a projection area of around $30m^2$. That means we would need a projector (or more likely projectors) to provide around 90,000 lumens!

Now the brightest projectors regularly being used in London's West End theatres in 2012 are rated at 10,000 lumens, so we would need a lot of expensive projectors to get even close to 3000 lux at our $30m^2$ screen. There has to be another way, and some possibilities follow:

Location of the screen to avoid spill and scatter. By placing the screen above head height, or giving it a frame that keeps stage light away from the projected image for example. More on this in Chapter 3.

Contrast and intensity in the content. Briefly, you can do everything possible to get as much light and contrast into the images as possible. More on this in Chapter 4.

Colour and texture of the rest of the set and costumes. This is another way of reducing, or at least controlling, the spill and scatter reaching the screen by choosing colours and materials that will keep the scattered ambient light to a minimum. A white floor, walls, furniture, or costumes will result in lots of scattered ambient light that will reduce the brightness of the images on screen. Reducing or eliminating white or other highly reflective surfaces, especially near the screens, with help to increase the perceived brightness of the content. You may even consider having the up-stage surfaces of set pieces (the sides the audience don't see) painted matt black to further reduce the amount of stray light on stage.

The effect of stage lighting – spill, bounce and scatter. Traditional theatre lighting often relies on most of the light coming from the auditorium, known as front of house. This can result in a good deal of 'bounce' light hitting screens at the rear of the stage and diluting the perceived brightness of the images. If it is possible to substitute at least some of the front of house lighting for light from the side of stage – known as cross-light or side lighting – and to keep the spill from this light away from the screens and off the stage floor (where it will still create bounce light) the situation can be considerably improved. Of course this is not always possible but close collaboration with the lighting designer will help. The key is to work together to make it possible for the lighting designer to achieve his or her design while making sure as little stage light as possible hits the screen, either directly or indirectly.

So basically, the better everyone involved in the production design understands what makes projected images effective on stage, the more likely it is that the video design will work.

Practical Set-Ups

To end this chapter, some illustrations of practical set-ups are shown on the following pages.

Single Projector, On Axis
mounted at about the same height as the top of the screen on the central horizontal axis of the screen

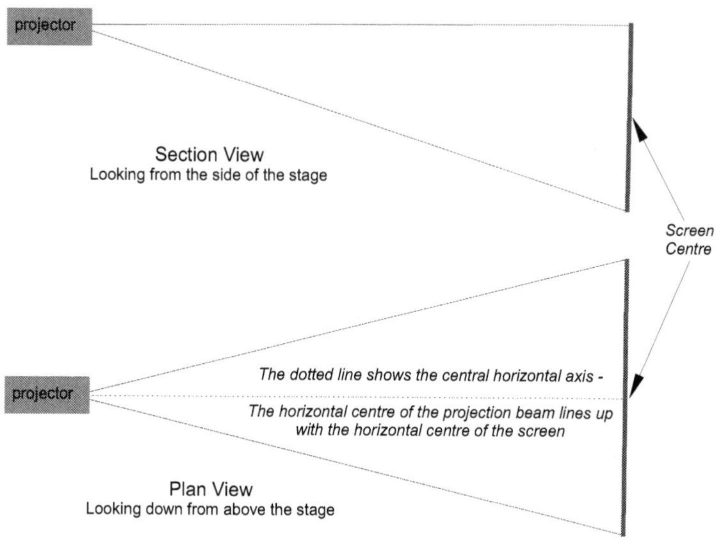

In this simple set-up, any distortion can usually be fixed with "Lens Shift" - accessible from the menu of the projector.

Where ever possible, use Lens Shift rather than Keystone Correction. This is because Lens Shift retains all the pixels while Keystone Correction inevitably looses some.

Double Projectors
"On Axis" and "Off Axis"

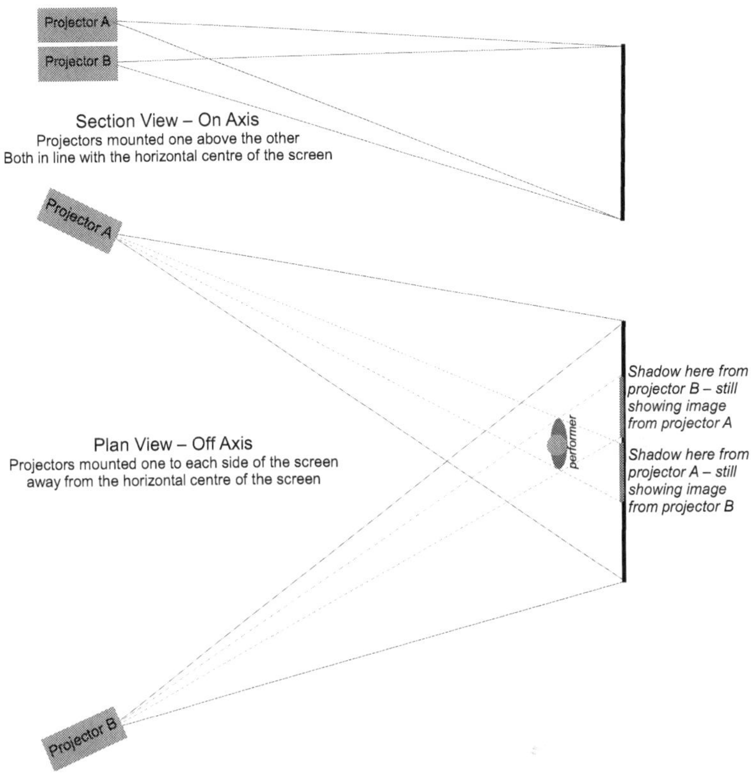

Doubling up projectors, each one showing the same image, is a fairly common way of getting additional brightness without the expense (and fan noise) of much brighter projectors. Lining the two images up can be tricky – projecting a grid can help.
If the two projectors are both "On Axis", then the "line-up" should be achievable using the "lens-shift" and "keystone" commands in the projector set-up menu.

In an "Off-Axis" configuration – so called because the projectors are not in line with the horizontal centre of the screen - the images will need some horizontal keystone correction to compensate for the distortion. This can be achieved in a number of ways (see chapter 4).

The advantage of this "off axis" configuration is that shadows cast by projector A are filled by projector B and vice-versa. This means that even when a performer is quite close to the screen image, the whole image is still visible. This can be a particularly useful set-up for a design involving projected scenic images in a studio space.

Single Projector, On Horizontal Axis mounted some height above the top of the screen

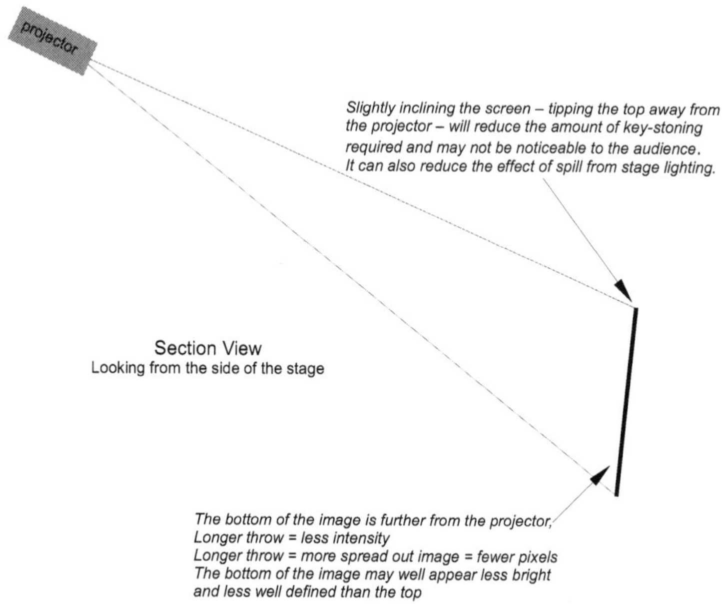

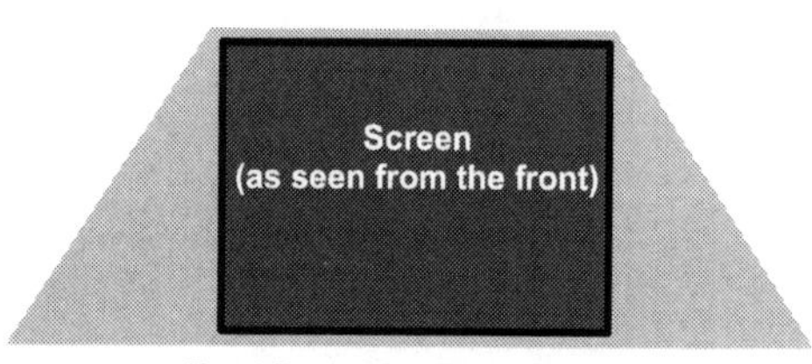

Total Projection Field (in pale grey)

With the projector mounted high above the top of the screen, to achieve a rectangular image on a vertical screen will need a substantial amount of keystone correction. This can be achieved in several ways (see chapter 4), but it is unlikely that the projector's built-in keystone correction will be sufficient on its own.

Back (or rear) Projection

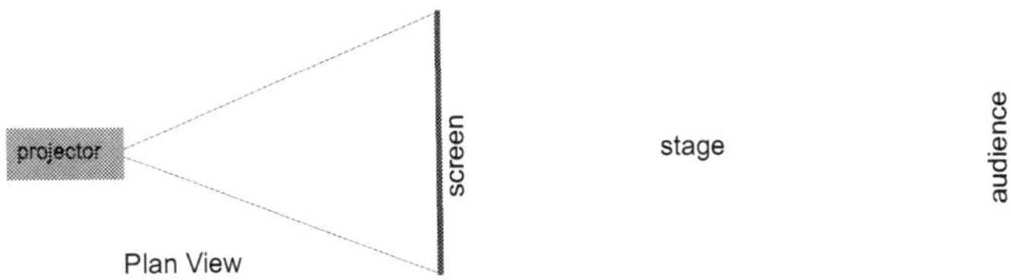

Plan View
Looking down from above the stage

Back Projection usually requires specialist screen material and a wide-angle lens (0.8:1 or wider)

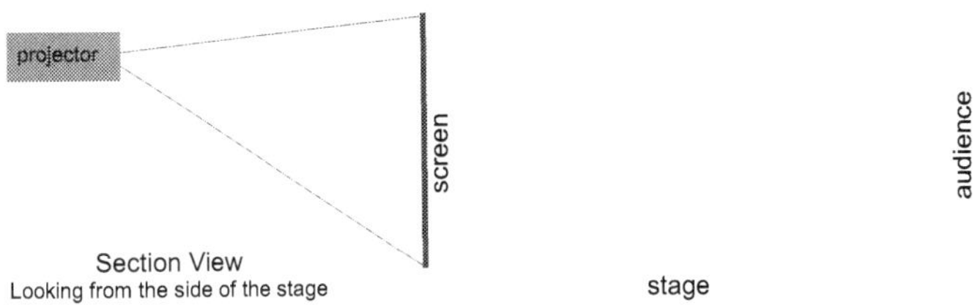

Section View
Looking from the side of the stage

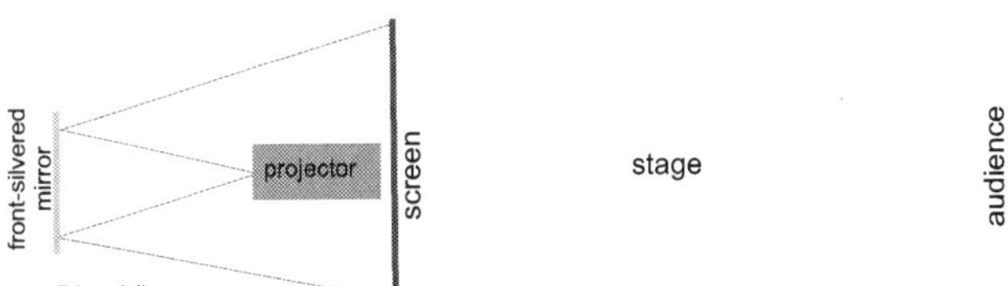

Plan View
Looking down from above the stage

When space is limited a specialist front-silvered mirror can be used to extend the throw of the projector. These can be expensive and difficult to keep clean.

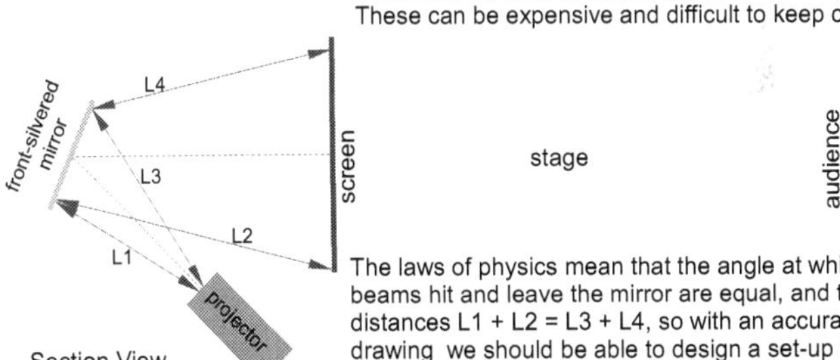

Section View
Looking from the side of the stage

The laws of physics mean that the angle at which the beams hit and leave the mirror are equal, and the throw distances L1 + L2 = L3 + L4, so with an accurate drawing we should be able to design a set-up that works. However, experience shows that working with mirrors is fraught with difficulty and usually best avoided

3 SCREENS AND SET DESIGN

Once you have decided to use video as part of a stage design, the next big aesthetic decision is "where will the images be on stage?" In other words, what will 'the screen' look like? For the moment, let's focus on video projection, rather than making use of display screens.

Perhaps the most important consideration is what do you want the whole stage picture to look like? What do you want the audience to see on stage? Ideally, the choice of projector and lens should come after decisions about size, shape and placement of screens have been made. That said, it should be clear now from chapter 2 that how bright the projector is and what lenses you have available will have an impact on the success of final design too.

Too often this is the point where technical considerations are allowed to dictate design – "the projector has to go here, so the image will be there" or "this is the size of screen we have, and this is where we hang it, so that is where it will be". Though there may be times when you have no alternative, this attitude rarely results in good production design solutions.

Despite its highly technical nature, the successful integration of video projection into stage design needs to driven at least as much by aesthetic considerations as by technical ones. Sure, any stage design has to be practical, but it also has to look right.

From Painted Backcloths to Video – a short diversion

For many centuries, as far as we can tell, the style of acting on the English speaking stage was what we would now probably call "over the top". It was certainly quite different from the much more naturalistic-looking acting style to be seen on most of today's stages. In the pre-electric age, stage lighting for the actors largely consisted of footlights from below the actor's face - which created unnatural shadows. The actors would then use heavy make-up to counter these unnatural shadows. Most of the stage lighting was used to light the 'settings' - usually large flown back-cloths and stage-flats - often cleverly painted to appear three dimensional to the audience. The main actors would tend to stand down stage centre, near the footlights and the audience. In any case they could not stand too close to the 'settings' without casting shadows on the flat painted scenery - which would of course break the illusion of reality for the audience.

No doubt all of this was a factor in making the grandiose acting style necessary. When commentators of the time did mention light on stage, it was usually in relation to some fantastical scenic transformation.

Many factors contributed to the emergence of a more natural acting style on the stage, but the change in style was certainly helped by the availability of better lighting equipment. Better gas lighting, and then electric lighting, meant actors could be seen clearly over more of the stage, without the distortions previously caused by the over-dominant footlights.

Slowly, from the final decades of the 19th Century, as more natural styles of acting on stage became the norm, theatre makers began to realise that the flat painted scenery they had been used to using no longer worked for the audience. At about this time, two new job-titles began to be seen in theatre, the 'director' and 'the set designer'. One of the main aims of many of these new directors and set designers was to create more believable worlds for the actors to perform in on stage.

Two-dimensional cut cloths and painted backdrops did not belong in the same world as these new more 'natural' performance styles. It is likely that the new art form of cinema made theatre-makers raise their game too. The cinema audience was beginning to see something like a heightened version of 'real life' on cinema screens, and many expected the same on stage. They were no longer content to watch grotesquely made-up actors do their stuff in front of what were clearly painted pieces of cloth 'pretending' to be walls or woodland.

In the early decades of the 20th Century sets became increasingly more solid and three-dimensional, with steps and levels becoming common. Typical examples of this new realistic/naturalistic style in theatre are the drawing-room sets for what became know as "the well-made play". At last the actors had substantial seeming walls and doors, with a 'real' fireplace and windows instead of painted ones.

Just as in the fine art movements of the early 20th Century, the new styles were not all about realistic representation. More radical theatre makers like Adolph Appia and Edward Gordon Craig designed abstract settings with multiple levels linked by steps, or stage spaces defined by large three-dimensional abstract shapes. Followers of these ideas were also interested in creating a unified world for the performer to inhabit on stage. The settings contrasted with the naturalistic drawing room sets, but they too gave the performers the opportunity to move freely throughout a believably three-dimensional stage world.

So what has this to do with video projection? Well as it turns out, quite a lot.

Without meaning to, some stage designs that use a lot of video projection force the actors to the front of the stage - to stop them casting shadows on the projected set, and fail in the attempt to convince the audience that the actors and the projected set are in the same place. What starts off as a good video-based design idea sometimes turns into a show where the actors are all too obviously playing in front of a cinema screen. When this happens, the world of the actors and the world represented on the cinema screen remain separate. The audience find it hard to "see" the actors as part of the projected world, or 'believe' in that world - just as their great grandparents found it hard to believe in the world of grotesquely made-up actors performing in front of painted cloths.

Documentary Content – News-Screens

There may of course be times when it is OK for the projected images to represent a quite different world to that of the live actors. One example of this is a theatrical device sometimes referred to as the 'news-screen'. This is often used for scene titles, locations and time. The news-screen can also be used for documentary material that gives an additional context to the performance. This is a design idea that many influential theatre makers used in the first half of the 20th Century. The German theatre maker Erwin Picator made use of something like this in his work with Bertolt Brecht. After World War II, on the British stage, companies such as 7:84 Theatre (founded by John McGrath in the 1970s) and Theatre Workshop (led by Joan Littlewood from 1945 through to the late 1970s) both made use of projected still and moving images to deliver additional documentary information to the audience. One of the best know shows from Littlewood's Theatre Workshop is *Oh! What a Lovely War*, which made extensive use of projected documentary material in the form of newspaper headlines and graphic black and white photographs. (The original production predates affordable video projection. Instead they used photographic slides and specialist scenic projectors.)

Shows such as the Royal Court's 2009 production of Lucy Prebble's play *ENRON* are a continuation of the tradition of delivering documentary information as projected content. Like *Oh! What a Lovely War*, *ENRON* used projection for other things too, but some of the contextual information that helped the audience make sense of what was going on in the play was projected.

Most stage and video designers seem to prefer their 'news-screen' to be outside the world of the actors. Most often, the content, text or pictures, is projected onto an area above the actors' heads. This is very often a technically simple solution, with at least a couple of big advantages.

First, if your main screen is above the heads of the actors, the stage lighting, both direct light for the actors and scattered bounce light, can usually be kept away from the screen without too much difficulty. This should mean brighter projected content with better contrast.

Second, since there is little possibility of an actor walking in front of a raised screen, you can usually mount the projector in line with the screen – just as the manufacturer intended. This means you probably won't need to apply any external key-stone correction to the images, which in turn will often significantly simplify both content creation and your playback system. No external keystone correction also means more useful pixels in your image, brighter images with better resolution, and the web-based guides to lenses are more likely to work for you.

If you want to present documentary footage and other contextualising information alongside the regular action of your piece – creating a screen above the actors, or otherwise outside the regular performance area makes a lot of sense. Of course if you go too far away from the regular action the attention of the audience may be diverted away from the live actors. The best solutions usually involve separating the images from the action but still keeping them within the central field of view of at least most of the audience.

In the production photograph from *Oliver's Army* opposite, a compilation of footage pieced together largely from clips posted on YouTube, was projected onto the top part of the back wall of the set. The content was from contemporary war zones and it served as a moving visual accompaniment to the song being sung in front of it. (The quality of the images was not great – most had been captured by soldiers in the field using their mobile phones, and the video designer had a lot of work to do to make the sequence acceptable. (There is some more about this in Chapter 4.)

The back wall of the set had lightly dappled texture painted over a pale background. This provided a reasonably reflective surface for the projections, while being a suitably neutral background for scenes without projection. Another way of saying this is, it provided a good screen area without shouting "I'm a screen" when it wasn't being used as that. The dappled texture did come through some of the darker projections – as you can probably see from the photograph. This did make some of the originally proposed content less effective. For this and other reasons, we decided to avoid content with a lot of fine detail, such as running water for example. You can also see how the strong blue colour of the some of the stage lighting bleeds through into the projected images. In this case the two sources of light – the stage lanterns and the projectors – work well

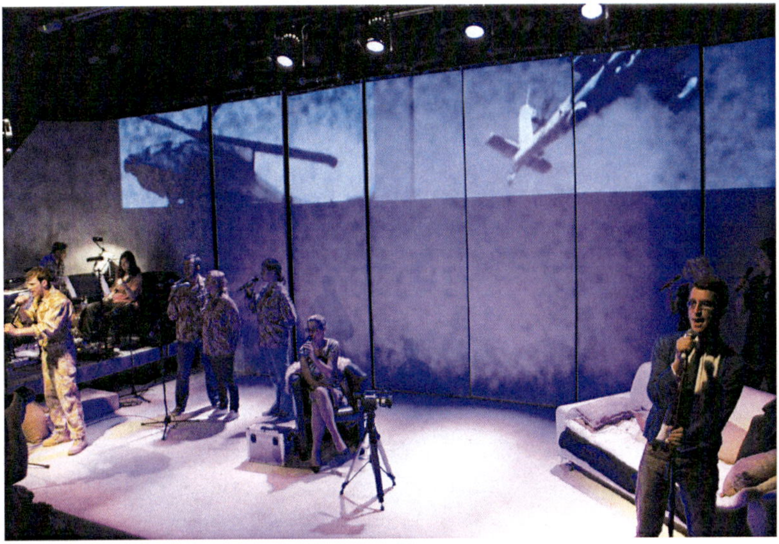

Oliver's Army, a studio musical staged at Central School in 2009.

Projected content serves to comment on the song they are singing on stage. The content is projected above head height, avoiding any chance of performer shadows. The dominant blue colour in the stage lighting bleeds through into the images, in this case helping to make the content more part of the world of the backing singers.

together, helping to unify the two worlds of the actors and the projection. When this happens it a rarely an accident and much more often an example of the video designer and the lighting designer working together for the benefit of the overall production design.

You don't have to use news-screens outside the regular performance area for documentary content. Below is a production photograph from The Edge, a piece of devised theatre looking at issues around how global warming is effecting communities around the world. At this point in the show, an animated collage of the names of places already threatened by rising sea-levels was projected over the cast during a choreographed scene-change. This was a very effective method of both conveying contextual information to the audience and maintaining the tension of the piece through an intricate scene change. The animation of the place-names – each of which moved around the whole-stage 'screen' – brought different names to areas of the stage that were good or poor 'screens'. Good screens included light coloured clothing or drapes, and flat areas of the back wall. Poor screens included dark clothing where brightness was reduced, and cluttered areas of stage where the image was distorted. When a place-name was on a good screen area, it became more legible for the audience. Otherwise it became part of a texture of jumbled letters. Place names popped out as they 'found' good screens, while places where a few names gathered together as part of the animation revealed the performers taking part in the transition. The animation also managed to convey a feeling of being overwhelmed, which linked to one of the play's themes, that of communities being overwhelmed by rising sea levels. This was a very effective piece production design, making creative use of video projection.

Projected Scenery and Screens

Let's return to using screens for projecting images that aim to evoke the particularities of a place – a space or a room; what we might call traditional scenic projections or projected scenery. What can be done to make this kind of projection effective and to stop it resulting in the

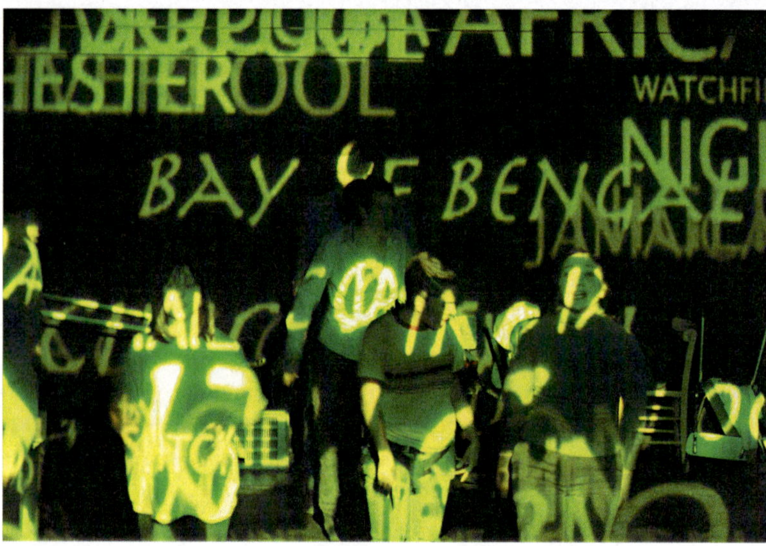

A scene from The Edge, directed by Douglas Rintoul and devised with students from Central School.

Projected place names move about the whole stage area. At in some places the words a readable in others they create texture, in others the illuminate performers or objects.

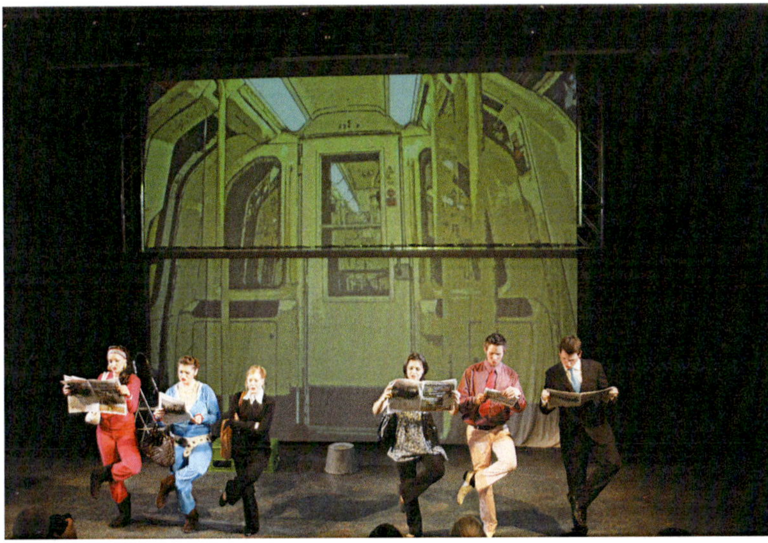

A scene from It Must Be Madness. Performers acting as commuters mime sitting on a train.

Even though the supporting projection is not what we would see behind people really sitting on a London Tube, it provides a suitable visual clue to support the mime, helping the audience to 'get' the gag.

'performing in front of a cinema screen' look?

Often the best approach is to get the whole creative team – all the designers as well as the director and writer, as available – to answer a few questions together, right at the start of the process.

Question One: What do we need these images to do for the production?

For me, this has to be the first question. In this section, part of the answer has already been decided – the images will indicate to the audience the location of each scene, and quite probably the time and atmosphere too. So further questions such as "how many locations/times of day/ atmospheres?" come next. It can also be important to discuss if there is a particular part of the story that will be told through projection – a flash-back or road-trip for example.

There are often many other questions that follow directly on from a discussion about what the images need to do for the production. One line of discussion might be "how important is it that all the audience know where we are all the time?" and "how much does the script tell them?" It's sometimes worth reflecting that Shakespeare's company evoked multiple locations, times of day and atmospheres largely through the words spoken by the actors. Times have changed a lot and with them audience expectations, but you may wish to challenge yourself as a designer or director by asking "am I doing this or that simply because I can and not because the production needs it?"

Question Two: Will you be using projected scenery throughout the piece?

If yes – one of the next questions is "how do the actors interact with this scenery?" Remember from chapter 1 – they can't walk up a purely projected staircase or climb through a projected window. Neither can they get too close to a front projection screen without casting their shadow onto it and taking some of the image onto their body and costume. The production design for *Re-Orientations* pictured in chapter 1 is a good example of a 'full time' screen. It is far enough away from the main acting area to cause few problems.

If no – then you need to think about what 'the screen' will look like when it's not being projected on. Often the simplest solution to this issue is to remove the screen. If you have the facility, maybe the screen can be flown out, that is raised into the space above the stage where it is hidden from the audience. It may be more practical to mount the screen on a movable scenic truck, and have that pushed or winched off stage – again, out of sight of the audience. Failing that, the screen could be dismantled after use – after all, it could be a simple as a bed-sheet between two poles, or a large framed canvas on an easel.

If none of these solutions suit, then the object that becomes the screen will need to have another scenographic function – another reason to be on stage – when it's not in use as a screen. This might be the back wall of the set for *Oliver's Army* pictured above, or the moving desks with their flip-up tops from *Consumed*, pictured later in this chapter. It will probably work best if what was the screen can dissolve seamlessly into the rest of the set.

Question Three: How 'real' do you want the projected scenery to appear?

The level or type of reality decided upon will frequently help to determine the size and location of the screen or screens and the style of the images projected onto them. The answers to this question are closely linked to discussions that arise from question one. Simply put, if the projected images need to be at the same scale as the performers, that will go a long way to determining the size and location of the screens, and the style of the content. Similarly, if the images need to dominate the performers, to appear to be from a giant world say, this will inform decisions about screens and content.

For some productions, the images provide strong visual clues to set-up a scene, but quickly become much less important as the focus of audience attention moves to the performers. This could mean that images must have an immediate or broad sense of 'real' and that detail is less important. For other productions however the projected images remain an important focus of audience attention throughout each scene. Here 'real' down to a high level of detail is likely to be important as the audience will focus on the images for longer. This could affect not only the choice of images and the resolution of the projection system, but also the position and quality of the screen – since all of these factors will have an impact of the quality of the final images on stage.

Look back to the two pictures from *Bad Girls The Musical* in chapter 1. The production design created a believably real prison hall on stage using projection onto an essentially flat up-stage screen. To achieve this scale of effect needs a lot of technical resources and creative skill – but most importantly everybody in the creative team needs to agree early on that this is what they are going for.

With any stage design it can be difficult to know where to start. However, if your production team can discuss these three big questions, and agree a general approach to the answers, at least you have somewhere to begin. After successfully addressing these big three questions, you will hopefully know where the screens need to be on stage, and how big they need to be. This will then give you some idea about what other practical problems you will need to solve, particularly where the projector(s) need(s) to be and the extent to which stage lighting is likely to have an effect of the perceived brightness of the image.

Believably Real? (another Brief Diversion)

What do we mean by 'real' on stage? The stage is, after all, a place for make-believe, play and fantasy. While we are watching the performance we buy into a lot of make-believe and pretence. For example, that the people on stage have real lives that continue outside the theatre rather than that they are characters played by actors; that the words they speak are spontaneous rather than written and rehearsed; and that the world we see on stage is as real as the one we live in every day - rather than not continuing beyond the walls of the theatre. We often do the same when watching a film or TV drama, or even when reading a novel. Theorists refer to the phenomenon as "the willing suspension of disbelief".

The theatre stage seems to be able to help the audience suspend disbelief to a far greater extent than most film or TV. Compare for example the film and the stage production of Michael Morpurgo's book War Horse. In the highly successful stage production - which began at the National Theatre in London - the audience allow themselves to 'believe' in the reality of the full-size puppet horses, even though they can clearly see the three operators inside each one. In Stephen Spielberg's film of War Horse, the horses are real horses. No one would consider using the stage horse puppets in a realistic film. The particular kind of suspension of disbelief that is makes it possible for an audience to believe in puppets on stage, is not really possible on screen. This has implications for designing video for the stage.

As a theatre audience, we are used to accepting collectively that most things we see on stage have a different kind of reality to the things we see in our everyday world. Flip back to the picture of three doors in chapter 1. None of them would be mistaken for a door and door fame from the everyday off-stage world. Yet each within its own stage set becomes an acceptable part of the world of that show.

In the same way, a traditional drawing room stage set representing a room in an upper middle-class house in a Scandinavian town in the late 19th Century is actually unlike any real everyday world room. To start with, it has a missing fourth wall, the one that the audience watch the action through. It probably also has other things that no everyday world room has too, and as the audience we know that what we can see is a stage set. Yet if the play is working for us, for the time we are in the theatre we believe that this room on stage is part of a house, which exists in its own world, as home to some of the people we are about to see, being played by actors.

This room on stage will have doors to other, imagined, rooms that we as audience can believe to be real - at least we do for the time that the performance asks us to - if the performance is good enough to hold our attention. All that is required for most audiences to maintain the 'willing suspension of their disbelief' is that the world presented on stage is believable enough and consistent. Most of the time the set designer and others will work hard to make sure nothing obviously challenges or disrupts the audience's 'suspension of disbelief'. For example the stage-set doors should open to reveal a space that appears to continue the world of the stage-set, and not onto the theatre back-stage.

Believably real on stage is often a very different thing to believably real in our everyday world. So its important to know what you as designer or director mean when you talk about your projected scenery being believably real? Do you mean, as if the things in the images you are projecting - the buildings, landscapes or whatever - were actually there? This is very difficult to achieve, and may be self-defeating. Very few adult audience members will believe you really have your actors performing in front of (say) the Taj Mahal or St Paul's Cathedral - they know that these buildings are 1) too big to fit on stage, and 2) exist somewhere else. But if you set up the situation in a way that allows the audience to suspend their disbelief then they may well go with you (even if your actors can't get too near the buildings without disrupting the image...). Avoiding the use of well-known landmark buildings and features can help maintain the belief that the projected objects are real - I dare say many of the audience for Bad Girls were happy to believe there was a real prison hall set on stage when in fact there was only a flat screen with an image projected onto it.

Screens that are always screens

If you are working on a design in which the screens will always be filled with a projected image, or where they will be flown out or removed from the stage in some other way when not in use as a screen, you can focus on making it the best screen it can be. Referring back to the section on screen material and brightness in chapter 2, this may well mean a grey screen, stretched tight to give a smooth surface. If you can afford it (or justify it to whoever holds the production budget) you might think about getting hold of some specialist screen material with a good gain. If that's not an option, experiment with what you have to hand – a clean bed-sheet for example, can work well. For a larger screen, calico and various grades of canvas can be purchased from specialist suppliers, who are likely to be able to supply cloth up to 2m wide, and sometimes wider. This can avoid or at least reduce the need for joins – which will show up as lines on the screen and probably in the images too. If you do have to make a large screen (over 2m wide for example) you will probably need to get a skilled machinist to join the panels together as neatly as possible. (Of course you could always incorporate the panelled nature of the screen into the design – making a virtue of necessity.)

To get a material screen as smooth and flat as possible it will usually be necessary to stretch it by attaching the material to a rigid frame. If you intend to use back projection, this frame will need to be made without any cross members – which can be limiting. Larger commercial shows often use a frame made from aluminium trussing of the kind used to support

5 x 4 Screen on a Truss Frame

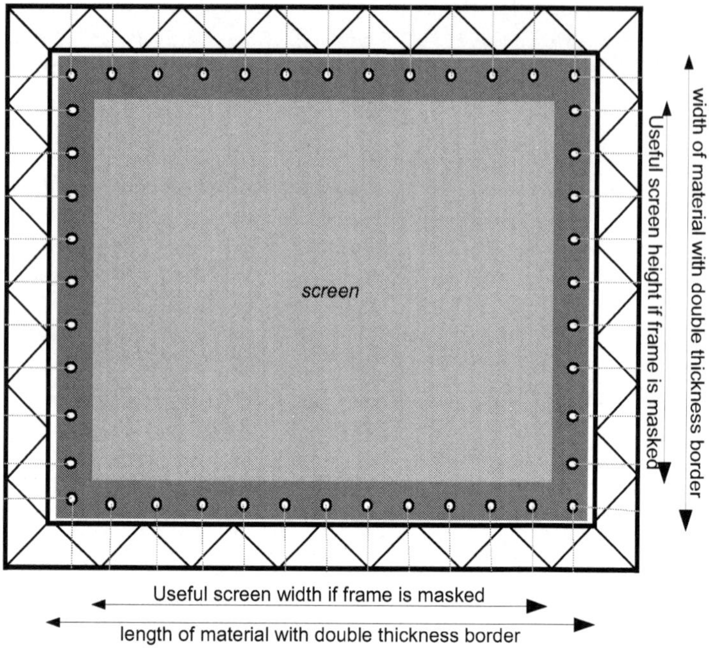

Truss Frame shown in Black
Lacing or Bungee cords shown in Light Grey

With appropriate material, this style of screen is suitable for front or rear projection

If the truss frame is not in keeping with the aesthetic of the production design it can be masked with flats or stage drapes

the lighting above touring concert stages and at music festivals. If your design can accommodate this style of frame for your screen, they can often be hired from a local lighting or AV supplier. Trussing frames for screens can be useful for larger screens even if they are not going to be used for back projection, as they can work out cheaper and easier to use than the usual alternative, constructing a timber frame.

Warning: screen frames made of trussing come in standard sizes and small adjustments are not possible since the trussing is made in standard lengths. Get in touch with the hire company early on to make sure that what they are able to offer will fit both your screen and the rest of the production design.

To make attaching the screen to the trussing frame neat and simple it is usual to insert eyelets at regular intervals all around the screen material – say between 15cm and 25cm – 6" to 9". You will need to make sure you have an eyelet in each corner, then evenly space out the rest. You will usually need to hem the screen material all round to create a double thickness of material in which to mount the eyelets.

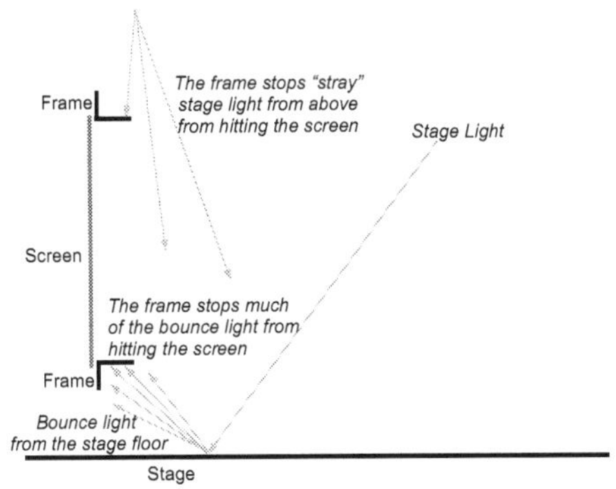

Section View
From the side of stage
Frame components at right angles to the screen can get rid of some of the stage light from hitting the screen.

If you are buying a screen made from specialist screen material you need to ask for all this to be done by the suppler. In any case, make sure you include the area lost to these hems (and joins) when you specify the size of the material for your screen.

Once you have eyelets round your screen you can lace it to the trussing frame with a suitable lengths of strong cord or lightweight rope, or use short bungee cords. Make sure that the screen sits centrally to the frame and that the tension is roughly the same on all sides of the screen.

If you are using a timber frame – perhaps an old stage-flat or something custom built – you can simply staple the screen material onto the wooden frame. Again this needs to be done with some care to make sure the material is central to the frame and that the tension is more or less the same at every point. Too much tension may result in the frame buckling or the material tearing. There are a number of text books and websites that can give good practical advice on covering a timber frame with calico or canvas – it is more or less the same as making an old-school canvas stage-flat after all.

If the stage screen is always a screen, it is possible to design into the frame something that will help to reduce the impact of direct and bounced stage lighting. This could be a solid component of the frame that is perpendicular to the screen itself.

Cyclorama Cloths

Technically a cyclorama is a solid wall at the back of the stage, but the usage has become much more general and now the word most often means a large white or grey screen, usually flown on the theatre flying system, at the back of the stage set – or up stage. The cyclorama forms the background for the whole setting, running the whole width and height of the stage, or at least as wide and as high as the audience can see.

Larger professionally made screens for use on stage are often referred to as 'the cyc' (short for cyclorama) or BP (BP stands for back projection, even when they are projected on from the front). These screens are usually made from durable plastics, and should appear seamless. Generally they have eyelets at the top for use with lengths of cloth tape to attach the screen to a fly-bar, pipe or truss. This can then be flown out to the correct height. There is usually a pocket in the bottom of the screen to take a scaffolding bar. This helps to keep the screen stretched taut, at least from top to bottom. It is often necessary to stretch the screen from side to side, and some screens have eyelets up the sides to help. If that is not the case, specialist cloth stretchers will be needed.

A white or light-grey cyclorama is often a feature of large scale set design especially for musical theatre, dance and opera. Traditionally it is there to represent the sky, or a distant horizon, and it is the responsibility of the lighting designer to use her skills to make it do just that. More recently though, cycs have become as much the province of the video designer as the lighting designer. Large scale projection onto a cyc can be very effective, but needs to be planned in just the same way that the use of any other video projection screen would be planned. We have already discussed how a large screen needs a lot of intensity to make the image bright enough for the audience. Although more powerful projectors will help, screen material with a good gain will help at least as much. It can be hard to decide between spending extra money on brighter projectors or a better screen in these circumstances. A video designer should give careful consideration to both options. As we have already commented, a good screen is better for showing fine texture in content such as water ripples.

Other factors that help to make a cyc 'good' include no visible seams, folds creases or ripples. Visible seams in a screen can undermine the power of big scenic images such as landscapes or skies – making them not quite believable enough. Set against that, in some situations and for some styles of production a cyclorama made from bed-sheets will be good enough – you will need to decide.

Ideally, the cyclorama should be set as far up-stage (that is away

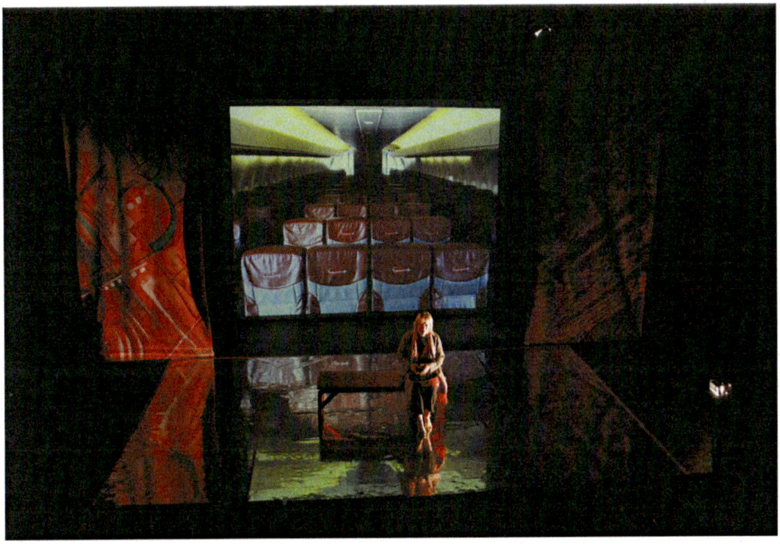

Re-Orientations, produced at the Soho Theatre by Border Crossings,

Extensive use was made of a large up-stage screen, in the same position that a traditional cyclorama might hang. However this cyc was a full time projection screen.

from the front edge of stage) as possible. This will reduce the chance of performers getting in the way of the projected image, and generally reduce the amount of stray stage light hitting the screen and diluting the projected image.

Images projected onto a cyclorama will generally fill the whole of the background to the stage action, something else that you will need to take into account as you plan your design.

Brick-Wall Cyc

Of course you may be able to make use of some existing element of the set or a part of the theatre space. If the set, or your stage, has a suitable back wall, the production design team could decide to paint this in a suitable way and just use part or all of it as the screen. The back wall of the stage space is likely to be painted matt black – which is not the best surface for a screen. However I have seen several productions that make very effective use of a black brick back wall as a projection surface – usually with high-contrast images and bold text.

Screens that disappear

If the production design does not want to use projection throughout the piece, you will not want to call attention to the screen, as a screen, when it's not in use. There are a number of options when this is the case. The illustration from *Oliver's Army* shows how it is possible to use the back wall of the set, painted a suitably light colour and only slightly textured, as a surface to project onto. The wall was not a dedicated screen, but performed the function of a screen none the less. This approach constrains the design of the back wall, not only its colour and texture but also its width, height and orientation. For *Oliver's Army*, the set back wall was parallel to the front edge of stage for the whole width of the performance area, almost as high as the studio space, and flat. There will be many occasions where this physical set-up is either not possible or not desirable, but where it is it can be made to work for the production design, and is well worth pursuing. A long flat back wall provides no obvious entrances. Doors would need

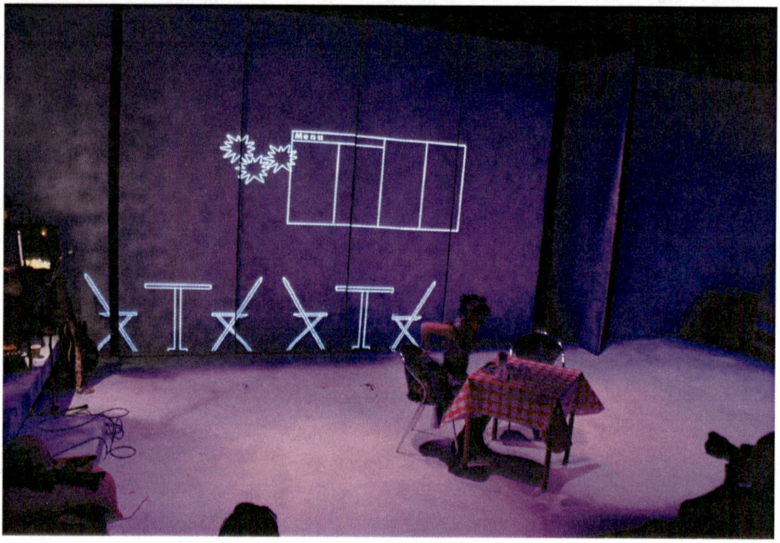

Another shot from Oliver's Army

Towards the end of a scene change into The Café, the projected outline of a menu board and some tables and chairs help to tell us where we are, even before the "real" table and chairs are set. The projection fades in the first 30 seconds of the scene to help pull the focus down to the "real" table down stage centre.

You can also see an entrance created by leaving the stage left panel in the back wall perpendicular to the rest.

frames and that would create disruption in the screen images that could interfere with the willing suspension of disbelief. (Imagine a military helicopter hovering over a domestic doorway? Although that is an image that might work well in another production, it would have anchored the number shown earlier in this chapter in a domestic environment that would have undermined it and reduced its power.) Instead of inserting doors and door frames the wall was made from five panels that each rotated about their vertical centres to create a range of openings.

There was no attempt at naturalistic recreation of rooms or other spaces by projection in this design. As you can see from the picture above, simple line drawings evoked rather than represented a particular space during the scene change then disappeared as the lights came up on the new scene.

The Edge used a quite different approach. The beams of the main projector for this production covered the whole stage. At various points during the piece large sheets of material, including opaque plastic and bed linen, were hoisted up on strings and ropes to provide screen surfaces. In the picture below, the performer is presenting using an improvised screen.

These improvised screens were chosen by experiment in the rehearsal room – the design team rigged up pulleys and provided various materials on which to try out ideas using a simple projector and lap-top set-up. Since all the chosen 'screens' were objects with another primary function they didn't really stand out as 'screens in waiting' or 'screens that have been used' in the way a conventional screen might do in a more conventional piece. Also, the period of experimentation in the rehearsal room provided a time to discover through play, away from the high pressure environment of a technical rehearsal, and for everyone to gain a good understanding of what could (and what could not) be achieved.

In *The Edge*, some scenes made use of full stage projection. In these scenes, there was some extent to which the impact of the images was randomised – it depended on un-choreographed movements as well as the staged placement of objects and people, and unmapped or untimed image placement, as well as some synchronised effects. With such a wide field of view for the audience too (the studio this show played in kept the audience very close to the performance area) at times the audience had to choose what part of the stage picture to focus on. Just as at some sports events it is likely that no two audience members got exactly the same impression from these scenes. While such an approach will not be to everyone's taste, it can provide some of the best examples of the fully integrated use of video as part of live performance.

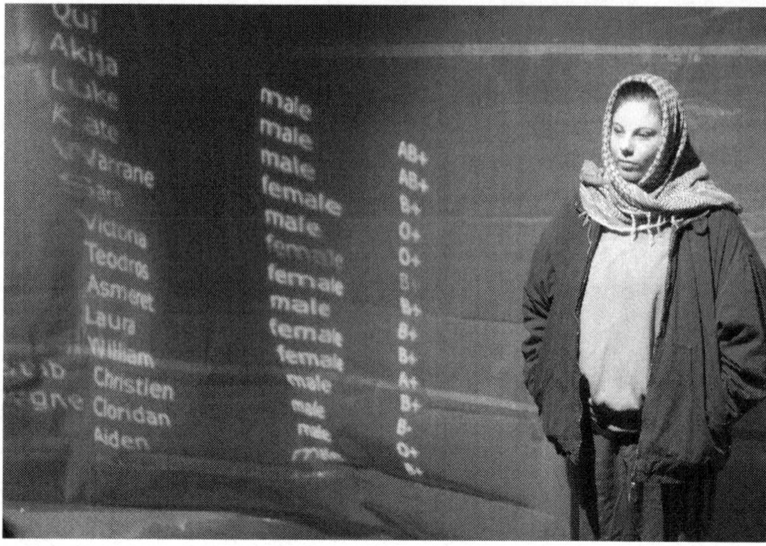

The Edge

The character in the photograph is delivering training for swimmers. The details of the information projected onto the improvised screen are not important for to the plot, and the fact that the words are not always legible helps to keep the audience focus on the performer

Video Projection Mapping

In several of the productions mentioned already, the beam of the projection system (or the **projection field**) covers the whole stage, effectively treating the whole set as a single screen. Content is then placed within projection field – onto what we might usefully call sub-screens – to appear on the selected element or elements of the set. This is called video mapping.

To cover a large area – a big set for example – is sometimes necessary to use more than one projector to achieve the desired brightness. When this is the case, the beams of the projectors are merged together. In most well resourced professional productions mapping and merging is achieved using a media server. Media servers usually consist of specialised software running on high-end, often modified, computers. They are expensive to buy or hire, and require specialist knowledge to make the investment worthwhile. The learning curve associated with professional media servers can be steep and it is likely to take some time for even the most adept first-time user to learn the ins and outs of media server software. Enter the video programmer, often a highly paid specialist who is able to make the magic happen. Detailed video programming for media servers is beyond the scope of this book, however there are alternatives to using media servers that we will look at a little later.

Mapping content onto selected parts of the set (or anything else for that matter) starts with a couple of basic tasks. Once the projector (or projection system) has been set up to cover the whole of our target area, we need to define the part of the beam that is hitting our chosen set element. This is often done by projecting a numbered grid over the whole target area and noting which sections of the grid correspond to each of the elements we want to use as a sub-screen. This allows the video programmer to create a mask, that makes sure projected light only hits the parts of the target area (e.g. our set) we have defined as sub-screens, and is masked from the areas we don't want to see the content on. There can be one mask for the whole show or multiple masks used at different times during the piece to map content onto different elements.

Once the mask or masks are made, we need to define the type and amount of predistortion that the content will need to appear correctly on

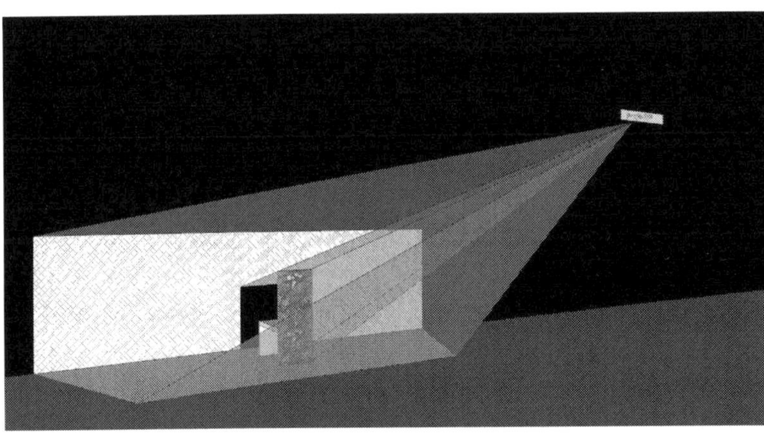

Schematic of projection mapping on Consumed.

The field of the single projector covers the whole stage (the area shown hatched in grey here). Content (a picture of grass and flowers here) is mapped onto the particular area of the field that will hit the desk/screen. It is also pre-distorted to correct for keystoning.

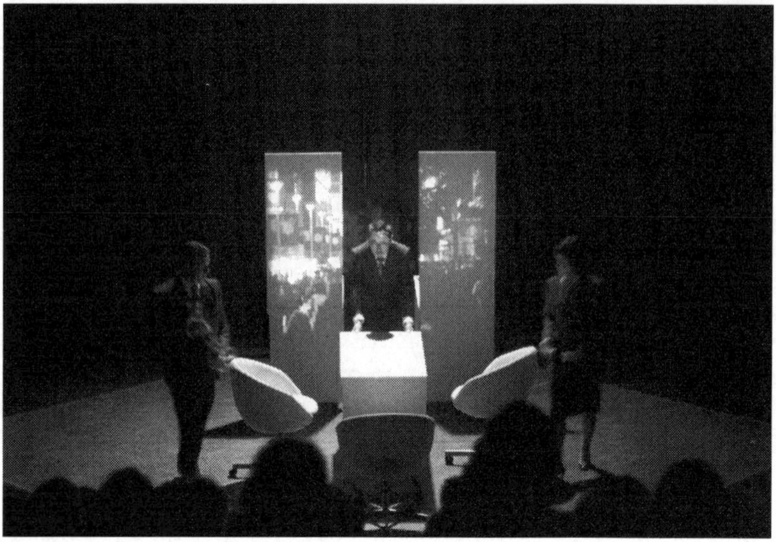

Video mapping for Consumed

The production design made use of video mapping to project content onto movable set elements – white desks on castors with flip-up tops. This video design was accomplished largely with Qlab software running on a Mac Laptop.

each sub-screen. This might be simple keystone correction – something we have mentioned already. If the element is not flat or/and perpendicular to the projection beam, the predistortion will be more complex. With the right video programming tools it is possible to make the content appear to be 'wrapped' around the element.

In the language of one of the leading media server programmes, this process of making the mask and defining the predistortion is known as 'making the mix'. A particular production or presentation may have one mix used throughout, or may use several mixes to match changing configurations of set elements.

The technology behind the kind of complex video mapping used in large scale events is very expensive, and well beyond the scope of this book. There are many examples of the creative use of video mapping on the internet, including some spectacular projections onto the Sydney Opera House and Buckingham Palace in London.

On a smaller scale, it is perfectly possible to 'map' content onto essentially flat mobile scenic elements using a single projector and software running from a reasonably well specified laptop computer. This is essentially the set up used to project a range of content in *Consumed*, a production I helped to design to tour studio theatres for the theatre company Border Crossings. The 'screens' were three IKEA desks modified to take castors so they could be pushed around stage. They also had a second top surface, hinged at one end, that could be raised by the actors to turn each desk into a tall narrow projection surface. In the rehearsal space, the director, design team and the performers devised 'landscapes' of raised and lowered tables for each scene. These where achieved through precise choreography. Video designer Dori Deng then used software running on a Mac lap-top to 'map' content to the appropriate positions on the scenic landscapes for each scene. As with *The Edge* above, the process was made possible by having the projector and other technical equipment in the rehearsal space. It was also necessary to make sure the table/screens were in the correct position each night for the video mapping to work.

Gauze Screens (or Scrims)

Gauze is cloth with a regular pattern of small holes in it. Theatrical gauze (scrim in North America) has been used to produce transformations on stage for many generations. In the right lighting conditions a theatrical gauze can be made to appear opaque one moment and transparent the next. If an image is painted onto the gauze, this can appear solid at first, and then with a change of the stage lighting, appear to dissolve away and reveal a new scene behind it. This is a trick still used extensively in classical ballet and pantomime sets.

More recently designers have used gauze as a projection screen. Images projected onto gauze can seem ethereal, ghostly, or even magical. Projection on gauze can help to reduce the high-tech look that tends to come with video projection, and make it seem more organic in some way. It has to be said though that it can also be a nightmare, and end up in major disappointments.

The two main things to consider when using gauze as a screen are first, how much light will be 'caught' and reflected by the threads of the gauze, and second, how much will pass through and where will that light end up? Both things depend largely on two factors – the construction of the gauze and the geometry of the projection set-up and the rest of the stage. Lets look at the construction of the gauze first.

The London-based specialist supplier McDougall's stocks nine different types of gauze, most in grey, white or black. The chief difference between

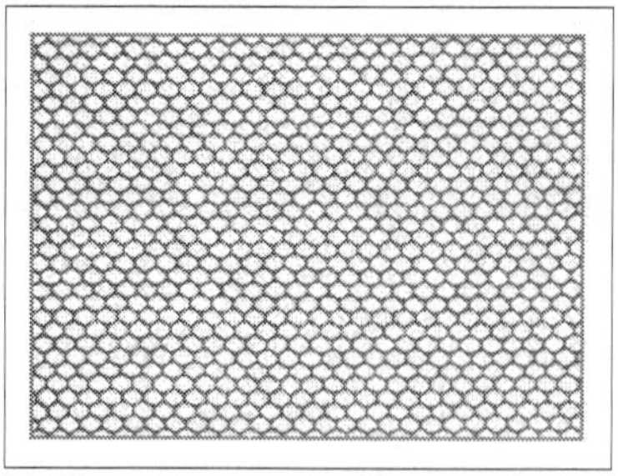

McDougall's Scenic Gauze is mostly holes, so most of the light that hits it goes straight through.

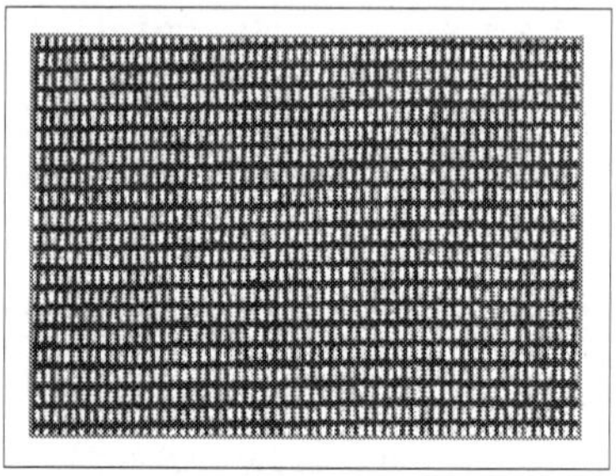

McDougall's Shark's Tooth Gauze, with smaller holes and thicker yarn, this gauze is more than twice as heavy as the scenic gauze. It has more than twice as much material to catch and reflect light.

The audience will see more of the image on a shark's tooth gauze than on a scenic gauze.

them is the size and shape of the holes, and the thickness of the yarn surrounding the holes.

As you can see from the illustrations, scenic gauze is mostly holes surrounded by thin yarn while shark's tooth gauze has smaller holes surrounded by thicker yarn. The shark's tooth gauze has more thickness – scenic gauze is almost two-dimensional while shark's tooth has some body. This means that shark's tooth is better at 'catching' light from a steep angle, which makes it the gauze of choice when the transformation scenes mentioned above – light from almost directly above a shark's tooth gauze can make it appear opaque. Projected light from video projectors can make shark's tooth gauze a very effective screen for steep angled projection.

So the choice of gauze determines how much light from the projectors is seen by the audience and how much goes through the holes – but where does that light go? The laws of physics tell us that it continues in a straight line till it hits something, and the geometry of the set up determines what it hits next.

Even a shark's tooth gauze consists of more holes than yarn, so it's worth bearing in mind that more of the light from your projectors goes through the gauze than goes back to the audience as the first image. If the 'next thing' the beam hits is quite close to the gauze, and has the same orientation, the second image will be similar in shape and size to the first. (Its colour and brightness will depend on the screen characteristics of the 'next thing' – as is the case for any screen.)

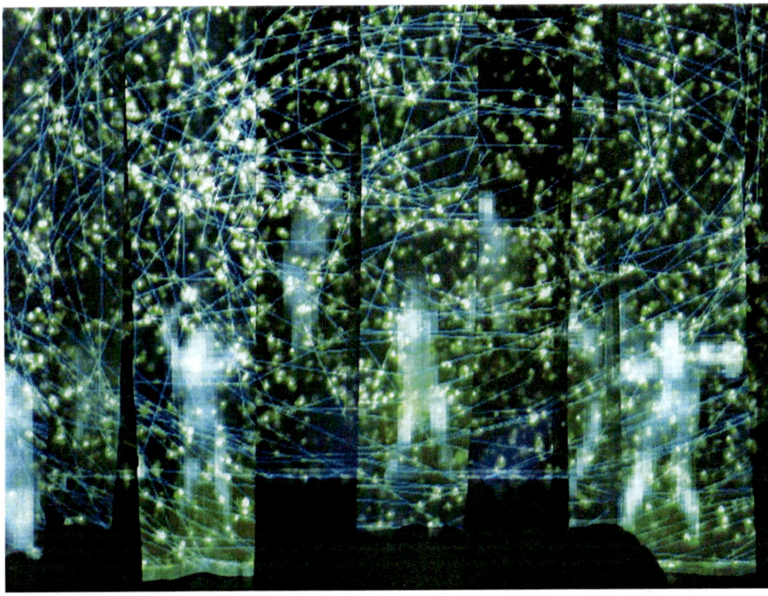

***A Midsummer Night's Dream* realised by Scott Palmer and students from Leeds University**

This ambitious production design included gauze panels, and an infra-red camera sensing the position of performers and feeding that information back into the computer system that interactively created the content for the projector. Photo: Scott Palmer.

Similarly, the size and shape of the image on each 'next thing' will depend on its relationship to the projector. If the next thing some distance from the first gauze, the image on it will be larger and will have less intensity than the first image. As discussed in chapter 2, if the "next thing is twice as far from the projector as the gauze, the image on it will be four times bigger and one quarter as bright as the image on the gauze. If the 'next thing' is not parallel to the gauze, say the stage floor in the drawing, the second image will be distorted."

If it is possible to make sure every 'next thing' in the path of the projector is not too close and more or less matt black, the second image can be made to effectively vanish. Making the first image stronger will also help to reduce the impact of any second images. This can be done by increasing the gain of the gauze – using a heavy or thick-yarned shark's tooth in white or light-grey will do this for you.

Projector Light and Gauze Screens

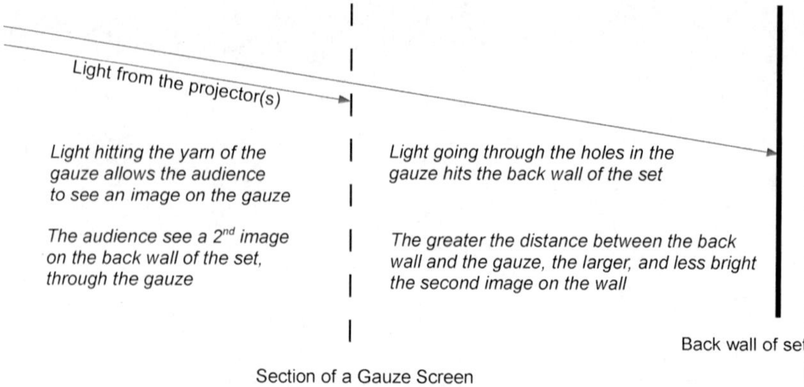

Straight-In or Shallow Angle set up
section view

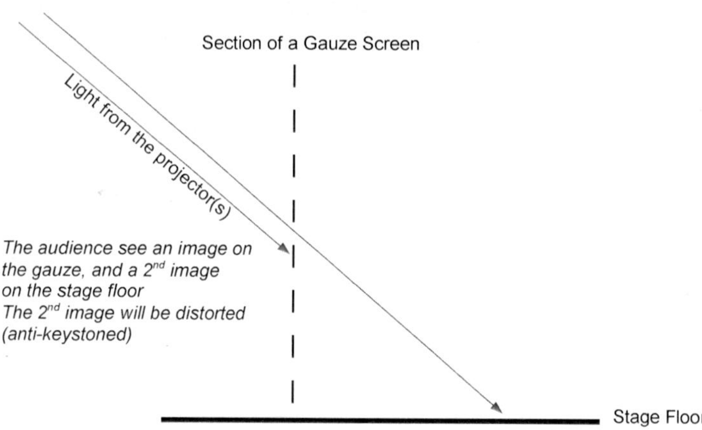

Steep Angled Set-Up
section view

Light that passes through the gauze hits the next thing in line, and creates an image on that. In these drawings that "next thing" is a wall and the floor. However anything that "gets in the way" will be lit by that part of the image that passed through the gauze.

A full stage gauze flown in front of the whole performance area (down stage) can give the scene behind it an ethereal misty quality. Using a gauze like this to reveal the set to an audience for the first time remains a popular stage design technique.

A full-stage gauze down stage can also become a screen for a pre-show video sequence such as the one shown in the four pictures below taken from the opening sequence of the Central School production of *Scenes From The Big Picture* shown below.

A montage of videos of silhouetted figures moving about in 'windows' was projected onto the front gauze throughout the time the audience were taking their seats. As the auditorium lighting faded down, these windows became more distinct, along with the moving silhouetted figures. Then the practical lamps on the set behind the gauze fade up, along with a blue wash of light. This begins to confuse deliberately the overall image. The climax of the sequence is a very loud sound effect of breaking glass which also triggers the final image. In the lighting blackout that follows, the gauze flys out as the projected image fades and the first scene appears on stage.

This was the only use of projection in the production, all over before the first word was spoken on stage. However, the way the projected material

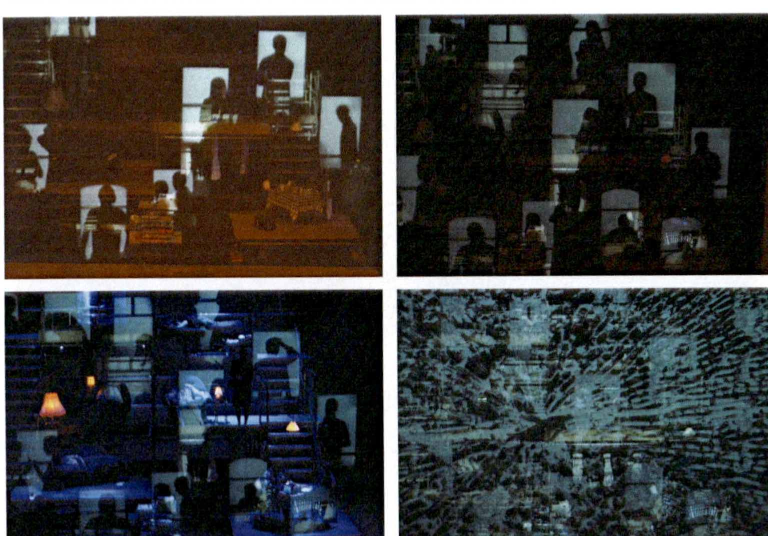

Scenes from the Big Picture for Central School in the Embassy Theatre, 2012

prepared the audience for what was to come, and the added impact of the visual of breaking glass, certainly justified the presence of a video designer on the production team.

So far we have been talking about the second image being a problem, but sometimes we actually want to make use of the extra image. Projecting onto multiple layers of gauze can create an almost three-dimensional look, each successive image slightly off-set from the first. This can be very effective, especially when used with less realistic content. If you want to try to create this kind of effect, its best done through experiment, ideally in the performance space since there are so many variables involved. The video designer will need to make sure everyone on the production team agrees about the importance of doing the experiments, as it could take up a good deal of time.

Screens the Actors Walk Through

Mixing projection and live action can be most effective when the actors appear to walk out of the projected image, or to step into the projected world. To achieve these effects the actors usually walk through the screen, and there are several ways of making this happen. These include making a screen with overlapping strips of a stretchy material such a Lycra, projecting onto a slash curtain, using vertical blinds or an industrial loading-dock door as a screen, projecting onto smoke, or even a screen of water!

Water screens really require good quality professional advice. Working with the large quantities of water needed, often near electric cables for lighting and other stage equipment, and with the constant threat of flooding and the damage that comes with that, is not something to be taken on lightly. (Of course the actors will be wet once they have passed through a water screen, but that may not matter.)

Smoke screens can be tricky too, but more in terms of reliability. Anyone who has perfected a stage smoke effect in rehearsal only to have it change dramatically once the audience fills the theatre will know how fickle smoke on stage can be. Specialist smoke curtains do exist. They require quite a lot of surrounding infrastructure, fans, ducts etc, and are usually quite limited in size. Some great abstract or semi-supernatural effects can be achieved by projecting onto clouds of smoke – from a stage smoke machine or from pyrotechnics, as long as you are not too concerned about how much of the content will be seen on any one performance. Smoke on stage is very dependent on how the air is

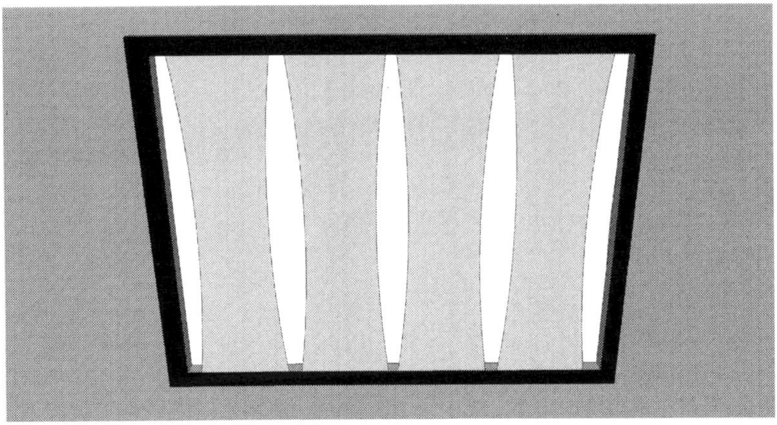

Sketch-Up model of a Lycra screen in a frame.

Alternate panels of Lycra are fixed to the front and rear of the frame, and overlapped to give the appearance of a continuous screen.

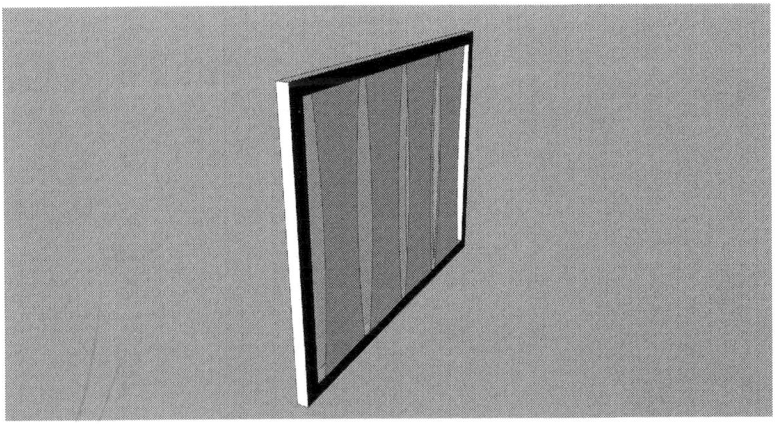

The same Lycra screen frame, viewed from the side to show a bit more clearly how it is made. The actors can enter or exit through the screen by pushing through the gaps between panels.

moving, both on stage and in the auditorium too. An effect that looks great one night may be totally missing the next because the smoke blew a different way. That could be caused by any number of things beyond your control – an usher opening a door at the wrong time, or the venue's air conditioning system deciding to work in a different way.

One other thing to bear in mind when using smoke and projection – the smoke (or haze for that matter) will make the projector beam visible. This can be massively distracting or a great effect in its own right. Visual artists have used the way smoke appears to make a beam of light solid to stunning effect. If you have the chance, take a look at the work of artist Liz Rhodes, whose installation piece *Light Music* is currently on display at the Tate Modern, or at Anthony McCall's piece *Line Describing a Cone*, which can be seen on YouTube.

A screen made from stretched Lycra panels can be a lot of fun to play with – for the performers as well as for the video designer. To stretch the material, you will usually need a rigid frame, or fixed battens top and bottom, to attach the Lycra panels to. You will need to overlap the panels because they will tend to get thinner in the middle as they are stretched.

A screen can also be made from industrial strip curtain, the heavy-duty curtains of PVC plastic panels used at goods entrances and elsewhere. These can be painted or treated in other ways to make them more or less transparent, or to match the rest of the set. They can also be sand-blasted to make them translucent – producing a gauze-like effect.

Coordinating the entrances and exits of actors through the screen with the content will be a challenge – as will ensuring that performers don't appear to change size – or costume – as they pass between the "live" world and the screen. (There are significant issues to be addressed when ever a performer appears live and on screen – whether or not they can walk between the two. Top of these is what do you do if the actor playing the role is sick and an understudy needs to go on in his or her place? There is a bit more about this in chapter 4.)

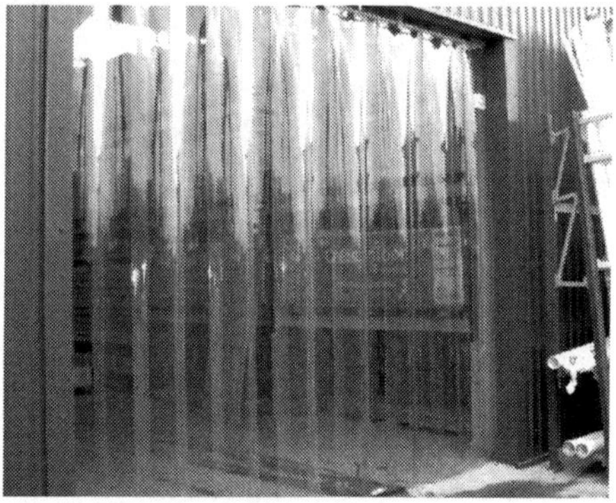

A Strip-Curtain door at an industrial warehouse. *These can be adapted for use as projection screens for performance. The PVC strips can be spray-painted for colour and texture, or carefully sand blasted to make them translucent - almost like a gauze. This type of industrial product does not have to be expensive, but lead-times from suppliers can be longer than you might expect for standard theatrical equipment.*

Fire-proof? I hope so!

In the UK, the professional building trade is much more safety conscious than it once was. Many of the materials they use are specifically made to minimise the risks in the already dangerous environment of a building site. The plastic sheeting used as an improvised screen in the production of The Edge pictured earlier in this chapter was salvaged from a building site. It had been used to cover materials on site and it was made specifically to be difficult to set fire to and to not to release harmfully chemicals if it did burn. The builders used this grade of plastic because it significantly reduced the risk of both fire and suffocation on their site. If bought new it would have been too expensive, but acquiring it second hand meant no fire safety certificate. To satisfy the licensing authority, a small spare piece was offered to the licensing officer to test with a naked flame. This was done some days before the final rehearsals. Once the licensing officer (and the venue's stage manager) were happy, the plastic could be used on stage.

One thing I haven't mentioned yet is a very important safety consideration – is the screen material a potential fire hazard? Screens are generally quite large and if one did catch fire on stage it could be a serious problem – for the performers and the audience. Some plastics and other synthetic materials can give off poisonous gasses when they burn, or even when they get too hot. A responsible theatre maker will take care to avoid taking unnecessary risks with the lives and well-being of cast, crew or audience, and the body licensing the performance will usually want to see proof that you have done just that. This can mean having to produce fire safety certificates for materials used on stage, including the material used for your screens.

Most materials from specialist theatrical or film suppliers – including plastic screen fabrics, canvas and calico – will be certified as non-flammable. Fabric from other suppliers may require treatment to make it non-flammable (which may make it more expensive to use in the end than material from the specialist supplier). Unconventional or improvised screen materials can be a problem, though it is often not as difficult as you might imagine to find alternatives that are acceptable.

There is a lot more to fire safety on stage than simply picking the right materials for your screen, but you can help everyone by being aware of potential risks in this area.

Conclusion

As with all the design decisions, as the video designer you will need to think through the consequences of the choices you make. First and foremost you will need to be sure that your choices still allow the video elements of the production to do what the production needs them to do (the first big question). Part of that will usually involve ensuring your screen or screens fit in with the chosen aesthetic and practical necessities of the production design, and are able to display your chosen content to the audience effectively. Now, as if that were not enough to consider, we need to look at making that content.

4 SO WHAT ARE YOU GOING TO PROJECT? – THE CONTENT

Content is the material that is projected or displayed in a video design. It can be still or moving images, pre-recorded, produced live, representational, abstract or any combination. Whatever the content is, the video designer will, at the very least, need to prepare it for playback during the performance. Most often he/she will also be responsible for selecting and/or producing the content too.

In this chapter I'll be looking at what needs to be considered when selecting content for a stage video design. I'll start with some technical considerations first, and then move on to the equally important area of aesthetics, looking at the 'art' side of video design.

Technical Compatibility and File Formats

Before you begin selecting and preparing content for projection, it's as well to have some idea of what formats will work best on the system you will be using to play back and display that content. Even if your system is relatively simple you will need to be sure that each still picture or video clip will successfully load into the playback system when you need it to, and display at the size and aspect ratio you require.

One of the things that frequently causes problems for users of digital video on stage is file compatibility. Digital images are stored as files of 1s and 0s. Your computer (or your DVD player, tablet or phone for that matter) uses software to encode those 1s and 0s for storage, and to decode them to turn them back into images. The software that decodes the 1s and 0s has to be compatible with the software that encoded them in the first place, otherwise the process doesn't work, the file won't open (or won't open correctly) and you don't get to see your images.

One way to find out which software had encoded an image file is by looking at the file extension, that is the last three or four letters of the file name after the dot. For example, Microsoft word files have the extension .doc or .docx. MS Word files ending .doc are produced by older versions of MS Word. Files ending .docx are produced by more recent MS Word software, and often cannot be read by older software – because it is not compatible.

To find the extension of computer files, try the "more options" icon in the folders you are interested in – for the current versions of Windows, select "details" and this will usually reveal the file type. If that does not work you will need to find the file properties (use "system help" on your computer if the way to do this is not clear).

The file format that a camera (still or video) is using to store images or video clips is usually clearer – and most have options to store and export files in a range of formats and resolutions, accessed through the camera's menu. Which option is best will depend on a number of factors, some of which are covered below.

The video designer needs to know which file format(s) she or he is using. However the way in which video pictures are sent from a computer, video camera, vision mixer or DVD player to a projector or computer display screen, also has a format. This format involves specifying, for example, the type of cable and connector required to link the output device (computer, DVD player etc.) to the projector or display screen, and maximum resolution of the video images. To try and avoid confusion I will refer to this as the video format.

There is more on video formats in Chapter 5.

A Note on Software

Making digital content almost always involves software and computers. Which software and which computer platform are questions with no single correct answer. While large scale professional projects use expensive software and media server packages, many shows in schools, on the amateur stage, and even small scale professional shows use basic slide-show software such as Microsoft's Powerpoint or Apple's Keynote. Both these programs (and others) can handle still images and short movie clips. Both programs will also allow you to specify the timing and nature of transitions between one slide and the next – that is the details of your video cues. The user interface is designed for someone making visual material for projection, and it is relatively simple to use. You can even do some basic image correction with these programs. If you have only one projector and one screen in your system, you would need a really good reason to use anything else.

If your system is more complex, if it involves live cameras, multiple screens or projection mapping for example, you will probably need to consider alternatives. You might be tempted to do that anyway, just to get some experience of the software used on larger projects. That's great – but don't underestimate the time it takes to learn the more sophisticated editing and playback software, and try to make sure you have someone you can call on to get you out of trouble too.

Generally speaking, professional software such as Adobe Creative Suite (which includes Photoshop, Premier and After Effects) will open just about any file format and output in just about any file format too. Professional media servers such as Catalyst, Hippotizer and ArKaos will cope with almost any file format, and give the video designer tremendous flexibility. Most professional video designers are more than happy to pay for professional software, and for the training courses required to become proficient with it. If you are a student or teacher you can probably find educational discounts, but the version of software you get may be limited. In any case, you will need to decide if you have the budget for this level of software, the time available to learn it, and the real need for what it offers.

With this in mind, I've tried to avoid too much focus on techniques that can only be accomplished with the expensive 'professional' software, but at times that has proved difficult. Very few of the free or low cost programs do keystone correction for still images as easily as Photoshop or for video clips as well as a good media server program for example. Your projector may well have the capacity to adjust for the level of keystone correction you need. If not, Powerpoint type programs can be used to distort images to create keystone correction, which is OK if you only have a few images to project. However, if you know that significant keystone correction is going to be a big part of your design, you may have to invest in professional editing software (which means Adobe Creative Suite for most of the people I've talked to) and/or media server software.

QLab software is a valuable alternative here, combining much of what you will need from an image editing software with the functionality of a media server. It offers image manipulation and cueing options in a relativity simple to use package. If money is tight, you can buy a licence for full capability for the duration of you production only rather than having to pay the full package price up front. It only runs on Mac computers (see below) however, which may or may not be an issue for you. I'll come back to Qlab in chapter 5.

Most media server software is usually tailored to a particular platform – Mac based media servers won't run on Windows and vice versa. (Mac users will no doubt be aware that they can run Windows on their machines of course, so this is not quite so true for them.) Some media server software makers offer stripped down versions at low cost or even for free in demo mode. Try them out, and check out the user forums too

– see what others say about each package, and see how much support for new users is out there. Again, you will probably find that the big-name (expensive) software has better support and bigger user forums, and more "how-to" clips on YouTube and Vimeo.

The big expensive photo editing and media server packages can have the disadvantage of offering too much choice to the first time or inexperienced designer. Also, in order to offer all that choice, the user interface can be daunting, requiring some days of training to even begin to understand how to use them. In all likelihood, these packages do many many things you will never want to do, and it can be quite hard to get to the stuff you do want to do. So often, even if you do have the money, the big name packages may not be the right choice. There are many things you can accomplish without recourse to expensive software, and for the most part that is what I intend to focus on here.

It has to be said that if you start off with a Mac computer, you will have more useful tools already on your machine (and generally a better graphics card too.) iMovie and iPhoto will allow you to do pretty sophisticated things with your content too, though Microsoft's latest built-in products are beginning to catch up in some areas. (Mac will also enable you to run Qlab, which Windows machines won't.)

Keeping Everything Technically Compatible

In most video system designs, it's usually a good idea to start with the projector(s) or display screen(s) as it or they will often be the biggest equipment cost to the production. The specification of your projector(s) and/or display screens are probably also the major factor in determining the quality of the images on the stage. It is for these two reasons that I've started this look at compatibility with the projector/display screen.

Try to stick to the video format that works best with the projection/ display system.

While it is possible to turn one video format into a different one, it is not usually simple or cheap to do this without losing quality, and it is best avoided. Also video systems are generally quite hard for the non-engineer to troubleshoot, so it's good to try to keep things as simple as possible when ever you can.

Get hold of the manuals for the projector(s) or display screen. If you don't have access to hard copies, search the web where you are almost sure to find the information you need.

In the manual, you are looking for "input format" or "input type". There may well be several options; hopefully you will be able to find one you can match to the output video format of the computer, vision mixer, camera or DVD player you are using to send content.

If there is a choice, make sure the video format you chose will work with the cables you have available, and over the distance you need. Many theatre video systems need longer cables because the projector is some distance from the operating position and the playback equipment. (More on this in Chapter 5.)

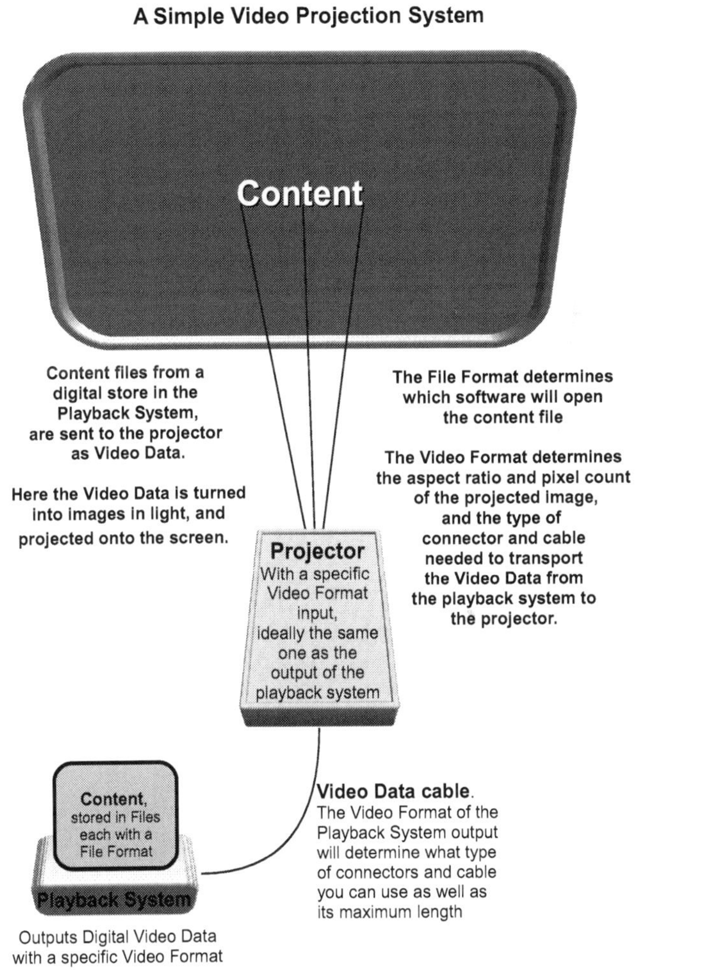

Figure 1: Video Data System

Make sure you have enough pixels

Next search the manual for the information on the resolution in pixels and aspect ratio: how many pixels wide by how many high will the full-size image be? Alternative inputs may be associated with different resolutions, so make sure the figures you are using from the manual are the true resolution for the video format you will be using. (See Chapter 1 for the definition of pixels and aspect ratio.)

Having found out the resolution and aspect ratio of the projection/display screen system in pixels, you will want to make sure all your content at least matches this. Most projectors are good at dealing with images that have more pixels than their standard resolution. although if the ratio between width and height is different this may result in a stretched image. In other words, if your projector wants a 4 by 3 image, make sure that is what you send it!

Bovril – squeezed into a 4x3 box

This image of an enamel advertising sign from the first half of the last century, has been "squashed" to fill a 4x3 frame.

This is what might well happen if you didn't take care when preparing your content.

You might also find noticeable degradation of the image due to the way the projector compresses it. Here you can see the straight lines of the V have become stepped, as have most of the curves.

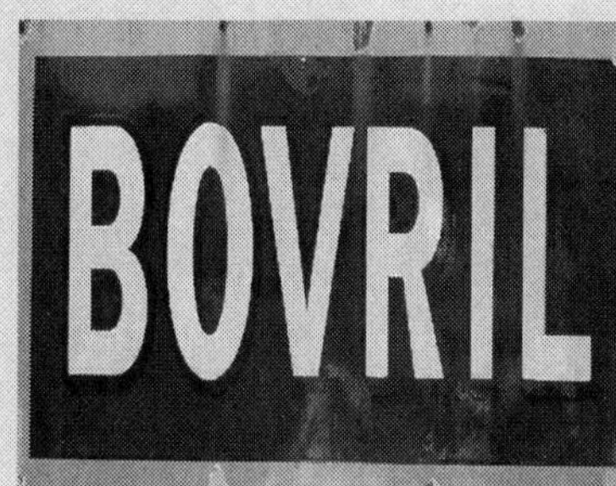

Bovril – undistorted, on a black background in a 4x3 frame

This is the same image at the correct aspect ratio. To keep the sign looking right in a 4x3 frame I have added a black background. Where the sign sits in the black background will of course determine where it appears on the screen.

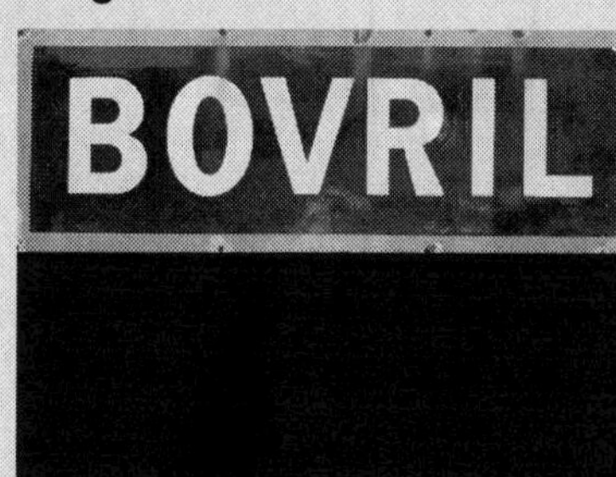

It's worth remembering at this point that very often a video design does not use the whole of the projection field. If you have already done the calculations that enable to to accurately predict how much of the projection field will be used for content, you might want to work out what that means in pixels.

A standard XGA projector has a resolution of 1024 x 768 pixels (ratio 4 by 3), while a high definition wide-screen projector sold to project HD movies should have a resolution of 1920 x 1080 pixels (ratio 16 by 9, and known as HD 1080p). My mid-price compact camera takes shots at a maximum resolution of 3648 x 2736 in JPEG format - so plenty to play with. I could crop out almost a third of the image and still have enough pixels for an HD projector running HD 1080p. However this is a 4 by 3 ratio. If I sent an unedited and uncropped picture from my compact to a XGA or HD1080p projector, in all likelihood it would be stretched in the display.
When it comes to video clips, you will usually want to use the highest resolution available to create the clip in the first place. This ensures you start off with the highest number of pixels, and the more pixels you have the more you can do with them. It's all too easy to 'lose' pixels as you edit and grade video.
The higher the resolution, the more pixels need to be stored, so the more memory capacity each image or clip takes up. If you want to use HD video clips in your production, you may well need to think about dedicating an external hard-drive to store the content. If you are creating and editing content as you go along, that probably needs to be at least a 1Terabyte hard drive.
The larger the file, the longer it takes a computer to open it or move it or begin to play it. If you are asking your computer(s) to deal with large files, you will need to have very fast computers as well as large external hard drives. The costs quickly add up, and before long someone will be asking you: "Do we really need all the content to be uncompressed HD?" (or you may be asking yourself). Experience will eventually allow you to know which projects need what sort of specification. Don't be afraid to stick with standard definition, it's fine for almost all small and mid-scale projects, and it is probably all that your projectors can cope with anyway. Once you are confident handling lots and lots of files of data and turning them into interesting show content, you can experiment with higher spec systems, and all the additional problems they present.

Most projector systems will cope well with files of higher resolution than the projector, but remember that to do this the projector is processing the image and compressing it. If your content involves significant detail such as small text, it becomes more important to match the resolution of content files and the projector. This is because the way projector systems compress images can lead to distortions in fine detail.

Check what file formats your playback software and computer can use

For still images – the JPEG format is pretty much universally read (though its worth remembering that every save of a JPEG file involves a new compression calculation by the computer saving the file, and this can lead eventually to a noticeable degradation of the image quality). Proprietary camera formats, sometimes referred to as 'digital negatives' or RAW files such as the .CR2 files from my Canon or Nikon's .NEF files, will generally be higher resolution and better quality, but usually require an additional piece of software (known as a Codec) for most computer programmes to be able to open and make use of them. (Full versions of professional photo editing software should come with these codecs built in, or easily available from the support website.)

For video files, the situation is considerably more complex. "Portable" is a term used to say that a file or file type is likely to work in a range of situations, e.g. on Mac and PC. MPEG, and particularly MP4 (files ending .mp4) is a relatively portable format for digital video files.

Almost all personal computers will open an image stored in the JPEG format. This is because software to open JPEGs comes with most personal computers, no matter what the operating system, so the format is "portable". Many digital documents are shared using the PDF format - PDF stands for Portable Document Format, and was developed by Adobe. PDF documents (which have the extension .PDF) will open and look the same on any computer with compatible reader software. Because this software is freely available (e.g. Adobe Reader) PDF is also considered a "portable" format - though most users will need to download the (free) Adobe Reader software in order to open PDF files. Other types of files will only open correctly on one type of computer, or in a particular software program (e.g. some Photoshop file formats). These file types are sometimes referred to as proprietary, meaning they are associated with one particular software maker or camera manufacturer. Canon RAW .CR2 from my DSLR and Photoshop .PSD are examples of proprietary file formats.

Windows PCs and Apple Macs currently come with software to decode and play most MPEG video files. It is however still worth checking that the particular MPEG files that your video camera produces are 1) compatible with the software you want to use to edit them, and 2) that the resolution is sufficient to display well on the projector system and/or display screen(s). Don't just assume this is the case, find out for sure. For example, the default setting for most camera-phones will produce video that will not fill a standard resolution projector or display screen. Mine defaults to 800x600 pixels, which means that a video from my smart-phone would only fill 80% of the screen at standard resolution, and less than half of an HD 1080p screen.

AVI video files are generally proprietary, that is specific to a particular camera or software manufacturer (like digital RAW files for still images mentioned above). In order to play or edit AVI files it is often necessary to download a Codec - that is a specific piece of software that enables your computer's software to de-code the AVI file. If you like to think of your computer as a 'plug and play' device, its probably best to avoid AVI and other propitiatory video files. If on the other hand you are happy seeking out, downloading and installing various bits of software, you will probably already know where to go to find the right stuff.

Check your editing software outputs files your playback system can use

In almost all video designs you will want to make some adjustment to still images or video clips to make them work better within your design. You do this with editing software such as Picasa or Photoshop for still images, iMovies or After Effects for video clips. Even if you plan to do most of your image manipulation in a media server, or a show control program such as Qlab, you will still often want to do initial preparations in another program. Straightening and cropping is often easier to do in a dedicated photo editor. Any cropping will reduce the resolution of your images, so it's good to start with more pixels than you need.

Most video and picture editing software gives you options when you come to finally save the files you will eventually use as content. File formats native to editing programmes (such as Photoshop's .pst and .psd files) cannot normally be read by other programs, so it is often best to save your files as .jpg or .tif (for still images) or .mp4 (for video clips). This is often the best point to do any conversions and to make sure your saved content files match the resolution and aspect ratio of the projector or display system, as well as the file type required by the playback system.

File Compression is the term for a number of different ways of processing data with the aim of reducing the size of the file. This is done to reduce the amount of space the file takes up when stored, and so that it can be moved from one place to another more efficiently. JPEG and MPEG are both ways of compressing data – JPEG for still images and MPEG for movie clips.

Compression can be our friend, but it can also be an enemy. It's a friend when, for example, it turns big files that only open in one software program into smaller files that can open in several programs. It's an enemy when it tales a high quality image with lots of fine detail – say a finely textured skyscape – and turns it into square blocks of blue and white, or makes smooth circles and diagonal lines into steps.

Two main factors determine the quality of images stored as JPEGs: dpi and quality. Most photo editing software offers options when you save your images as JPEGs, though you may have to search for these options in some programs.

dpi or Dots Per Inch was originally a setting for printers – the more dots per inch, the smoother and higher quality the resulting image. The range usually starts around 75 dpi, and goes up to 300, or even 600 dpi. Matching pixel width to dpi setting can be useful, if you can face the calculations. Most people use trial and error, or stick to a particular dpi setting they know works. The dpi setting can define the size of an image on screen, and some software displays the choice in centimetres or inches instead of dpi. If you are lucky, the software will display the pixel count of the resulting image. This makes it relatively easy to choose a dpi setting that gives you enough pixels for your use.

Quality is often represented as a sliding scale from 1 to 10 or from 1% to 100%. Quality relates the directly to the level of compression used on the data that makes up the image file. Low quality corresponds to high levels of compression and very small file size. High quality corresponds to low compression and large file size. Low quality settings and high levels of compression lead to smooth lines becoming stepped, loss of detail in areas of the picture with fine texture and some loss of richness in colour.

Defects in the compressed image are referred to as artefacts. Most of the time you will want to reduce or eliminate artefacts, though from time to time they can become a useful creative effect.

For video the process is more complex, but based on more or less

> *Wherever possible:*
> *Limit the amount of compression of your image files until the final save. When using JPEG compression for example, keep the dpi setting high (e.g. 300) and the quality setting high (e.g. 85-95%), until you make the final save of the file.*
> *And keep a copy of the uncompressed or best quality file as a back-up.*

the same idea. Either way, if you care about preserving the image quality of your content then it is important to understand what you are doing when you are saving files in a compressed format. Once you have lost quality by saving a file in a compressed format, you can't get that quality back. Naturally though there is limited advantage in preserving quality that can't be displayed by your projector or display screen, as you will end up with larger files than you need, using more disc space and taking longer to open and edit.

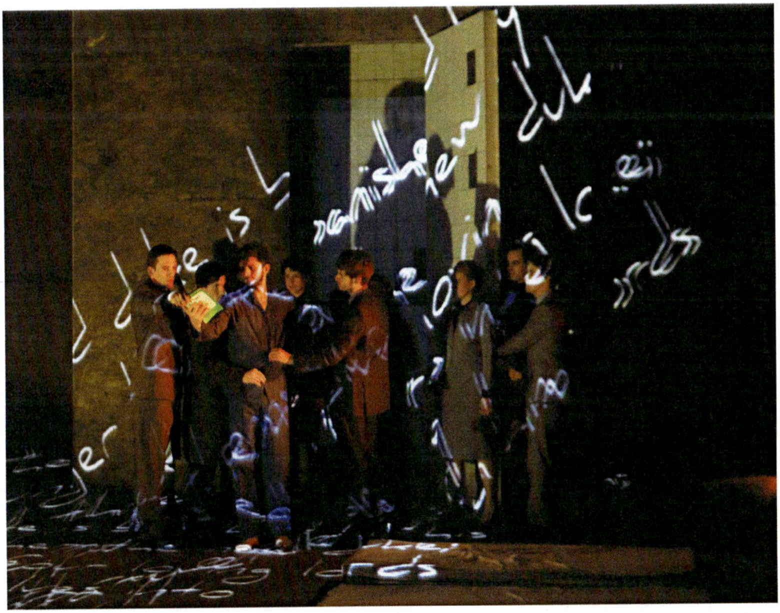

As You Like It: 3861 by 2896

High Resolution production shot of As You Like It, which used projected text and video mapping as part of the production design.

This image is 3861 pixels wide with a file size of 5.7MB.

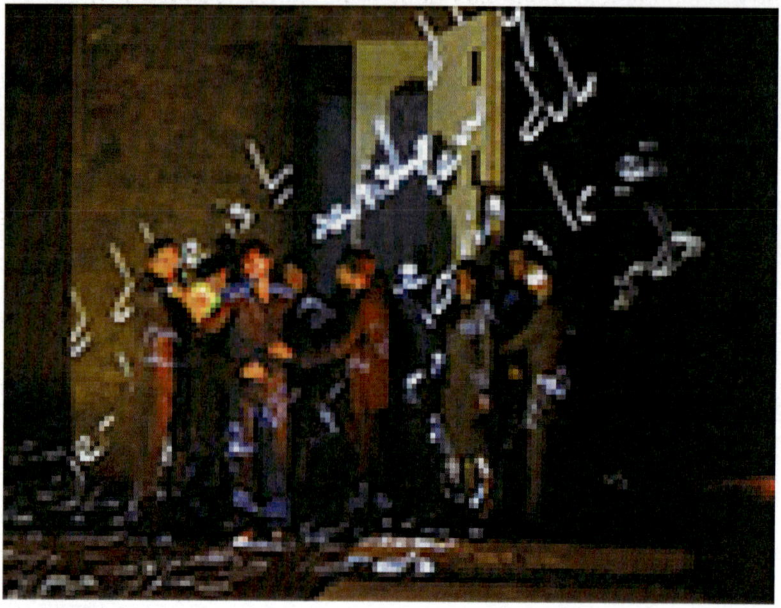

As You Like It: 322 by 214

A very low resolution copy of the same shot. Note the loss of clarity and focus, and of artefacts, due to the high level of compression.

Check the images you want to use are compatible with the editing software

While you are looking at the specifications of your editing software, check what formats it can use. There is no point in shooting high quality images in a proprietary format (such as CR2) if the editing software you are going to use won't be able to use files in this format. If in doubt, try it out. Pick some trial images to edit, making sure they are of the file format you want to use, and see if the edit program works with them. Then see if the resulting edited files work with the playback program. You can also look for help on how to make still image or video files compatible with editing programs on the web, but don't expect miracles!

Check the video format of the output of live cameras

What you are looking to check here is both the video format *and* the cable connector type will be compatible with all the other parts of the system. Older video cameras may not have a digital output for example, and the signal from them may need to be converted (see Chapter 5). If you plan to use USB cameras connected to the playback computer, be aware that your playback software may have a limit on the number of live inputs. QLab for example can currently handle up to two external USB camera inputs. Most current media servers will need additional capture cards to cope with more than one external camera.

Although there is no pre-editing to do with live content, you will still need to plan for how it will work within the design – technically as well as aesthetically.

Don't be tempted to put off finding out this kind of basic information. It defines what content you can use, and what your system will and won't be able to do with that content. Being thorough and gathering all the information before you begin making content can save hours of wasted effort and frustration later on.

Video Connectors and Cables – a brief note

This is by way of an aside. The main section on this is in Chapter 5.

Unfortunately, there are a great many different cable types and connector types used in digital and analogue video. Almost all video system designs will involve changing from one cable type to another at some point. At this point, what you need to be aware of is that some of these conversions are simply changing from one connector to another, while others involve changing the video format.

The first type of change can usually be done simply by buying an appropriate adaptor. You are probably familiar with adaptors for the various types of USB and micro USB connectors. Another example is the SCART leads that are used to transport video, sound signals and control information in older home systems. The main function of a SCART lead can be duplicated by three RCA phono leads, one for the video signal, the other two for stereo sound. You can buy an adaptor to convert SCART into three phono and vice versa. The video format stays the same, all that has changed is the connectors.

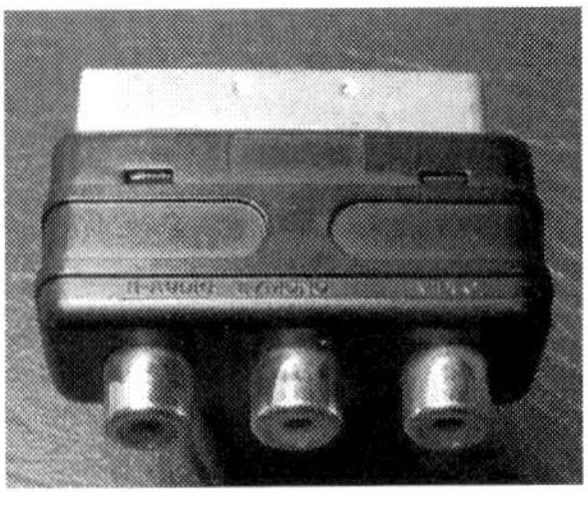

Composite Video to SCART adaptor

This is a way to get composite video signals into older domestic TV screens, or out of older DVD or VCR players. The quality of the video signal is not likely to be very high.

The second type usually involves a 'box of tricks' that converts the video signal from one video format into another. For example, If you want to get the video output of a computer onto an old fashioned cathode ray television set, you would need to convert the video format of the signal coming out of the computer. In this instance you would need a box of tricks called a scan converter. A good quality scan converter will offer a range of input and output video format options, and probably options to enable almost any input format to be converted to almost any output format.

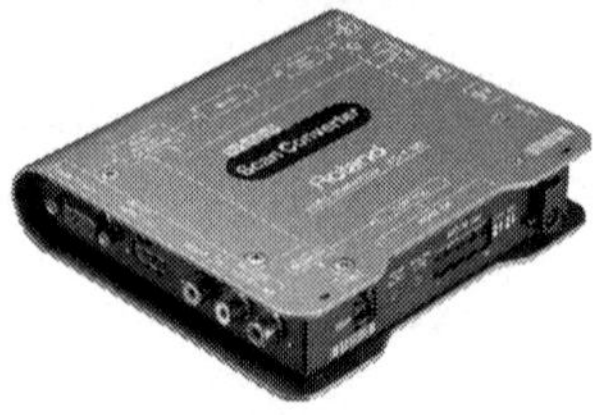

Scan Converters

This sophisticated scan converter has a range of inputs and outputs, and a number of setting, most of which are the province of a video engineer

How a scan converter works is well beyond the scope of this book. What it is important to realise however is that while anything like a SCART to phono converter is simply about joining the pins of one connector to the right pins of another, devices like scan converters involve processing the image. This can introduce distortions and time delays, and other problems that are really the province of the professional video engineer.

Quick Technical Check List:

Hardware:

- What video format will the projector accept?
- What connectors are available on the back of the projector?
- What is the video format of the output machine?
- What is/are the video output connector(s) on the playback machine?
- Are the two video formats compatible?
- Are the connectors compatible?
- Will you need adaptors or converters?
- What cables have you got available?
- Do they have the right connectors – at both ends?
- Are they long enough?

If you are using live camera:

- Is the camera's video format compatible with the playback computer?
- What connector do you need to get the camera output?

- What are the connector(s) for camera input on your playback machine?
- Are the connectors the compatible?
- Will you need adaptors or converters?
- Are the cables long enough?

Software:

- What file formats does your playback software accept?
- How much file storage space is available on your playback machine?
- Will you need an external storage device?
- What file format(s) does your content come in?
- Will you need to convert the file format of any of the content?
- Have you got the software to do the conversion?
- Will you need to apply distortion such as keystone correction, to the content?
- Have you got the software to do that?

If you are using live camera:

- Do you need any special software to use the camera with the playback machine?

This list is by no means exhaustive, but hopefully it will give you somewhere to start.

Aesthetics or 'Visual Compatibility'

Having defined the technical constraints of the video and projection design, we will now turn to what is usually thought of as the more creative aspect: what the content will look like on stage. In this section I'm going to take a quick look at the theory of looking – what is it that makes something appeal to our visual senses, what makes images work well together and what is happening when they don't? If you like, what makes one piece of content 'visually compatible' with another, and what makes all your content visually compatible or work aesthetically with the rest of the visual (and other) aspects of the production?

Traditionally, aesthetics is the study of art and beauty, and also of the mechanisms of human perception of these things. The definition in most dictionaries has two concerns – describing "that which is pleasing to the eye" and describing what makes it pleasing. This double meaning is not always useful, and does perhaps contribute towards what has been called "the lure of beauty" in very many video design – but more of that later.

Visual aesthetics have probably been argued over and discussed for as long as humans have had language, and of course ideas of what is visually 'right' or appealing are quite subjective. What gives me visual pleasure may disgust someone else. What the general public find pleasing or "aesthetically right" in one context may be completely wrong in another.

Classical writers devised rules that defined what was visually beauty in fine art, architecture, and the human body. The rules might concern themselves with the proportion of one part to another, the thickness of this or that feature in relation to the whole, the relationship between foreground and background. All of these considerations are about how a part of the work relates to the whole, but there were also some absolute rules, defining the colour of shadows for example, or setting out what was appropriate to include in different genres of painting.

The renewed interest in the classical world and its philosophical rules in the European Renaissance (beginning in the 14th century) began an academic process of codification of aesthetic rules for fine art and architecture. An understanding developed among educated people in Europe regarding these rules of aesthetics. The rules defined what could be painted, sculpted or built and how these things should look. The rules attempted to define what was, and what was not, art.

Although many writers on aesthetics through the ages have thought their rules were universal, we can now see that they are in fact quite specific to the time and tradition of the writer. Perhaps we can see this most clearly in the works of art that were influenced by these rules of aesthetics. For example, paintings of female or male beauty from a particular time and place tend to focus on similar shapes of body, face, poses and compositional details – they are all obeying the rules of aesthetics of their time and tradition.

A collection of works of art from the same time and place, can be said to have an 'aesthetic unity', they 'go together', demonstrating a common idea of what is "pleasing to the eye". For example, paintings from almost any period in history have many similarities to other paintings from that same period. If the artists are from the same place too, the similarities are likely to be even more striking. Dutch Old Master painting refers to works produced in a particular part of Northern Europe at a defined point in history. The Dutch Old Masters, whilst each exhibiting their own individual style and execution, have all made similar choices in what they have chosen to depict and the way they have gone about depicting it. Through these choices they are expressing a common understanding of aesthetics from their time and place.

Jump forward in time to paintings from mid 19th century France. Paintings from this era too have many similarities to our eyes. This was perhaps the last time and place in the West when academics writing on the aesthetics of fine art were largely in agreement about 'the rules' and were taken very seriously by artists. However all that was about to change with the arrival of (among others) Edouard Manet and the Impressionists. Both challenged the academic aesthetic rules of their time and worked in an alternative aesthetic. The aesthetic approach they chose gives much of their work an appeal to us now that many rejected at the time. It is interesting to compare French painting from the 1830s with the major works of those artists born about that time, Manet, Monet and Degas for example. The work that these men made has a very different aesthetic when compared to the paintings that were being made when they were young.

The works of Monet and Degas were not to the 'taste' of many of their contemporaries. Manet's work too was a radical departure from the academic aesthetics of the mid 1800s. A good example of how much taste in art changes over time is Manet's painting Déjeuner sur l'herbe. It caused a scandal when it was first exhibited in 1863. In several ways it challenged the aesthetics of its day. Although his work came to be much praised in years following this, less than 100 years later his paintings were described by some as 'chocolate-box' art, rather too sweet for modern tastes.

To some extent we can only try to understand why work by these painters so upset the established view of what were the 'correct' aesthetics for a painting. The world has changed and the aesthetic of Manet, Monet and Degas seems quite natural to us now, even old fashioned.

Today we no longer live in a world where there is a single universally agreed set of aesthetic rules for painting, or anything else for that matter. Many different art and cultural movements exist at the same time, and each has its own approach to aesthetics. Added to that, the internet has made the work of almost every art grouping or cultural movement from almost every part of the world and from the whole of art history available to almost everyone with an interest in looking. Without a single codified set of rules, it can be difficult to define a single aesthetic for the time and place in which we live. (It is quite possible however that cultural commentators of the future will look back on our times and be able to do just that.) But this does not mean that aesthetics has become a redundant term, far from it.

Contemporary discussions have extended the use of the word aesthetics beyond the fine arts and "that which is pleasing to the eye". Cultural critics and others now use the concept in discussions about almost all aspects of the way we describe all kinds of things: a single work of art, a whole exhibition, a city redevelopment or indeed a production design. And a good aesthetic does not always have to be pleasing to the eye, at least not in the traditional sense – think of great war photography or industrial landscapes for example. Neither are praised for their classical beauty, but still valued for their power, and sometimes the ugliness of their aesthetic.

The Aesthetics of Stage Design

A stage design that consists of a realistically detailed and ornately decorated room might be said to have a 'high aesthetic' or a 'naturalistic aesthetic'. If this set accurately reproduces the style and taste of a particular period, it might be said to have that period's aesthetic, perhaps a mid-Victorian upper-class aesthetic, indicating that the design choices have been made by following the rules of taste and style that mid-nineteenth century upper-class English people would have considered correct. This approach will have involved the set and costume designers (and in all probability a good many other makers and buyers too) in a great deal of period research to discover exactly what 'fits' the aesthetic of this particular time and place. This helps them to make sure that every choice they make helps the audience (and the actors too) 'believe' in the particular 'world' on stage.

Making choices in stage design is about more than just getting period detail right

A set featuring a representation of a bikers' café from the 1950s might be part of the 'greaser' aesthetic of the production. If that production is *Grease* the teen musical – it is likely that the production design will want to follow a 'clean, cool preppy-greaser' aesthetic. By contrast a piece based on the iconic 1950's film staring James Dean, *Rebel Without A Cause*, would probably be looking for a 'dirty, gritty, more authentic greaser' aesthetic.

Whatever the time or place being evoked on stage, the designers, makers and others responsible for a production are all working to create a believable world for the performance. The aim is often to make sure everything on stage 'fits' or 'goes with' everything else, and that nothing disturbs the sense of place and time – for the actors as well as for the audience. This could be described as working towards an aesthetic unity.

Stage designers, writers and directors often use words associated with particular artistic style or period or architectural or cultural movement, to bring to mind the visual (and perhaps other) aesthetics of that style, time or movement. Initial discussions about a production design will often include lots of these types of words.

Early discussion about staging a play in a set using material salvaged from skips and demolition sites might be described as having 'a rough aesthetic' or maybe a 'brutalist aesthetic'. While rough is a general term, brutalism is a word associated with a particular style of mid to late 20th century architecture; London's National Theatre building is an example of this style. Knowing this might help you as a video designer when you select images for the video design (and when making choices about screens too for that matter).

As the video and projection designer, your work will need to be in keeping with the aesthetics of the overall production design. If the desired aesthetic of the production design is 'preppy greaser' or 'brutalist realism' your work – the screen and content choices – will need to take this into account. You will need to research each term, probe what the writer, director and other collaborators mean by these terms, and come to an understanding of what each term means for you too. How will working within a 'preppy greaser' aesthetic affect the content choices you make? Where will you go to find content that works with this aesthetic?

Be aware too that you will frequently need to take into account the historical and/or geographical context of the terms used to describe an aesthetic. For example, in the late 1970s the punk aesthetic was subtly different in New York and London, but on both sides of the Atlantic it was largely based on home-modified second-hand garments assembled by the wearer, or bought from obscure specialist shops (some of which became famous later, towards the end of the original rise of the movement). 1970s punk was dirty, smelly and intensely 'anti-everything'. By the time a punk style resurfaced in the 1990s the emphasis was on brands (Converse, Levis etc.) and a look largely bought pre-distressed from main-stream stores. 1990s punk was distressed but clean, and rarely smelly. So the single word punk has a different aesthetic connotation depending on the time (1976 or 1993) and place (London, New York, Boston or Leeds). As with so much of what we do when making design choices, and so much of any discussion about aesthetics, context is everything.

All these considerations play directly into any discussion about the content choices made by a video designer. If the aim is to achieve a particular period aesthetic, then the things in the pictures – if you like the content of your content – will need to match that aesthetic. *Grease the Musical* for example is set in and around an American High School in the 1950s. To research your ideas for content you might well be looking at pictures of iconic items from that time and place – buildings and objects, clothing and hair-styles for example. You might also be looking at the style of photographic image typical of that place and time, images relating to the newly emerging teenage consumers of the story for example. You might look to replicate or evoke the glossy, crisp and smoothly lit advertising billboards and magazine adverts as part of the content design – lots of depth of field and bright almost saturated colours.

If instead of supporting the world of early pop songs and teenager Greasers we are in the hard-edged adult world of the Tennessee Williams play *A Street Car Named Desire* (written in 1947 and filmed in 1951) the aesthetic of the stage design will almost certainly be very different. The cars, buildings and other objects captured in the images might be the same as in those used in the design for *Grease the Musical*, but the style of the pictures is likely to be quite different. As the video designer, you might research the film of *A Street Car...* and find links to the film-noir movement and black and white documentary film-making inspired by post-Second World War French cinema. This would probably lead to content choices with a quite different aesthetic than that used by a designer working on *Grease the Musical*. Rather than the Technicolor hyper-reality of 1950s advertising you might be inspired by news and documentary images of the time, and work by the photographer's collective Magnum. You might also be looking to reduce your colour palette, perhaps even working in black, white and greys.

It is even possible that video designers working on these two shows might chose some of the same images as content, and merely be treating them in different ways, make the same image work for each design. Think of a picture of a classic car of the period, parked in working class street. The design for *Grease* might up the colour saturation and simplify the image by removing background detail – the houses – to bring more attention to the car. Meanwhile the design for *A Street Car...* might reduce the colour saturation and use an etching style overlay to make the image read in quite a different way. Both treatments could be achieved relatively quickly in (for example) a layer based photo-editing program such as Photoshop or one of the many much cheaper digital photo editing programs such as Picasa. Although we begin with the same picture, simple editing can produce two images that will be read in quite different ways – each with its own aesthetic, each fitting with quite a different stage design world.

Working with the aesthetic of the rest of the design

Thinking again about a design for *A Street Car...* the choice of a reduced colour palette in the projected content would work well if it was also part of the aesthetic of the set and costume design. The use of high-contrast lighting and shadow within the video content might then be picked up by the lighting designer in the approach to lighting the play. When it all comes together on stage the effect should be an aesthetic unity across all aspects of the production design, helping to create a believable world on stage.

There are other aesthetic consideration too, that will help the screen and projected content to work well as part of a production design. It may be that referencing the classical rules of aesthetics will be helpful here, particularly the ones that refer to proportion and scale, and relationships between foreground and background. If a set is composed largely of rectangles with a particular aspect ratio, the screen(s), and perhaps the content too, will probably want to use the same aspect ratio for example. Similarly if the set contains lots of ovals, you would probably be looking at oval screens.

If the set has elements with a distorted perspective (like the central door pictured in Chapter 1), the video design will usually want to reference that same distortion, in the screen design and in the content.

Similarly if elements of the set are over-sized – giant doorways or windows that tower over the performers for example – the video content will want to echo this too. But if the setting is naturalistic, the content design will usually strive to achieve a naturalistic feel too, striving for an overall wholeness of production design, an aesthetic unity.

Of course, it might be that the creative team decide that the video design is there to contrast with the rest of the production design. For example in a naturalistic setting, the video design might present a distorted fantasy world, maybe the world of dreams or the subconscious. Alternatively, video might present a "normal" perspective in an otherwise distorted stage world. These are all valid aesthetic choices.

Colour Palette

In most cases the aim of the team responsible for the production design will be to have the shape and proportion of the screen and content to fit in with then rest of the production design. To achieve an aesthetic unity this approach will need to extend to the colour palette too. If the set (and costume too perhaps) are coloured in muted tones, then to fit in with this the content will also need to use the same muted tones. This can be achieved the way the images are originally made, in the editing software, or by a combination of both.

The process of altering images and clips to have a particular look is called grading. Feature film grading is a really big deal. It includes things like enhancing weaker shots by highlighting foreground elements and boosting the impact of shots, perhaps by adding sparkle effects to water or deepening the blue of the sky.

Grading and colour correction also involves processes that give an aesthetic unity to the film as a whole. The result of this process can be seen in the bright clear crisp look of an MGM Technicolor musical such as *The Wizard of Oz* (where the impact of colour is used to great effect to contrast Oz with Dorothy's Kansas home) or in the muted brownish look of many so-called Spaghetti Westerns.

The look of a movie is to do with far more that just the grading of course, and is one of the main responsibilities of the production design team and the director of photography. However, the grading of a full-length film is an important responsibility, and can provide a strong visual style to the film. Something like grading is available on most digital cameras – often called photo style or scene. These are some of the choices offered by my mid-priced compact camera: portrait, soft skin, transform, food, party, candle-light, baby, pet. These settings will change the way the camera flash responds and the settings of shutter speed, aperture and ISO for the shot, and probably change the way the image is recorded, adding an effect layer to part or all of the recorded image and changing the colour space or colour temperature. In a set of portrait photos shot with the camera set on soft skin, one shot using a different scene will stand out, and look odd. Try this with your own camera.

Very often what we are trying to achieve when creating video content for the stage is to make a set of images or clips that have the same look or feel. If I'm making a set of still images that will evoke or signify say, different rooms in the same house, or houses in the same part of town, I'll want them to all have the same look or feel. I will not want any images to "look odd" – at least not by accident. (If I do want one particular room or house to look odd, for reasons to do with the plot say, then I'll take care to make all the rest "look" even more the same.) I'll achieve this similarity of "look" in part by applying the same grading to all those images. Taking the example below from *It Must Be Madness*, the grading might be the application of sepia, and the same level of grain and glow, or it might be applying a similar contrast boost, and the same level of pencil sketch. Alternatively it might be shooting all the content in a very controlled way, with the same lighting conditions, same lens settings, etc, or applying the same colour correction recipe to all the images.

I began this section writing about the aim of matching the colour palette of the set and costume with that of the content. This can be achieved in part at lest through grading and colour correction, however, difficulties can arise once you get your content on stage. Sometimes content that appears to have the same colours as the set and costume on a computer screen when projected or displayed no longer matches the set and costume colour palette. In a projection system this may be due to the screen colour, or to coloured stage lighting reflecting onto the screen. It may also be due to the set-up of the projectors and/or display screens. If the shift is down to screen colour, you may need to re-process your images to compensate for that, but it may be worth just checking the colour settings of the projector(s) and/or display screen(s). These settings are usually accessed via the menu, often using the remote control. It is usually best to start any tweaks of this kind from manufacturers' recommended settings, and make small changes from there. If you are unsure what to do, check the projector or screen manual.

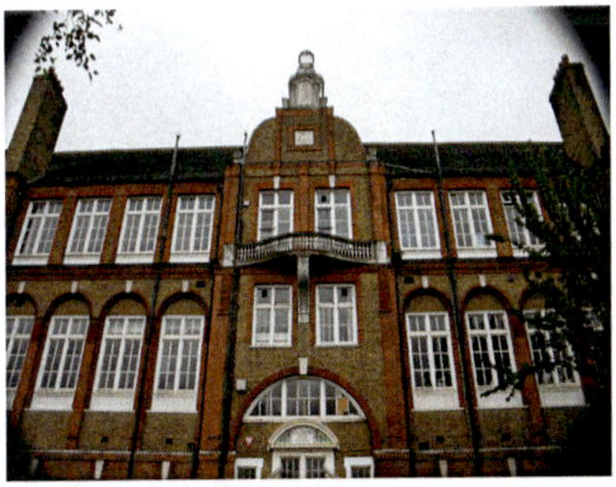

1: School no effect

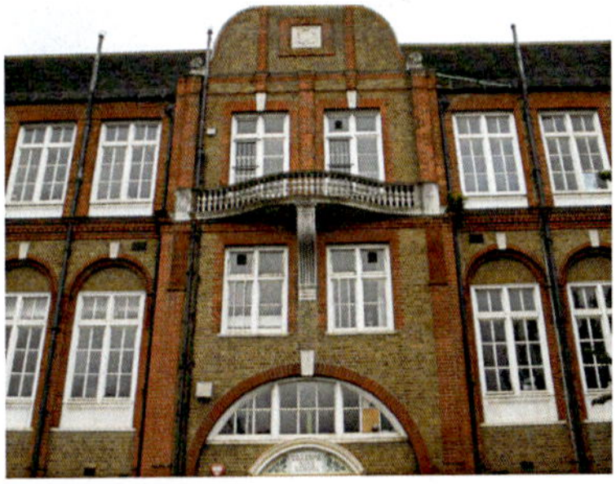

2: School Straightened & Cropped

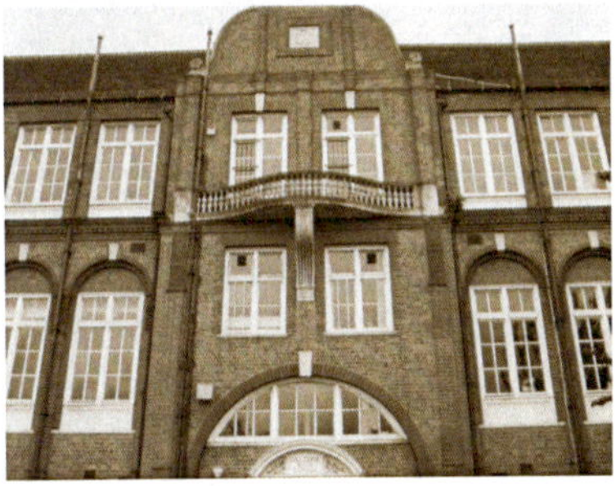

3: School Sepia, Grain & Glow Effect

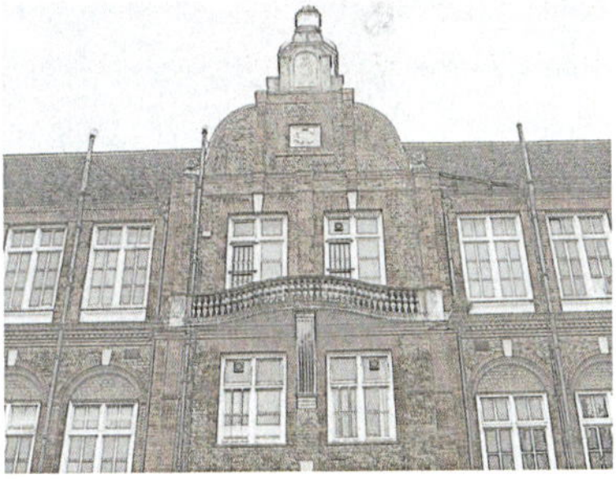

4: School Pencil Sketch Effect

When the projected or displayed colours are radically different, it is usually down to a technical fault with the projector or screen, or with the video cables. If this is the case, no amount of tweaking will help, and you (or someone else) will need to do some video system fault finding.

A case study from *It Must Be Madness*

For the song Baggy Trousers in the studio musical *It Must Be Madness*, we wanted to create a number of images that would be projected as the scenic background. Although the content for the spoken parts of the show was largely realistic, we made the design decision that content for musical numbers did not have to be.

1: We started with a wide angle shot looking up at a typical London primary school building. Almost every London neighbourhood still has at least one school built in this style, even if some of them have now been converted into apartments. The architecture is familiar to a London audience, and others. When used as a background it will help to set the scene, reinforcing the idea of 'primary school'.

2: First the image is slightly straightened up around the central verticals. (It is possible in Lightroom or Photoshop to completely square a shot up, but this would remove some of the vertiginous feeling of domination that the diverging perceptive lines give the image.) Then the image is cropped - to remove the trees and the lens hood, but also to make it fit a 4x3 frame. Always straighten first, then crop.

3: Next, contrast is slightly increased and a sepia effect is applied to give a nostalgic feel, since the song reflects back to the singers' time at school, we wanted to enhance a feeling of the past. To further enhance the nostalgic feel, some film grain is applied, and a glow effect. In Picasa, both these effects come with faders to vary parameters. Play around with the parameters until you achieve something you like, but don't forget to note the settings so you can apply the same effect (of grading) to all the images you want to have this 'look'.

4: Alternatively, the picture could be rendered as a pencil sketch, an different way of creating a nostalgic feel. Again, in Picasa the effect comes with parameter faders. I found a setting that enhanced the outline of the building against the grey sky. Having found that, I noted the parameter settings, and went back to the original image and re-cropped it to include more sky and the whole of the central roof feature. Finally I re-applied the pencil sketch effect using the parameter setting from my notes.

Below is a shot of the number from the final dress rehearsal, without the school buildings!

By the time we opened the show, it had been decided that the Baggy

Trousers number would be played with no curtain in front of the band. This curtain was the bottom half of our 4x3 screen, so our school building content was suddenly not going to work. This picture shows one of a number of 'blackboards' we used instead. The company had great fun creating these on large sheets of white paper with black pens. Co-designer Cate Blanchard then reversed the images, making the black white, etc, and cut them into an interesting sequence, interspersed scans of snap-shots the cast brought in of themselves as primary-school children.

In spite of all the planning, we still needed to improvise a solution almost at the last minute. This is normal!

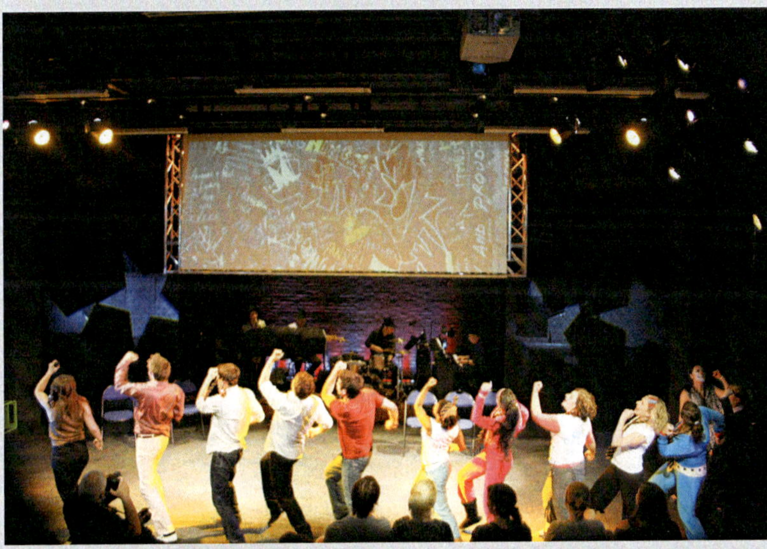

It Must Be Madness at Central School

A picture taken during the dress rehearsal of the number Baggy Trousers. The images of the school building have gone, to be replaced by blackboards full of graffiti. This change became necessary because the creative team decide to reveal the band for this up-beat number, taking away half the 4x3 screen.

The number worked much better with the band visible, and so the video team had to adapt their design ideas for this scene. This is a normal part of the process of taking a show from rehearsal room ideas onto a stage in front of an audience.

Now let's briefly consider getting it wrong. Suppose the content got swapped in two of the productions mentioned earlier, *Grease* and *A Street Car Named Desire*. They can both be set in 1950s USA, at the same time and place. But how would projected content made for a teenage musical work in a gritty play about missed opportunity and betrayal? Surely it is important that the video content works with the text of the play, and with the rest of the production design? Well perhaps not always, because it is possible to make performance with contradictory messages coming from each element. However, in most mainstream work, and most other work with a clearly defined story to tell, all the elements of the production design will usually aim to have a similar aesthetic. The video content will belong to the same visual world as the rest of the set, costume and lighting, support the same sonic world as the sound design and perhaps most importantly support the performers and the text.

Brightness and Contrast

As a video and projection designer you will usually want your content to be bright. As discussed earlier in the book, for humans, 'bright' is a relative term. What is bright outside on a dark night might be dim in a well lit room and invisible back outside in the daylight. Also, what our visual systems are good at picking up is rapid changes in contrast, sharp black letters against a clean white page for example. Low contrast makes it harder to distinguish between foreground and background – think about how hard it can be to make out detail in a distant view on an overcast grey day when the contrast between objects is reduced. Contrast helps too when it comes to distinguishing foreground and background. Without sufficient contrast it can be difficult to read an image, difficult to make out what is in the picture being projected. There is little point in getting the aesthetic of the content right if the audience can't actually make out the pictures.

When your content is projected (or displayed on a display screen) it is made of light. To project an area of white in the content, every pixel is "fully on" in a particular area, and that is as much light as the projector or display screen can produce. Similarly, in areas of the content that are black, the pixels are 'fully off'. That means no light from the projector hitting the screen in that area, and no light leaving that area of the display screen from the projector. All the colours and shades of grey are produced by pixels being something in between fully on and fully off. As we have already discussed, the colour of the screen and the way we humans process images in our brains can also make a difference to the way we see content.

Most of the time, when you are designing content for projection, you will be wanting to optimise brightness and contrast. This might start with making sure the white in your images is as bright as it can be without losing information. This means that the white areas of the projected images will be using all the available light from the projector – the pixels in the white areas will be 'fully on'. Making this happen could be as simple as increasing the brightness. With single pictures this can be done in even the simplest editing software, and can make a dramatic difference to the result on stage. Even for a movie clip, increasing the brightness is usually not too difficult, though a lot will depend on what software you are using to play the clip.

Increasing contrast between foreground and background can be trickier. Again though, for single pictures, there may be a simple parameter adjustment in your editing software, or it might need you to play with two or three parameters, for example, fill light, highlights and shadows in Picasa. What you can do without losing too much of the important detail will depend on the original image – and of course you have a lot more control over that when you shoot it yourself.

Histograms

The intensity of a digital picture can be represented as a type of graph known as a histogram. Intensity is represented on the horizontal axis and the amount of information recorded at that intensity is shown by the height of the bar at that intensity point. Bars at the extreme ends of the histogram indicate that there are areas of the image with no information. Pixels that are either fully on (over-exposed) are represented by lines at the extreme right, and pixels that are fully off (under-exposed) are represented by lines at the extreme left. Over-exposed areas are white with no detail and under exposed areas are black with no detail.

Intensity is represented as four separate channels, 'white', or the overall intensity, and three colours channels, red, green and blue. The histogram shows the amount of information stored at each intensity level for each channel or a combination of channels. In Picasa, the histogram shows all four channels together. The intensity faders are under the second tab (the sunshine symbol). As you play with the intensity faders you will see the histogram change. As you increase intensity the curves on the graph move to the right; eventually they begin to move off the graph, indicating detail is being lost, as areas of the image become white or over-exposed. Similarly as you decrease intensity (by decreasing any of the faders in Picasa) you will see the curves move off to the left. As you take this further, areas of the image again lose detail, but this time they become black or under-exposed.

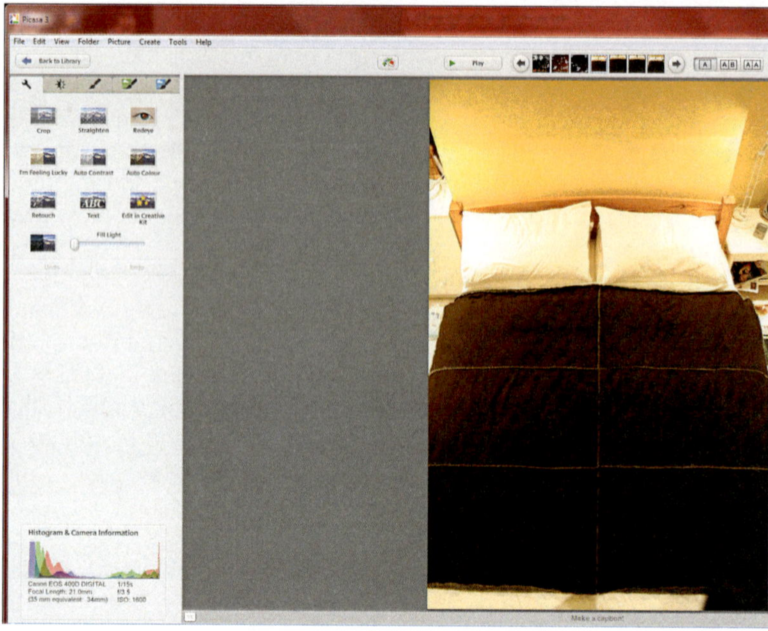

Screen Shot 1

Screen shot from Picasa 1: this is the unedited image of a bed for the production It Must Be Madness, used in the scene pictured in Chapter 1. The histogram is at the bottom left of the screen.

As you make larger adjustments using the intensity faders, you should also notice the histogram becoming spiky. This indicates lost information too. What is happening is the software is 'making up information' in some areas of the picture, and you are losing quality. Quite quickly after you first see the histogram become spiky, the image will be visibly degraded. It may become what is known as 'solarised'. How important this is will depend a lot on what you want to do with the image and on the style you are working in. In one of the pictures from *Re-Orientations* in Chapter 1, the large projected head of the performer on screen is slightly solarised, and in the context of that production design it is a decision that works. That won't always be the case, and sometimes the original image is just not good enough to do what you want it to do, no matter how much tweaking you do in the edit.

While high quality images for magazines and adverts will usually reject any image with under or over exposed parts, they can be a useful for

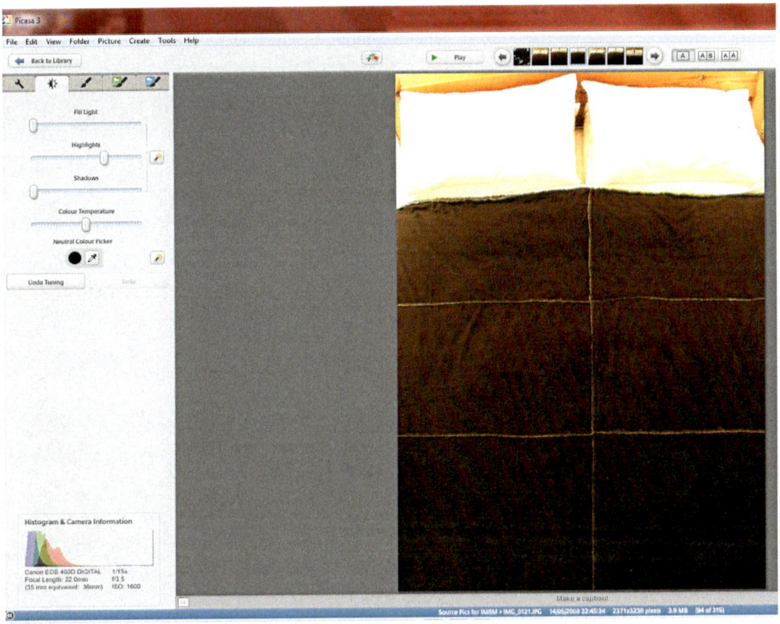

Screen Shot 2

Screen Shot 2 from Picassa: the edited image. Straightened, Highlights increased to "blow" the pillows (which will help these areas light the faces of the actors "on the bed"). Comparing the histograms you can see that, in increasing the Highlights and "blowing" the pillows, we have lost some of the highlight detail (information) from the highest intensity area of the graph, on the right. This area represents brightest areas of the image.

The image has also been cropped to improve its readability by removing potentially distracting detail at the foot of the bed.

the video designer. The second screen shot from Picasa shows the image with pillows 'blown out' (another term for over-exposed). When this image is projected the pillow areas will be as bright as they can be, lighting the faces of the couple in the bed. (See production shots from *It Must Be Madness* in Chapter 1.)

On Line and Off Line Adjustment

Deciding what level of brightness and contrast is best for each video design, and each piece of content within that design, is very often a process of trail and error. As mentioned earlier there are any number of factors that will affect the brightness perception of the audience. For any given scene, these factors include how much stage light is in use at any particular moment, how much was in use just in the last scene, how much of the stage is illuminated, and whether the rest of the performance space is lit too. In the final stage rehearsals, as the whole of the production design comes together, the video designer may well need to adjust brightness and/or contrast for particular images, groups of images, or for the whole show. Some playback programs will allow some level of adjustment in the moment, or on the fly. Changing the image using the playback software (be it Powerpoint, Qlab or a dedicated media server) is on-line editing. It is usually quick, but can be quite crude. Too much on-line editing can lead to losing the unifying look of a set of images, and undermine the quality of the design.

Even with video systems using the most sophisticated media servers, there is often a need to re-edit still images or clips to adjust brightness contrast, colour balance or grading in another program – off-line. This can take longer (though in a set up with an editing machine networked to a playback machine, it need not be) but the results are generally better, both for the look of the material being edited and the overall quality of the production design. After all, if you have spent time debating over what level of pencil sketch or glow you want on a set of images, that was presumably to make each image do its job within the overall video and production design. You don't want to spoil the unity of what you have created by crudely increasing the intensity of one or two images!

Rendering

To produce the final file as a high quality JPEG (for stills) or MPEG (for video clips) editing software goes through a process called rendering. This is essentially sorting out all the information and making it into high quality an image or set of images. It takes time – for still images and short standard definition clips, not that long, but still a noticeable amount of time. When software such as a media server applies a complex set of effects to a video file, that file too needs to be rendered to make it playable, but the media server is doing this in real time, and so it is taking short cuts when ever it can, and sometimes this results in a noticeable loss of quality.

Real time rendering, as performed on-line by media servers will not yet produce as consistently good quality images as off-line rendering by most photo and video editing packages. So if you need to apply complex effects to your raw content, it is best to do that off line and let the edit software render the file. Then the media server can do the final tweaks, without any loss of image quality.

It is worth knowing that it is a rare video design that has all the same content at the beginning of rehearsals through to opening night. There will almost always be a need to find new clips and still images. This new content may well need to be graded and colour balanced to fit with the look of the scene or the overall video design. Try to remember this as you are preparing your content. Make notes of what you have done to achieve each look. Note down the grading and colour balance recipes you have used, the settings you went for with effects, and what you were aiming for with the contrast and intensity adjustments you made. All of this information will help you create new content in rehearsals to seamlessly sit along side the painstakingly achieved stuff you made in advance – and help each element of your content to work aesthetically with the rest of the video design, and the production design too.

To Make It Yourself or To Find It?

This is one of the defining questions for any video design. Even if you know the answer, it might still be worth thinking one more time about the pros and cons of make-it-yourselves and find-it for each element of the design.

There are some types of content that it's just too expensive – or maybe impossible or unethical – to make yourself. For example large scale explosions, natural or man-made disasters, extreme realistic violence or vintage newsreel. Examples of this type of clip can be found in the public domain but often the production will need to pay a royalty to the copyright holder to access high quality clips. (See the Appendix on Copyright.)

There is a long history of using stock footage on stage, dating back almost as far as the invention of the movie itself. Everything from a moving background behind a stage car 'driving' along, to romantic cutaways of waves crashing on a shore or a train going into a tunnel.

Stock footage can be found in libraries on line, some of which may require a fee before you can even search everything they have. You and your production team need to be aware that decent footage is unlikely to be free. If you need good quality, high resolution clips from a library that charges, it is as well to alert the rest of the team to the potential costs as soon as possible, to avoid disappointment all round. Unfortunately, it appears to be increasingly difficult to negotiate affordable royalty payments for even small-scale and school productions, but who knows, you might be lucky.

Public domain video clips found on the web are sometimes of sufficient resolution and quality for projection on stage at standard resolution. Even when this is not the case, there may be ways of making a feature of the poor quality within your design. (See the projection design of helicopter action in the production of *Oliver's Army* mentioned in Chapter 1.)

Once you have decided to use stock footage, got hold of it and paid any licence fees, there may still be a need to colour balance and grade it, and to adjust intensity and contrast. After that though, there may be little else you need to do other than make sure it runs on cue, in which case turn now to Chapter 5.

If you decide that the design is better served by content you make yourself however, there are many more choices left, and most of them will still involve spending money.

If you are shooting material for you content – movie or static – here are a few things you will need:

A camera. Sounds obvious, but let's face it, any image you capture can only be as good as the camera you use. Things are looking up here though. I have been told of at least one major concert tour with video content shot on an iPhone and edited in iMovie, and not just for effect either. So a lot depends on what you want to shoot and where. As a starting point, make sure your camera produces images with a resolution at least as big as the projector or projection system.

A searchable catalogue of images – there is no point taking great shots if you can't find them on your computer. As you gather the material that may become your content, you need to catalogue it. Some people rely on re-naming their picture files with a name that says what the picture is of. Others use parameters such as "title" or "comment" and set their computer to display these fields. Others (like me) aim to tag every picture they shoot or collect with Key Words that indicate what is in the shot. I can then find all my pictures for (say) shots of trees in snow, by searching for the tags "trees" and "snow".

If you only plan to have a few different images on stage, and they are not complex, you can probably put them all in one folder and sort them by file name. If you are planning on making a lot of content, you will probably need to be much more organised and create a file structure – that is a set of folders and sub-folders on a hard drive that makes it easy to find what you are looking for. The illustration shows the file structure for *It Must Be Madness.*

Access to an editing program. Professionals use professional software packages such as Photoshop or Lightroom (for still images) or After Effects (for video and animations). However it is possible to make

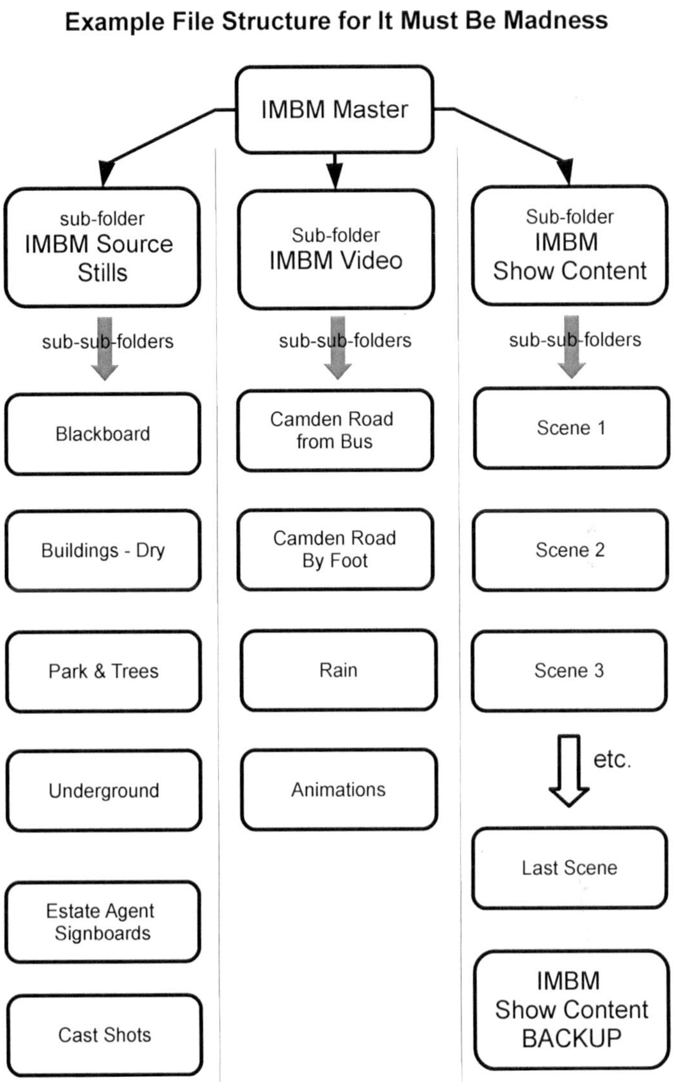

Figure 2: Video File System

perfectly acceptable content for standard definition projection using free or inexpensive packages such as Paint in Windows or Picassa (from Google) for still images, or iMovie for video. Free packages provide fewer options and some things take longer to do, but don't automatically think you have to use expensive professional software to make great looking content.

Projecting Backgrounds

Let's look first at content that is there to depict, evoke or indicate a particular space; projected landscapes and rooms are a good example.

There are many style options open to the video designer when it comes to depicting, evoking, or creating the world of the performance on stage. Deciding the style of the images will have a big impact on the overall production design.

Photo-realism – these are images that look like a full page picture from an expensive magazine or footage from a slick wildlife documentary. The prison hall from *Bad Girls* in Chapter 1 is a good example.

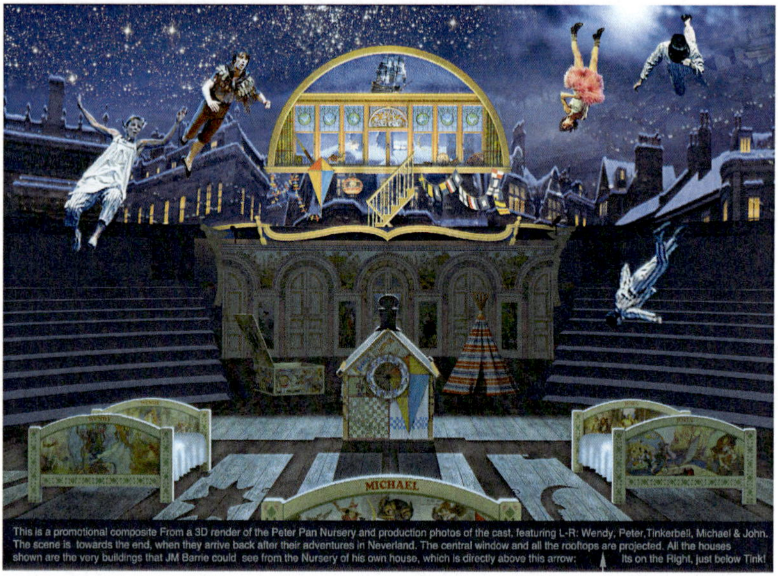

Peter Pan Pictures from Bill Dudley

The production design for Peter Pan is an examples of the work of William Dudley, one of the top practitioners working in this kind of 3D projection for the stage.

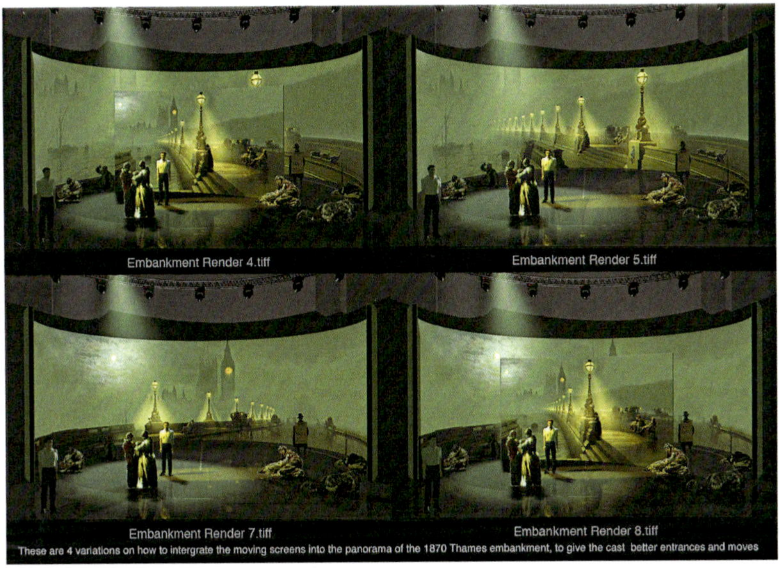

Woman in White pictures from Bill Dudley

Computer renders from the production design for The Woman in White, from 2004/5 (with thanks to William Dudley for these images)

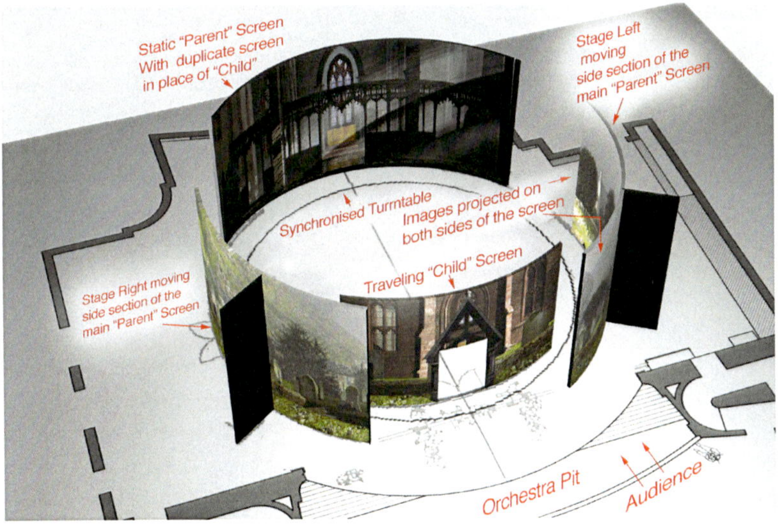

Hyper-real 3D – images that evoke games worlds or other digital spaces, or the worlds of computer animated film. Above is an image from the spectacular production of *Peter Pan* produced in a specially constructed tent in London's Hyde Park, and from the London production of *The Woman in White*. The production designer William Dudley is one of the foremost exponents of this style of design. To produce work at the scale of this production is well beyond most company's budgets and technical capabilities, but its worth looking at what can be achieved with enough of both!

Drawn – anything from monochrome outline sketches to full colour, fully rendered drawings, from child-like art through various comic-book and graphic novel styles, to renaissance sketches or whatever your digital pencil can come up with. There are examples of simple drawn content from *Oliver's Army* in Chapter 1.

Making Digital Scenic Backdrops

Very often the video designer is asked to produce content that gives the audience the impression of a particular place. This might be by projecting a background landscape (static or moving) on a single large screen or multiple wrap-round screens, or by suggesting a view through (imagined) windows, mapped onto an otherwise featureless wall, or in dozens of other ways. The point is that for the illusion to work – for the audience to 'get' the location on stage – the images need to work as indicators of the location within the aesthetic rules of the production design. For *The Woman in White*, those rules meant flat surfaces were seen as moving three-dimensional panoramas. For *Oliver's Army* the rules meant white line drawings could indicate a café table and chairs and a menu board.

The images also need to present objects, the city-scape or café tables or whatever, in such a way that the audience allows their 'suspended belief' to see them as a real enough background to the action on stage. The video content needs to show the scene as if the objects in the content – the Thames Embankment of *The Woman in White*, or the café table of *Oliver's Army* were the actual background to the scene played out in front of them. This means the photograph, drawing or computer animation needs to depict the objects from a similar point of view to the one the audience would see if the objects were really there. This usually means the images need to appear to be at a scale that fits with the rest of the stage and the people on it, and it usually means the point of view used to produce the image (be it photographic or not) is what film theorists sometimes call 'neutral'.

The neutral point of view for camera is generally a shot taken at around head-height, looking more or less straight ahead, with a lens that neither overly magnifies or miniaturises the scene, and gives more or less the same perspective distortion we are used to seeing in our day-to-day lives. The aim is to produce a picture that looks similar to the view from

War Horse Exhibit

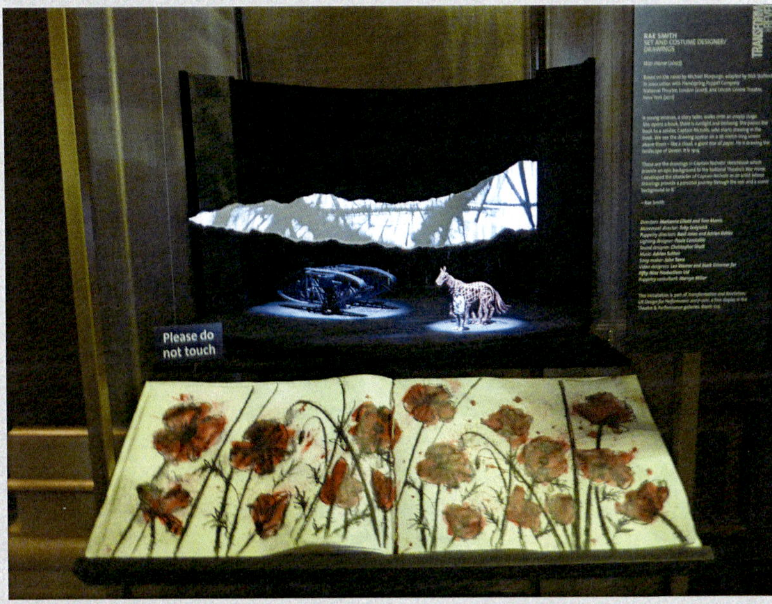

A model showing elements of Rae Smith's design for the UK National Theatre's production of War Horse.

Projected on the "torn paper" screen behind the man, horse and tank, is a fragment of a watercolour sketch of a view from the trenches, a location for several key scenes in the play. Below the model is a drawing of poppies from one of Rae's sketch books which were also used as video content for the show.

The video design for War Horse, by Leo Warner and Mark Grimmer of Fifty Nine Productions, is an example of projection mapping. In order to achieve enough brightness, several projectors are directed onto stage. The content is "mapped" into the required area of each projector's beam using a Catalyst Media Server.

This model was part of the SBTD exhibition Transformation and Revelation at the Victoria and Albert Museum in London, in 2012/13.

that spot of a normally sighted person. A 50mm lens on a full frame DSLR camera or a 35mm lens for a sub-full frame is usually considered to be the ideal for taking this kind of shot. If the image is to be projected onto a screen more or less perpendicular to the centre line of the stage – say a traditional cyclorama or a flat back wall for example – the shot would normally be taken looking straight on to the major elements of the image, keeping the horizon, and any other horizontal lines, parallel and horizontal in the final image. The school building shot earlier in this chapter is one example, the prison hall from *Bad Girls* in Chapter 1 is another.

Even when a projected background is not attempting to represent or evoke a realistic landscape, it is often best to use this neutral PoV – as if the thing being projected were actually there. Designer Rae Smith makes use of her own evocative drawings and watercolour sketches as projected backgrounds in the production design of the National Theatre's *War Horse*. The 'screen' is a scaled-up representation of a piece of a page torn from an artists sketch book. The video design incorporates sketches and drawings projected onto the torn paper screen, as you can see in the picture of the set model, exhibited at the Victoria and Albert Museum in 2012.

Say I want to indicate to the audience that the action on stage takes place in front of a building. I'm going to project an image of the building that is a realistic as possible, without grabbing attention. It needs to just say to the audience "you recognise this type of building and you know the type of place where we now are" and that's all. I'm creating a background and I want the image to largely disappear from the audiences' consciousness once they 'get' where the performers are. To do this I'm going to try and use the most neutral image I can – something that looks right, but is unremarkable.

I would take shots of the building at about the same distance from the building as I want the front row of the audience to believe they are. If the stage is raised, I might tilt the camera slightly up to help continue the natural perspective of the audience. I would shoot the building absolutely straight on, to make sure all the horizontal lines, such as window sills, gutters rows of brickwork, etc remain parallel and horizontal in the captured images.

I'd shoot the image with my zoom lens set around 35mm (because I'm not using a full-frame camera, and that is closest my equipment comes to matching the view I see with the view through the camera.) Remembering how big I'm going to want to make this image – it needs to be crisp and sharp with no sign of shake! With this in mind, I'd use an

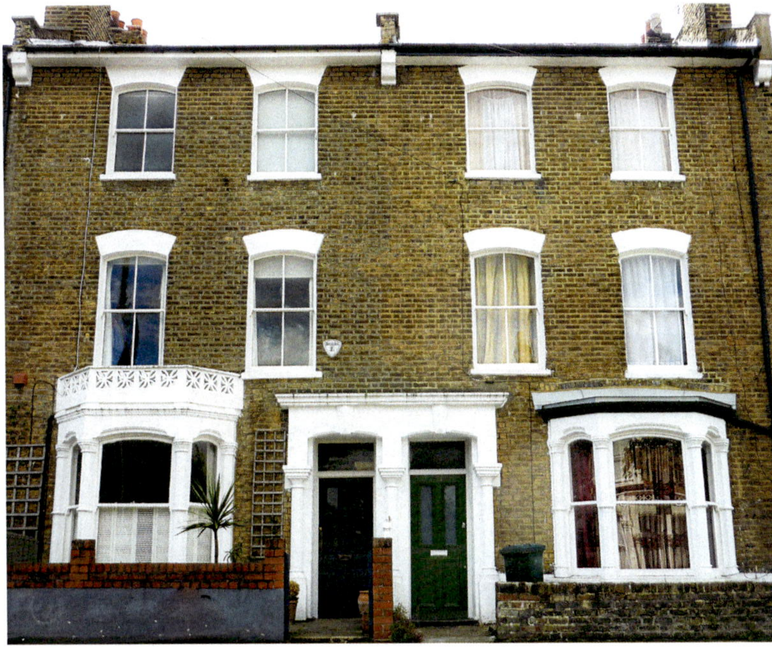

Street Backdrop: a digital photo of London Terraced Houses, with some editing to prepare it for use as a scenic backdrop.

I have removed some distracting damage from the grey front wall, and the house numbers in Lightroom. To make the image more unremarkable further edits might include making all the windows black (to get rid of coloured curtains and reflection) removing the cables, and possibly the palm tree (though this would take some time to do well).

aperture setting to give me a good depth of field – say f-8. Ideally I would capture the images on a slightly overcast day, to avoid strong shadows that might create visual distractions in the captured image or cause me other problems later on. This might mean using a slowish shutter speed because I would also want to use lowish ISO (or film speed) setting to get the highest quality images. If I was using a shutter speed below 1/125s I'd probably use a tripod.

I'd also aim to shoot the images when the building is at its least used – perhaps mid-morning if it's a residential building or before the working day starts if it's a commercial one. This reduces the possibility of people appearing in windows and causing distractions in the final image.

Point of View (PoV)

PoV is a commonly used term in TV, film and cinema – short for Point of View. For a film-maker, PoV is a way of describing some types of shot. For example a thriller or murder mystery film might mix shots from the PoV of the killer that is as if we were seeing through the eyes of the killer with shots from above – which we might call a 'bird's-eye' PoV. Each PoV gives the audience a different perspective on the action.

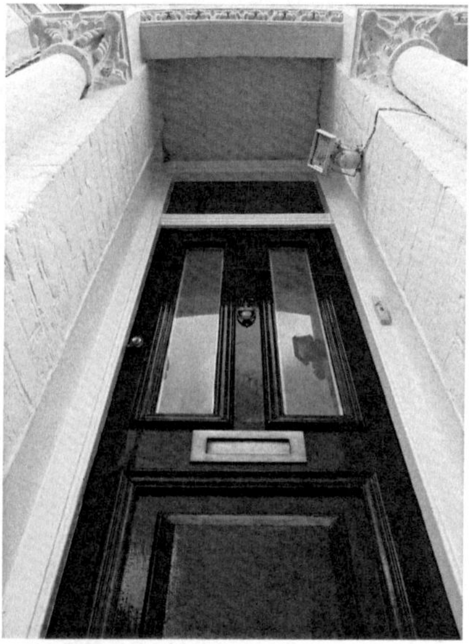

Front Door Mouse PoV

A Front Door, as it might look from the PoV of a mouse (again, edited to remove the house numbers)

PoV is one of several choices that need to be made whenever images are captured through a lens, whether shooting still photographs or movie clips. Cinematographers and film theorists have other terms for shot types, and if you are interested in making film (for stage or for cinema or TV) the handling of PoV, especially as an aid to storytelling, is one of the most fundamental skills of cinematography. It is also an important consideration when designing content, especially if that content is representing real things, such as buildings, landscapes or people.

For the video designer on stage, the PoV can radically alter the way the audience not only sees the content on the screen, but the whole stage picture. The neutral perspective mentioned above makes use of an eye-level PoV. If instead of striving to make the background unremarkable the video designer wants to make it imposing, the shot choice would be quite different. If I wanted to do this I might choose a wide angle lens looking almost straight up the building – which we might describe as the PoV of an ant or a mouse.

Including cast members in content

There are many reasons why you might want to include images of cast members in video content. To show them doing something they can't do on stage for example, or simply to show them in a picture, for example from a newspaper. Sometimes the image will be created live, perhaps at the side of stage. The only real considerations then will be to do with making sure there is enough light for the camera (without any spilling onto stage if its not wanted there) and making sure the background of the shot is appropriate. You probably don't want to project images of a stage hand relaxing in the background of your shot for example.

If the cast images are to be recorded before hand and played back for each performance, it will be necessary to agree a date, place and time to "shoot" the content. This can involve some interesting negotiations, and there are two additional considerations. First is, will the right costume be ready for the shoot? The performers will need to wear something and if the idea is to create a look that is consistent with the way they look on stage, they will need to wear the right costumes, and the right hair-styles, wigs and make-up too for that matter.

The second consideration is will understudies or alternative cast members be available for the shoot too? What happens if the cast member(s) featured in the content is/are unwell for a performance? The video designer will want to have images of the replacement ready to substitute for the content that features the missing person. If the content features several principal performers, all with understudies or substitutes, the number of possible combinations can add up fast and lead to a lot of shooting and a lot of alternative files. Sorting out the right one to play on any given night can be an issue too!

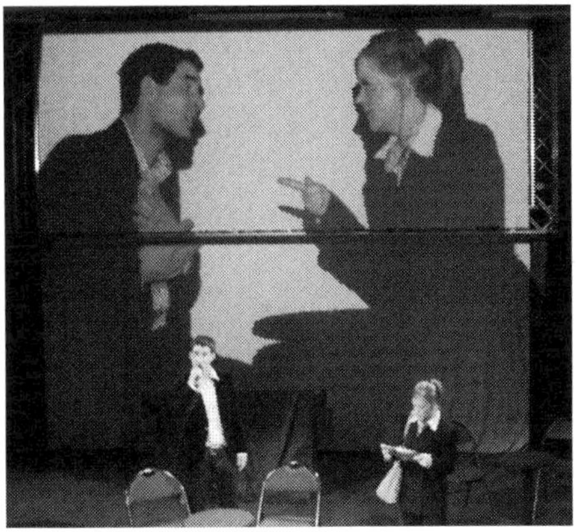

IMBM Cafe Row 1

A still image of the start of the argument became the background for the number 'My Girl's Mad At Me'.

The shot was taken with both actors in costume and make-up, against a white sheet, using a flash gun to make a double shadow.

All this aside, when you are involved in setting up a shoot, try to remember that performers can get quite tense and nervous in front of the camera. Allow plenty of time for setting up too. If you have not lit for camera before, try to get help from someone who has. Usually you will need a much softer light that generally used on stage, for example. Perhaps surprisingly, this means that bright sunlight is not the best for still video camera.

Finally, check what is going on in the background of your shot, especially if you are shooting outside in a public place. It can help if you can control the depth of field of your shot (that is have only the main subject in sharp focus with the background out of focus). This leads to the background, and especially the distant background, becoming indistinct. Sometimes though, it is necessary to rig your own background – though naturally this adds time to the set-up and potentially complicates the lighting.

Abstract content – if you can make it digital you can project it

Video content does not have to be representative, realistic or photographic. We know that you have to get your content to the projector as a digital video signal. Beyond that, the constraints on the designer's choices are few. Can you digitise the image? This might mean photographing with a digital camera, scanning it, or videoing it with a digital video camera. As long as the output can be turned into a file that your playback machine can read, in principle you can project it.

Suppose you are making abstract patterns with coloured oils on water – as the 'old school' projecting artists of the 1960s and 70s did for New York Art Happenings and early concerts by The Pink Floyd. Light it, set up a video camera to record it (or play it live) and project the result (or show it on a display screen).

Of course you might make the images in the digital world of a computer graphics program, in which case the only issue will be file compatibility. Some really interesting work involves taking an infra-red security camera to monitor the stage, and then using that output as part of the projection. This can be a way of mapping content, live, onto performers' bodies, or cutting holes in the content so that there is no projection on them, but all around them. The production of *A Midsummer Night's Dream* from Leeds University, pictured in Chapter 1, used this idea.

At large scale, this kind of set up is still expensive and technically difficult to achieve. However at smaller scale, you can do lots with a Wii. If you are technologically minded, it is not too difficult to make use of the output of a Wii in a small scale video design, but you will need to be aware that the device was built to track objects in a domestic room, so a stage of any size might be too much for it.

One of the main pioneers in the field of interactive video design are the dance company Troika Ranch in the USA. Their production designer Mark Coniglio has developed a program called Isadora, which is really good value for what it does, and relatively easy to use. A full description of what Isadora can do would be a whole book in its self. There is lots about Isadora on the web, but a good place to start is Troika's website http://troikatronix.com

Next Steps

So far, we have looked at screens, projectors, lenses and now content. The next step is to put all of this together and start making the production on stage. The video designer will usually want to see what the director and performers are doing in the rehearsal room. Have ideas about the piece changed from the initial meetings? Have new ideas about what video can do for the piece begun to emerge, or has everyone forgotten they have video? It is important for the video designer to stay in touch with these kinds of developments if they are going to actively and usefully contribute to the final production design.

The video designer will also want to stay in touch with the set designer, to ensure the realisation of the set is still on track and that the screen or screens will still work (aesthetically and practically). She or he will want to make sure the costumes have not changed too much as well, especially if some of the content design involves shots of the performers in costume. The video designer will probably be interested in how the colour palettes of both the set and the costumes are coming to life, and make sure the content design is still in the same aesthetic world.

Inevitably there will be technical considerations too. If any equipment needs to be hired, there are more questions. For example, has the right specification gone to the hire company, and can they deliver it? Are the cables really the right length? Do they work? Do they have the right connectors on each end?

It is increasingly common practice to set up the video system in the rehearsal room, in the final few days of rehearsals. This has many advantages. It gives everyone a chance to see what the content will look like, and this can be especially important for actors. If a lot of the set is projected behind them, they will usually gain confidence through seeing the content that is helping to create the world of the performance. It also gives the director and all the designers a chance to discuss any changes that are deemed necessary before it is too late to make them.

5 PUTTING IT ALL TOGETHER

Fit-Up, Technical Rehearsals, Dress Rehearsals, and Performance

A good technical rehearsal, or 'tech' as it often abbreviated, is one where at the end everyone knows what they need to do to make the show happen, and everyone is still friends! If you are familiar with the process, skip through to the next few paragraphs. If you have never encountered a technical rehearsal or you are unsure about cues and cueing, read on.

The Purpose of Technical Rehearsals

Very often on stage we want to make it appear to the audience that they are seeing something special happening for the very first time. Of course this is rarely the case. In a murder mystery play, the surprise on the faces of the actors when the victim is killed or the killer is revealed needs to look spontaneous every night. This is achieved through the skills of the actors and rehearsal. The dancers who fling themselves across the stage apparently at random do not end up in each other's arms at exactly the right point in the music by chance, but only after a good deal of trial and error to develop the dance and practice to get it perfect. If the video design involves something like helping to reveal the killer, or highlighting the final move of the dance, making that happen in the right way and at exactly the right time every performance will also take some experimentation and practice. This is the purpose of technical rehearsals.

Working through the show, section by section, all the technical and design elements are tried out and put together. When the desired outcome has been reached, everything that needs to happen to arrive at that outcome is recorded so that it can happen exactly like that again, and the company move on to do the same for the next section.

The majority of technical rehearsals happen on the stage or performance space where the first shows will happen too. It is likely that in most cases the performers will arrive at the technical rehearsal almost ready to perform for an audience – indeed this is usually considered necessary. However, very often this will be the first time that everyone has seen (and heard) some significant elements of the production design all in one place. Adjustments will very often need to be made in the run up to the technical rehearsals. Ideas and concepts of individual designers may need tweaks to ensure their individual or team contributions work better with the production design as a whole. Sometimes technical adjustments will need to be made – perhaps accommodating some part of the building that was left out of a drawing or simply finding a way to make a not-quite-long-enough cable long enough with a bit of creative adjustment. For a video designer in particular, there will almost always be changes to be made and it is prudent to be well prepared for this.

Cues and cueing

Cues coordinate all the elements of live performance. Actors learning their lines also learn the *cue lines* that come just before theirs, the lines that give them the *cue* to speak, move or whatever. Dancers learn their *cues* as part of learning the dance – they may take *cues* from the music, listening for a particular phrase on which to start a set of moves, or watching for someone else to do or say something that *cues* them in. Singers on stage take their *cue* to start singing from particular beat in the music, often signalled by the conductor. To keep a performance working as planned, all the performers perform *on cue.*

And so it is for the technical and design elements too. Coordinated changes of the set, costume, light, sound and video all happen *on cue* in any planned performance. These *cue points,* that is the point where the change begins, are agreed during rehearsals, usually first in the technical rehearsal, and then refined through dress rehearsals and early performances (previews). Each change is given a *cue number,* and the situation that results from the change is often called the *cue state.*

It is important to distinguish between *the cue point* – that is the point in the piece when the change begins – and *the cue state* – which is the result of the cue having happened. However, most theatre and live performance makers use the word *cue* when talking about *cue states* and *cue points.* So if your director talks about this or that *video cue* they may be talking about particular content (the *cue state*) or the point in the show when that content appears (the *cue point*). It can be confusing, but the context will usually tell you what is meant.

Here is an example of how you might think about just one *video cue.* Imagine a production that includes the following line and stage direction:

> *Sasha*: "I heard the waves crashing on the shore" (the sea is seen through the open window)

Through discussion with the director and others, it is agreed that a video clip of waves should slowly appear on the screen through the window, so that by the time the audience hear Sasha's line the waves can clearly be seen. Before the appearance of the waves, this screen has no video image on it.

The state of the screen being blank might be called *video cue state 1* and the state with the waves clip running might be called *video cue state 2.* By the time this line is spoken the clip has to be on the screen and running, so we will be in *video cue state 2.* This means that the cue point – *video cue 2* – will need to be some little time before the line so that there is time for the video clip to appear slowly. But we don't want to distract the audience, or give away too early what is about to happen, by having the waves appearing too early. We will probably also want to supplement the visual effect of the waves on the screen with a *sound cue* and to change the lighting state on stage too, perhaps to isolate Sasha as he remembers, or simply to take stage light off the screen so that the waves can be seen. All three changes will need to be coordinated – the time taken for the transition between each *cue state* to be decided and each *cue point* defined.

All this coordination helps to determine how the audience understand or 'get' what is going on on stage, and how they respond to it. If the production aims to make this moment poignant (perhaps Sasha is remembering some tragic loss) the transitions will be set with the aim of helping to create that feeling in the audience. The placement of the *cue points,* and the time taken for each transition between one *cue state* and the next (the *cue time)* will all be decided with the aim of helping the actor playing Sasha to gain the sympathy of the audience.

But suppose the piece is a comedy, and the short scene ends with a bucket of water being thrown over Sasha from off stage. It is likely that the timing of at least some of the transitions will be quite different. (It might also be that the *cue states* will be quite different too. It's interesting to think what might be the difference between a video clip of waves used to gain sympathy, and one that might make the audience laugh.) The point is that just as the choice of video content – or *cue states* – will have an impact on what the audience 'get' from the production, so too will choices of *cue points* and *cue timings.*

In the tradition of North America and the UK, these stage *cue points* are *called* by the deputy stage manager (DSM) or show caller. This person has a large copy of the script (or the score for shows with music) *marked up* with the exact position of each *cue point.* In other traditions, each operator learns the show, and learns all their own *cue points.* Both ways of working have advantages and disadvantages. It's a good idea to decide early in the production process which model of practice you are all going to follow.

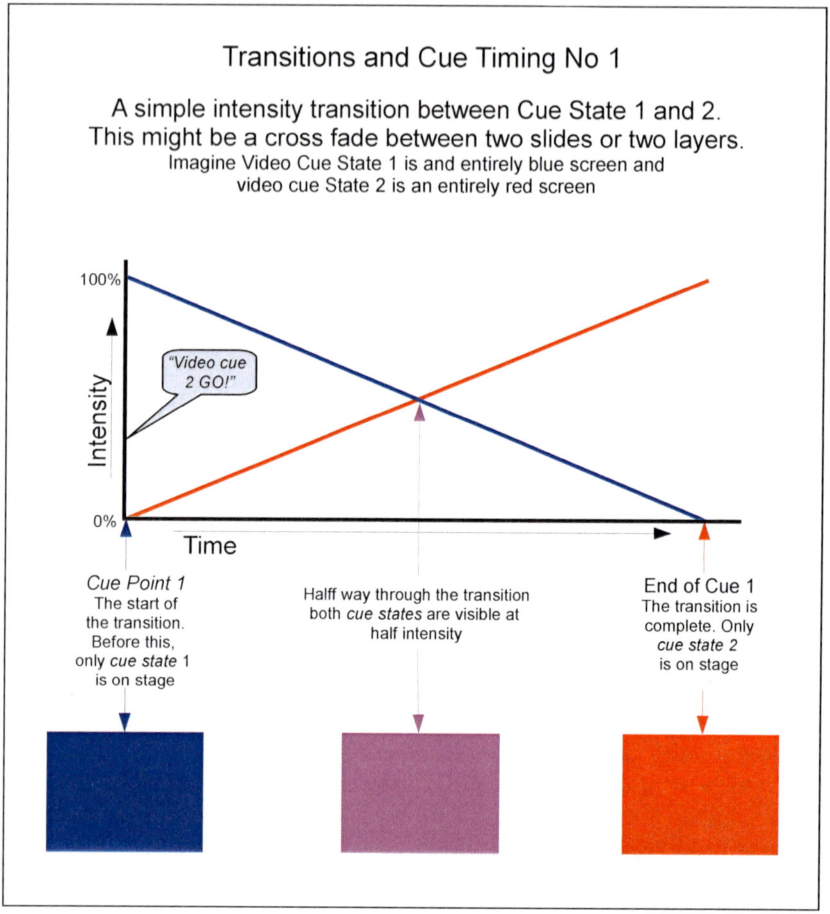

Before the Tech Starts: check that all your kit works!

Time on stage is usually very precious and should not be wasted. If at all possible, before technical rehearsals begin, all the technical elements will be thoroughly tested and made ready. This is particularly true for video systems. As equipment is rigged in the performance space small errors in planning drawings can become quite troublesome. Perhaps the projector will not fit where you had planned, or there is a speaker hanging between it an the screen! Poor communication over preceding weeks can suddenly come to light – perhaps the 20m cable you ordered turns out to be only 20 feet long! Try to make sure you have enough time and access to additional resources to be able to cope with as many of these issues as you can, without raising your stress level – and that of anyone else.

Expected Colour vs. Projected Colour

It may become clear that some elements of the content no longer fit with the overall concept and will need to be changed. Perhaps the colour pallet of the set and the projected content aren't as close a match as you and the set designer had hoped for. Projectors produce colours in a different way to computer monitors. Added to this, old tired projector lamps can change the colour of the projected output too. If you find that the colours coming out of your projector(s) are not what you expected, the first thing to do is to find out what needs to change. Check the projector is working OK by projecting a test image – for example a test card – and compare the projection to a known original. You will often be able to check how old the projector lamp is and to adjust the colour balance of the projector output through the projector menu.

Once the projector is as good as it can be, if there are still colour issues you will probably have to adjust the content to make it match the set.

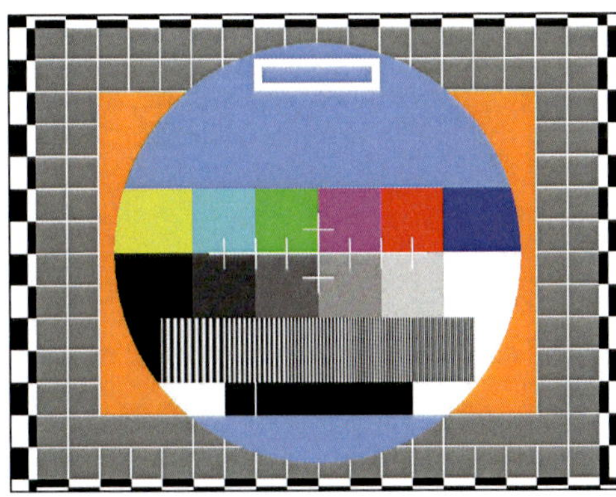

This is the Colour Testcard of RTVE (Radiotelevisión Española) from around 1980, downloaded from Wikipedia Commons.

It is a good idea to download something like this to help you diagnose colour and other problems with screens and projectors. You may also want to print off a copy on a good quality colour printer for comparison.

(Remember: If you are using a coloured screen, this will effect the colours you see. Use a white screen to set the colour balance of your projector(s). A plain white sheet draped over the screen will do.)

Colour is not the only thing you may need to adjust in your content once you see it on stage. You may need to increase the contrast of some content to make the images more readable on stage. Text may be too small to read and may need adjustment. (Of course the actual text may need to change too.) Vertical, horizontal or other dominate lines in content may need to be tweaked to line up with set elements. It is for these reason, and others outlined below, that it essential to be prepared to make changes to your content during the technical rehearsal period, and to have access to editing programmes you are familiar with.

So, as the video designer, you should aim to have a complete working video system ready in good time for the scheduled start of technical rehearsals. You should also aim to have briefed any additional operators and/or programmers on both the system and your design ideas, so that they can work as efficiently as possible with you to realise the video design as a coherent part of the overall production design.

If you have live cameras with operators – make sure they have time to get to know their equipment. If you have the luxury of a programmer, that person will be more useful to you and the production if she or he knows something about what you will be trying to do with video. Try to make sure too that there is time to prepare and check out all the equipment the programmer will be using.

Make sure you have a copy of the script (or score or whatever) that you can make notes on. That way you stand a much better chance of always knowing where in the piece you are working, and recalling exactly what you did earlier. This is somewhere a storyboard comes in handy too as it will be a reference for you and the team. You can use it to remind everyone what you planned to do for each scene as it comes to be rehearsed. You can also use it to show what is planned for future scenes, and a reminder of what each past scene looked like. Technical rehearsals for complex performances can go on for days or even weeks. In these situations it can be easy to forget exactly what you have done before, or the order in which you did it.

Finally, prepare yourself physically. Try to make the space you (and your colleagues) will be working in as comfortable as possible. Poor seating and an uncomfortable workspace will not help you all to concentrate and do your best work. Try to be well rested and fed prior to the start of the technical rehearsal too. It's generally much easier to be creative when you are alert and not hungry. Make sure you have all the power sockets you need, including one for a work light and another for the charger of your mobile phone – you'll need both.

Playback Machines

At the heart of any video system for live performance is the playback machine. This is where the content is accessed, processed and sent to the projector(s) or display screen(s). Whatever form the playback machine takes, its main job is to get the right content to the right screens at the right time, preferably without causing too much stress along the way. The playback machine will usually be programmed to play video cue states in order. It will also usually be possible to program the cue timing and other specifics of all the transitions.

The playback machine could be a laptop computer, or even a tablet or smart phone. In some circumstances the playback machine could be a professional DVD player with the ability to cue and loop, or it could be a dedicated media server, based around a high-end personal computer running custom software, with additional high-end graphics cards. If the design uses mostly live cameras, the machine at the heart of the system could be a vision mixer. It feels a bit silly to call a vision mixer the playback machine, but in some stage video systems that is the job it does.

What about the content? Well, this will almost always be either digital video files, or the output of live video cameras. Thinking just about the digital video files for now, they have to be stored somewhere, hopefully in a logical way, so they can be accessed by the software in the playback machine. The content store might be built into the machine – say the RAM or built-in hard drive of a personal computer, or the store may be separate device, say an external hard drive (or a stack of DVDs if your playback machine is a DVD player).

When the playback machine is a computer (which includes tablet computers or smart-phones) the key to what makes it do its job is the dedicated software. The next section looks at some pros and cons of different software.

Presentation Software

This includes Keynote (for Apple Mac) and Powerpoint (from Microsoft, running on Windows) as well as several other programs that allow the user to create *slides* and to play them back in a given order. To be useful to the video designer, it is good to have a lot of flexibility over each transition from one slide to the next, but for a simple show, this may not be necessary.

For some, these programs do not have the glamour of the dedicated video software we will come on to, but they do have a number of significant advantages:

- They have a familiar feel. Because these programs are designed to be part of a suite of office software, the user interface is similar to that of the programs used for day-to-day stuff such as writing. Most of the production team are likely to be able to make the software work, which means if the video designer has to go off to do something specialist, others can playback cues or even make new cues with new slides.
- They work reliably! Keynote and Powerpoint are made by big corporations and used all over the world by millions of people; if these programs have bugs they get found by thousands of users and generally get sorted out quickly. This is not to say that specialist video design software does not work reliably, but there is a lot more general support with most presentation packages than with even the best media server program.
- Easy to set up. There is very little faffing around trying to get the right images on the projectors or display screen. These days, the computer's operating system will do lots of set up for you – *providing you use the right cables* (see the technical appendix relating to VGA and DVI cable systems).
- What you see is what you get. These programs are designed to display the finished slide in the same way that you see it on the screen of the computer you make it with. This is not always the case with specialist video software.
- You are much less likely to need expensive accessories to get your system working.
- You probably have at least one of these programs already.

With presentation software, generally you make a slide for each video cue state. You can use text, pictures, photographs, and video clips as content in your slides. You can place that content where ever you want it within the slide too, and you can insert backgrounds for each slide, or for the whole slide show. If you want your content to disappear completely for a while, put a black slide into the show for that point.

Through trial and error it is even possible to do some simple projection mapping this way. Of course it won't be as simple to achieve good results as it would be using a dedicated video designer program but once you have got one slide right, you can use that as a master for all the rest. (There are some more tips on simple projection mapping later.)

Once your computer is 'talking' to the projector(s) or screen(s), and your content is made and stored as a set of slides, the final thing to look at is getting the right content to the screen(s) at the right time, and in the right way. Video system cues become *transitions* in presentation software. Transitions define how the video output changes from one slide to the next. Parameters include:

A: the time taken for the next slide to go from not being there, to being the only thing there (sometimes called the *in time* or *reveal time*).

B: the time taken for the first slide to go from being the only thing there, to not being there (sometimes called the *down time*. These two times need not be the same).

Any delay between A starting and B starting (or between B starting and A starting).

The way in which the change happens e.g. fading evenly across the whole screen, or from the bottom first, or wiping across, or from top to bottom, in from the middle outwards etc. There are lots of options!

See following diagrams overleaf.

Although both Powerpoint and Keynote have defaults that can get in the way of creativity, but with a bit of patience it is usually possible to find a way of doing most things a video designer needs to do. For example, the programs usually assume that you want the same transition between each slide – but you probably don't. With a bit of investigation you can find settings that define timings, fades and other parameters for each transition (and remember all those users mean there is almost bound to be someone out there who has tried doing what you want to do and can help). Once that is done, you can set up the program to change from one image to the next at the click of a mouse or the push of a space bar, or with a little technical creativity, the GO of the lighting console or even some action of a performer.

> *Technical creativity* in this context often means understanding MIDI – the communication protocol developed for digital music making. Many lighting and sound consoles can be set up to send and receive MIDI signals and there are several inexpensive boxes that allow laptop computers to do the same. The details of the set-up will vary from console to console and from MIDI box to MIDI box. The usual aim is to have the lighting console send a "GO" message to the computer running the presentation software – to synchronise video and lighting cues, but you can just as easily synchronise the video to the sound system.

Transitions and Cue Timing No 2

A split intensity transition with a delay time between Cue States 1 and 2.

This might be a cross fade between two slides or two layers

The *Delay Time* is the time between the *cue point* and a secondary action, in this case, the beginning of the appearance of *cue state 2.*

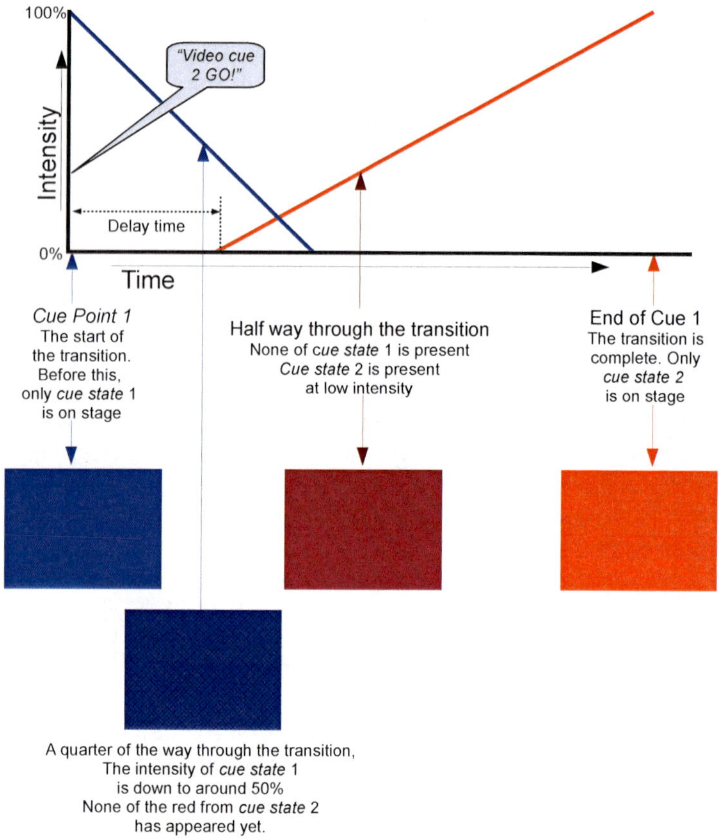

Transitions and Cue Timing No 3

Another split intensity transition between Cue States 1 and 2.
This might be a cross fade between two slides or two layers.

Again the Delay Time is the time between the *cue point* and a secondary action, in this case, the beginning of the disappearance of *cue state 1*.

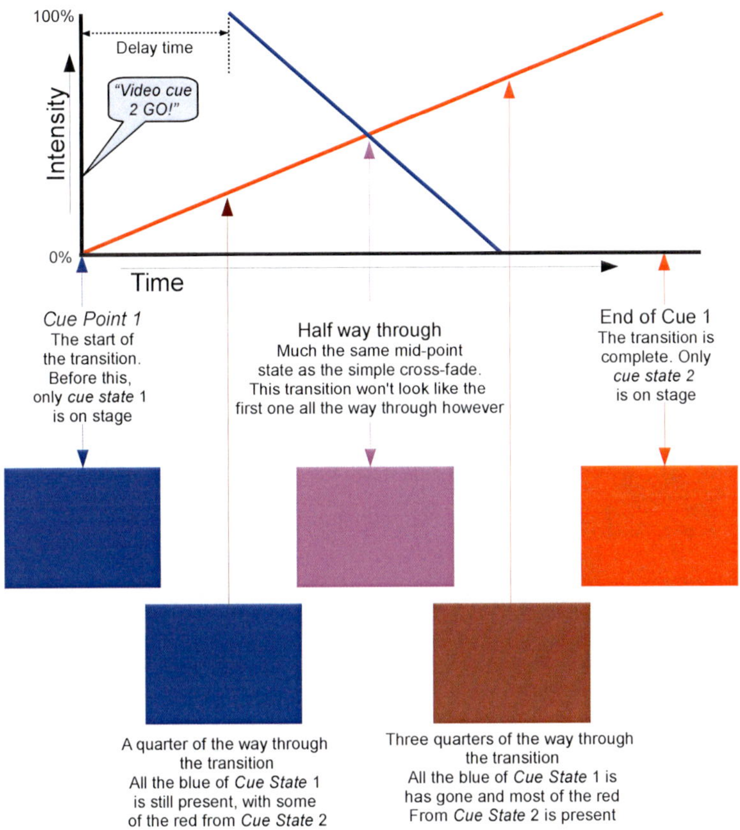

Transitions and Cue Timing No 4

A vertical wipe transition between cue states 1 and 2.
This might be a cross fade between two slides or two layers.

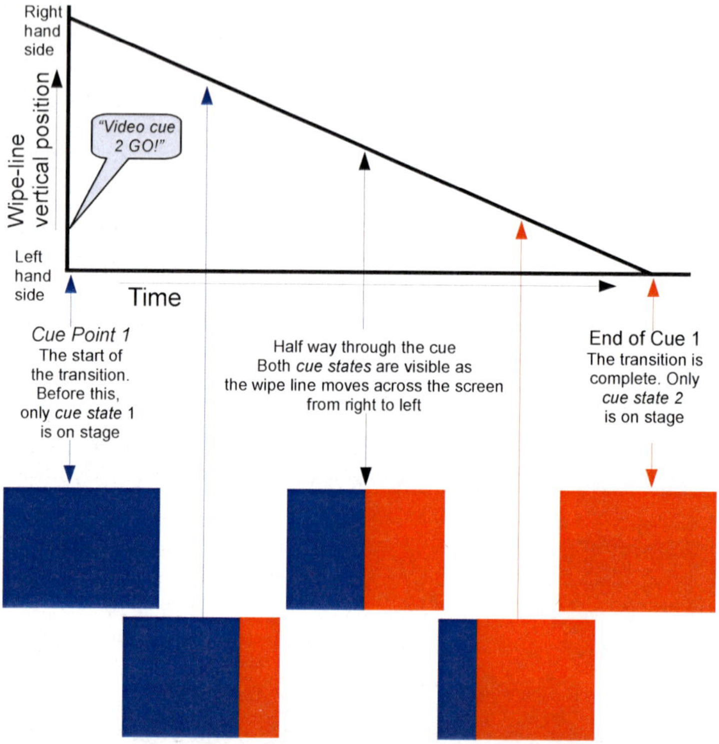

Wipes are an 'old school' vision mixer effect. There are many variables for the wipe line, including its start and end point, its shape and its thickness.
It need not be a simple line either – it could be a diamond or a circle that grows from the centre of the screen, or from a user defined point.
Most presentation software offers the user a range of wipes, dissolves and other transitions.

Another option is to have a device on stage that lets a performer trigger the video cues. In some situations this could be the computer running the software. The reason this practice is not common however is: "what happens when it goes wrong?" Is it fair to ask a performer to learn how to correct anything that goes wrong and still do all the other things she or he needs to do? (If you ask me, no.) Instead, we can set up some thing that sends a MIDI message to the show machine. That leaves the show machine with the technical crew, who should have a bit more head-space to respond "when it goes wrong".
This *thing* could be a musical keyboard. Some bands do exactly this with a keyboard player triggering video content with MIDI signals. There are many other *things* that can be made to send MIDI signals. Triggers could include a foot switch, or a security pad or even breaking an infra-red security beam. Just be sure that the time effort taken to make this work does not compromise any other part of the video design process. (Better still, make it someone else's project!)

Even with this relatively simple system, there are a couple of technical things you will probably need to get involved with. This is because you will often be using the software in ways that are slightly different to the expectations of the software makers. For example, a stage video design will often want many more full size images than a standard presentation for teaching or business. More importantly, everyone will want to know that the transition will always start when space-bar is pressed (or whatever trigger you are using) and not some moments later. To ensure this happens it is a good idea to make a few system tweaks.

First is related to image file size. Remember the more pixels wide each image is the bigger the file size. Big files take longer for your computer to process and take up more *working memory*. This can mean when the file size of an image in a slide is too large the computer appears to freeze as it is opening the slide. There are two simple ways of getting round this problem.

First, don't use big images files! Remember that a standard definition projector image is between 600 and 1024 pixels wide. Any images that are larger than that will get compressed down to fit the video format at some point, so there is no point including higher resolution images in your final content. (The good thing about stating off with higher resolution images is that you can selectively cut into them or process them in other ways and still end up with enough pixels to project, but you don't need 3000+ pixel wide images if you are using an XGA projector with a

Use your editing software to compress larger images - to your own specification - before you put them into the slide show of a presentation program (or most other video software for that matter).
If you don't have HD displays, don't use HD formats to store the final version of any video clips. Instead, make show versions of the video clips at the resolution of the display equipment (projectors or display screens).

maximum resolution of 1024 x 768 pixels.)

The same goes for video clips. There is nothing to be gained from using a high definition video clip (say with a resolution of HD1080p) with an XGA projector which cannot project in high definition. All that happens is that computer processors have to work harder and the computer uses more memory to decode the HD video file, which tends to make it slower at doing other things, like processing your slide transitions for example. Sending an HD1080 clip to an XGA projector will not make it project an HD image.

Most of the presentation programs have an option to compress all still images, including backgrounds, in every slide. The details of how to do this varies from program to program and from software version to software version, but you should be able to find out how to do it in the program you are using with through "help" "compression". However this may not always do what you expect, and it's usually a better idea to try to create images that are close to the right pixel size before you put them into the slide.

Second thing you can do is to increase the size of the graphics cache for the program. You will probably find settings for this in "options". If you are not confident tweaking these kinds of settings on your computer, it can be helpful to write down all the setting before you change them. That way you can always go back to the original settings if things get worse instead of better.

Disable Screen Save, Back-up, and other Background Activity

One other important thing that you will need to address if you use any software for a show is making sure the background programs don't interrupt your show. This means turning off things like screen savers. You don't want your content to be replaced by your screen saver in the middle of a long scene. It may also be worth looking at any programs that automatically access the web for updates, as performing these functions will slow down your computer's ability to execute your show cues.

If you don't need access to the internet to do the show, turn it off. You want the show playback machine to be doing the show and as far as in possible, nothing else. (It may seem obvious, but doing nothing else includes not playing games, even when the video system is between active cues, before the show or in the interval. Several shows have run into trouble because a board operator has been playing a game in the background on the show playback machine, and crashed it, so it wasn't able to do its show job!)

Keeping it simple

The process of putting a show on stage can be very stressful. When video is a key part of the production design, it is highly likely that the video designer will need to be thinking of all kinds of creative and technical issues, answering questions and making changes, throughout the process. While all that is going on, it's probably not a good idea to be trying to learn new software at the same time. One big plus with presentation software is that it is relatively simple to program and operate. The familiarity of the user interface means that the video designer is less likely to be the only person in the room who can run cues and make changes. Being able to delegate simpler tasks to someone else at stressful moments can be a huge relief, and leave the video designer free to make creative decisions.

Presentation software is often the best tool to use for your first video design, and for many others after later on for that matter. These programs are designed to make it easy to create slides and display them in a fixed order. It's also easy to change the order of the content, simple by changing the order of the slides, and to change the content, by editing a slide or making a new one. Once the system is set up, there is little need for specialist technical knowledge. Simply turn on all the machines, open the software, load the right slides, turn on presentation mode, and hit space-bar every time there is a video cue. Why over complicate things?

QLab

Sometimes – very often in fact – the production design calls for more than one projector or screen, and the kind of content manipulation that is simply not possible with presentation software. Made specifically for theatre and live entertainment by Figure 53 in the USA, QLab started life as a program for editing and playing back sound effects. The basic software still does just that, and a version can be downloaded for free from the Figure 53 website. The video control side of the package has become increasingly sophisticated and it is currently a very cost effective

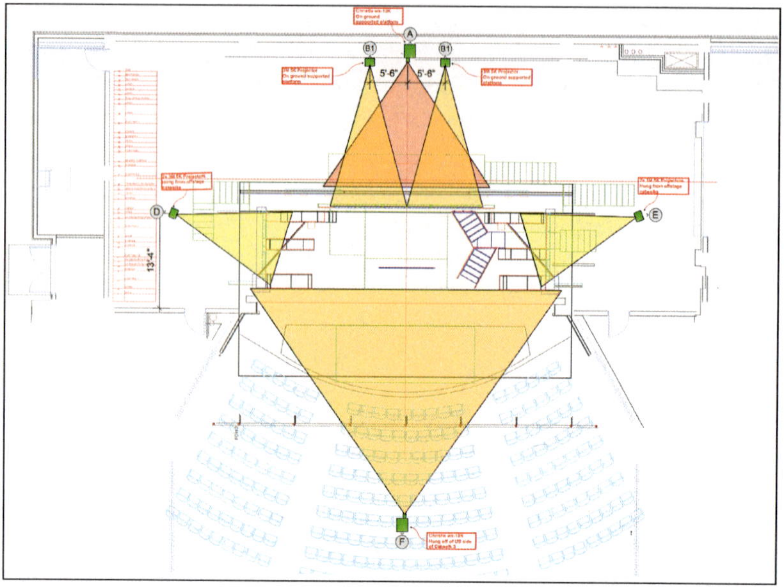

A Plan View of the projectors and screens for One Night with Janis Joplin (video design by Colin Lowry).

The content for all six projectors was cued from a Mac Pro running QLab.

way to run even quite complex video systems since a licence can be purchased for a specific amount of time. It only runs on Apple Mac.

The software allows the video designer to map to one or more screens within the projection field, managing all the necessary keystone and other distortions, presenting the video designer with a set of *video surfaces* to create content on. Once created, the content can then be saved as an ordered set of *video cue states* and played back with pre-defined timing and effects, using a simple GO button. The software accepts most video and still image formats. The current version accepts up to two live camera inputs. The output resolution is limited only by the video graphics software installed in the Mac computer. A video output several thousand pixels wide can be mapped across several projectors and/or display screens with relative ease, again providing the right cables are used.

QLab has a relatively straightforward user interface and good support, both from the makers Figure 59 and from user forums. It has been used to make school and college shows and ambitious video designs for national tours and Broadway shows.

If the video set-up is similar to a basic lecture system, that is one flat screen and one projector – no external key-stone correction necessary, and no external inputs such as live cameras – then presentation software is ideal. For anything more complex, QLab offers so much more than the presentation software can, in an easy to use reliable package.

QLab, like all good software, is continuously developing. In the 12 months or so since I began writing this book, QLab's capabilities have significantly expanded. You will find more about what it does right now on the Figure 59 website and about its current limitations (such as they might be when you read this) on user group forums and the blogs of video designers.

VJ software

> Wikapedia says: *VJing is a broad designation for realtime visual performance. Characteristics of VJing are the creation or manipulation of imagery in realtime through technological mediation and for an audience, in synchronization to music. VJing often takes place at events such as concerts, nightclubs, music festivals and sometimes in combination with other performative arts. This results in a live multimedia performance that can include music, actors and dancers. The term VJing became popular in its association with MTV's Video Jockey but its origins date back to the New York club scene of the 70s.*

The key thing here is real-time visual performance – if you want to work with pre-determined cue states and transitions then VJ software is probably *not* what you want. If however you want to play with some ideas in rehearsals, or make quick responses to what is going on on stage, then VJ Software could be for you. The entry-level versions of popular products – such as Module8 and Arkaos – currently cost around €300. For trying things out in rehearsals you can probably get by with demo versions at first.

VJ software manipulates content. Most of the programs come with some pre-loaded content, and have libraries on line. However just as most good DJs are avid collectors of music and sounds, good VJs have their own ever expanding store of clips and still images.

Good VJ software is truly impressive. Not only does it let you to mix clips live, it also makes it possible to change the shape, colour, contrast and almost all the other properties you have met in video edit programs,

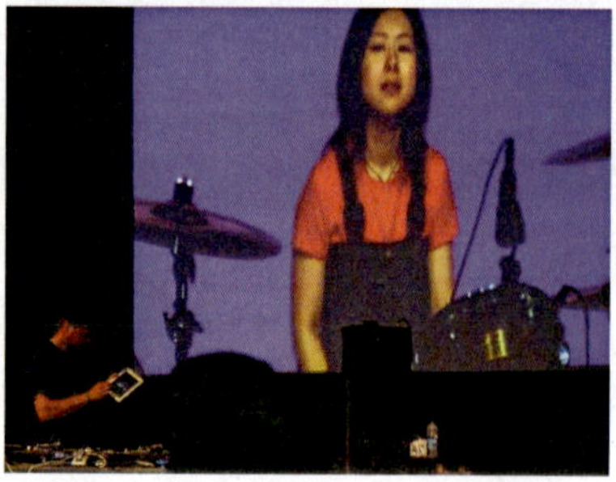

VJ Cheeba using an iPad to play a You Tube clip of a Japanese American girl playing drums as part of his extended set at WOMAD 2013.

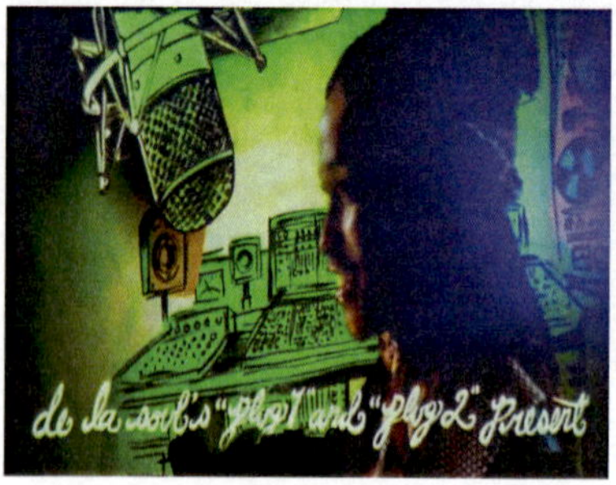

A 'mash-up' of a hand drawn cartoon background, a video clip of a vocalist, and some animated text, from another section of VJ Cheeba's WOMAD show.

live. Apart from being a way to make exciting live content in a club, this can be a great way to try out effects and demo them – for yourself and the rest of the creative team – in your studio or the rehearsal room. VJ software may not have the ability to produce the most finely rendered images, but it can create dynamic and fluid images that (with a good operator) can tightly synchronise to music and/or movement on stage.

Most VJ software offers on-screen buttons, faders and wheels as the user interface: the way to select files, create the effects and make the changes to the output. A good quality touch screen can make using these a lot more fun than trying to access the controllers with a mouse or keyboard short cuts. Alternatively, there are several MIDI controllers that offer programmable faders, buttons and wheels. These can be plugged into the machine running the VJ software, usually via the USB port, and give the VJ hands-on control of whatever parameters appeal to them.

To make VJ software really *fly,* you will need a lot of practice. *Playing* VJ software along with a live performance is a lot like playing an instrument in a band. You need to get beyond thinking consciously about *how* you do most things, it has to become instinctive. One way you might get in some practice (and possibly get paid for it too) is to offer your services at your local club or dance venue. Of course, you will need to have made at least a small investment in kit (and content) before you can do that.

Most but not all VJ software runs on Macs, making use of the generally superior graphics processing. If you run on a Windows machine, make sure you have a very good graphics card. This is because VJ software is rendering the final image live (see the end of Chapter 4 for more on rendering). Without good graphics processing, don't expect the highest image quality, especially if you are asking the program to do a lot of processing. To a large extent, the quality of the end image (that is how well it is rendered) and the responsiveness of the controls (how quickly you can change lots of things at once for example) depends on the speed and memory capacity of computer you are running the software on too. Machines sold to play computer games are usually the best choice – high speed processing, lots of on-board memory and a high-end graphics card with plenty of its own memory. The cost can soon add up. If you are about to make an investment, you need to be pretty sure that the high level of interactivity and live control offered by VJ software is the way you want to go.

Good VJ software can do video mapping which as we know from previous chapters can mean a number of different things. Some of the

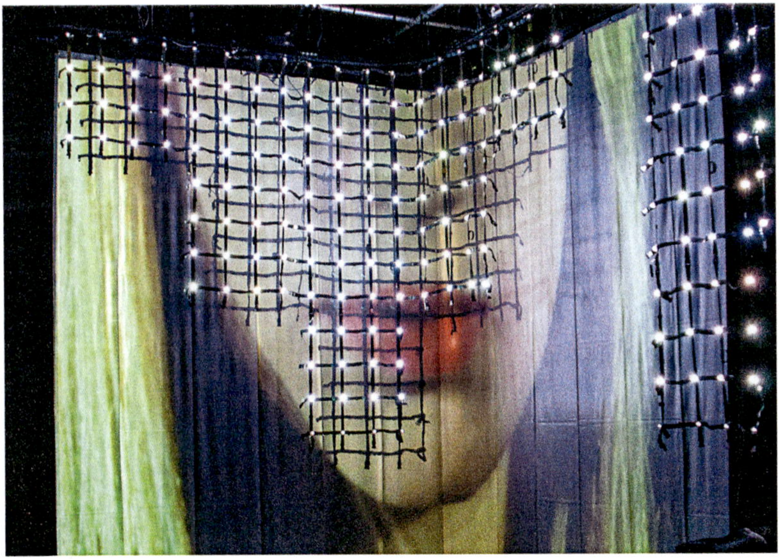

This experiment with projection and a product called Pixel-Net shows two types of Video Mapping.

The female face has been 'wrapped' onto a screen set into the corner of the room. The software in the playback machine does all the necessary calculations to predistort the projected image so that it appears undistorted on this screen.

Meanwhile, another module of the software maps a different image onto the Pixel-Net. Another module then turns the video signals in DMX data which is then fed to the Pixel-Net controllers.

most popular programmes can do it very well, *wrapping* images round regular 3D objects *and* user definable 3D objects. This can be a very powerful effect. If this kind of mapping is key to your design, check exactly what each program can and can't do in its current version, and how easy it is to do it. User forums are often the best place to get the kind of information you need. (For more on video mapping and VJ excitement in general, search on line using the term *Mapping Festival*.)

It is possible to *cue* VJ software, and some programs have this facility built in (e.g. Module8). If the VJ software you are using does not have cue stacks, the next best thing is probably to make use of an external MIDI controller, and write cues for that on a lighting console. Transitions can then be programmed on the lighting console with pre-recorded cue-times. In this way a set of video cue states can be played back in repeatable ways on stage, under the control of a lighting console. Not the most straight forward way of working, it usually needs the skills of a good lighting console programmer to make it happen. However, if what you have available is VJ software, and you want at least some parts of the show to include changes run to programmed times, it's good to know that it can be done.

Experiments with a Light Organ

Further on in the Wikipedia article on VJing, there is mention of synaesthesia and experiments from the last century with a thing called the light organ. This all has to do with the way the brains of some people automatically link musical notes to particular colours and/or patterns. The idea of the light organ was to enable someone with this gift to *play* coloured light on stage, in response to music. With the right video system, including VJ software linked to a MIDI keyboard perhaps, this could easily become a 21st century reality. If you see particular colours when you hear certain notes, and even if you don't, this may be something you will want to make your own experiments with.

Media Servers

A media server for live performance is simply a computer running a specialist software package. They are complex and specialised programs, requiring high levels of skill to program and sometimes to operate too. Because of this their use is largely confined to larger scale professional shows.

Media server programs usually run best with a lot of additional memory. If the system has multiple projectors there may be a need for additional high performance graphics cards. Because of this, most professional media servers use desk-top machines rather than lap-tops, because it's easier to add memory and graphics capability. Many large scale video systems for live performance make use of at least one media server.

A good media server for live performance needs to do at least three things well:

- Manage content – a large scale opera such as *Death of Klinghoffer* pictured earlier might use several terabytes of image data organised in several hundred files. A good media server needs to help the programmers organises this, first so that alternatives can be found quickly during rehearsals, and secondly so that the cues run smoothly during the show (avoiding embarrassing pauses while the computers find the right files for each cue).
- Manipulate different content, together or separately, so that *video cue states* can be programmed and stored. The software needs to offer lots of alternatives to the programmers, in logical ways, so that things can be tried out quickly, decisions can be made and cues recorded.
- Playback the programmed *video cue states* and transitions – rendering images live as required. Again, the computing power of the graphics cards will be at least as critical here as the choice of software.

In addition, any up-to-date media server will have advanced video mapping capabilities. This means not just putting the image in the right part of the projector beam so that it hits the desired screen elements. It also means actively distorting the images so that they look *right* on each element.

Media servers are usually designed to be programmed and operated from a sophisticated lighting console (though most have their own user interface built in too). This means that the ease of use of the media server is to some extent dictated by the lighting console you have with it, and how well the programmer/operator knows the server and that console. This added layer of complexity (and cost) is another reason why at present media servers are mostly found as part of larger scale professional systems for theatre, opera, live concerts and events.

There is a diagram of a large multi-server video system at the end of the technical appendix.

Layers and Transparency – a Brief Diversion

Media servers, like some VJ software, Photoshop and other editing programs, work with layers. If you are not familiar with the concept, you can think of layers as a set of images stacked on top of one another. If we are talking about still images, then it's easy to think of each layer is a piece of clear smooth plastic sheet with the image drawn or printed onto it. This is normally how layers are explained in tutorials for still image editing programmes such as Photoshop. It's not that different when the image is a video clip, even though no one has quite come up with a clear plastic sheet that can display video clips – yet (2013).

Layers have parameters, and media servers and editing programs allow you to change the parameters by layer or globally. Here is an example of how you might use layers, either in an editing program (off-line) or in a media server (on-line).

Say you have a great shot of a castle you want to use as a background. It works well for the daylight scenes, but now a night scene has been added. There is no time (or budget) to go back and shoot the castle at night, but we can apply a 'night-time' layer – either in Photoshop or in the media server. This layer could be a preset, with parameters that allow you (for example) to reduce overall intensity or contrast and de-saturate colours (we see colour less strongly at night) all by variable amounts determined by the value of the layer parameters. This layer can now be added to the original image for night scenes, and removed for daylight scenes.

In layer-based editing programs and media servers, you can use a layer to cut round some part of the image you want to change in some way, and then apply that change only to the cut out area. So with the castle scene you might apply a 'night-sky' effect to the sky only, by making a cut out that is just the sky. The rest of the layer would be *transparent* – this means that part of the layer is still there but it has no effect on the image.

The amount of effect can be varied across the layer (or the cut-out section of the layer) too, and this is another parameter (or more likely set of parameters). So with the night sky behind the castle, we might make the effect quite weak near the horizon, and gradually stronger higher up the sky.

Transparency is another important concept when dealing with layers. There is a difference between a normal and a transparent background. An isolated image from a camera or an editing program will normally have an overall rectangular shape which will include a solid background. This will be the case whether the image is a still photo or a video clip. Even if you have cut an image out and put it on a plane black or white background, that is not the same as it having a transparent background. To use that image as part of a composition, without its rectangular background, the

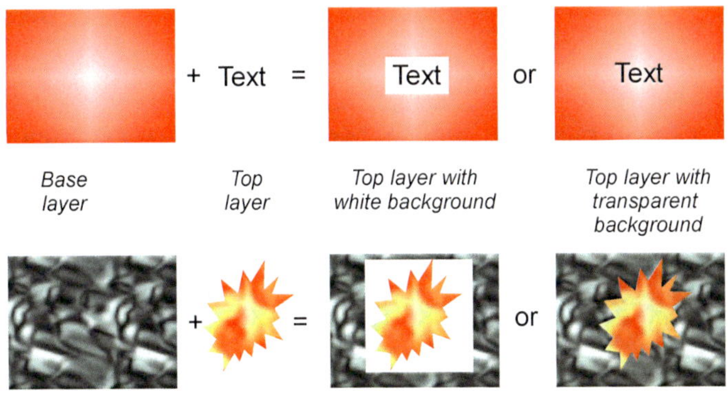

Figure 2: Transparent Layers

images will have to be changed so that it has a transparent background. You can sometimes see when this has not been done with elements of a web page for example. Select the whole web page. If text that sat on the

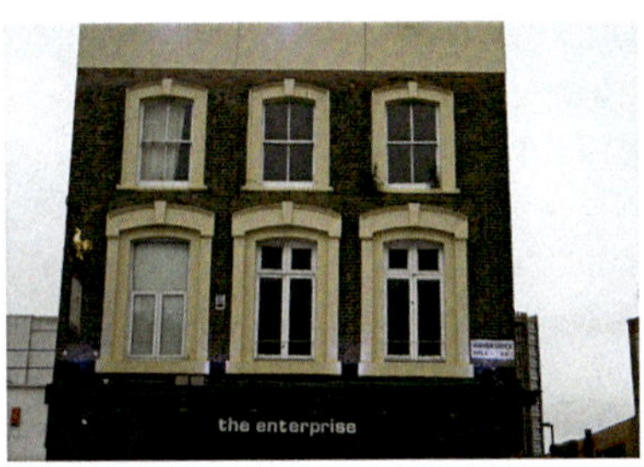

This largely unedited image of a well-known Camden pub was shot to be part of a number of images for backgrounds for the studio musical It Must Be Madness. It needs fixing in a number of ways.

First it needs to be levelled.

Then to make the image more present on stage we need to crop it to make it fit the aspect ratio of the screen and to remove distractions. Then we can make further adjustments to give the image more presence when projected.

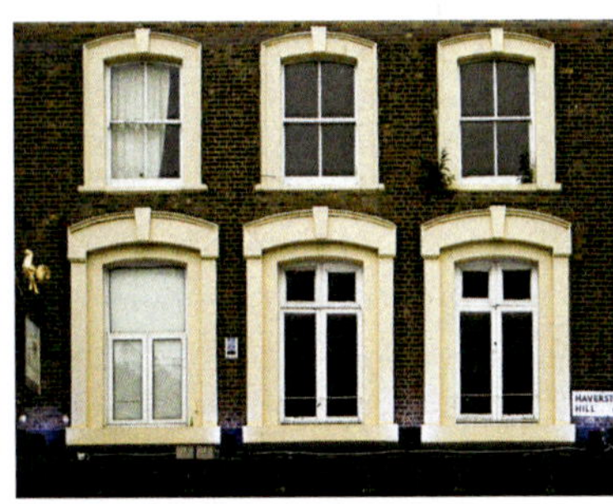

This edited version has been levelled and 'stood up' in Lightroom, using the Straighten and Upright tools. It has then been cropped to completely fill the 4x3 screen. This gives the building a more neutral perspective, and removes otherwise distracting wedges of almost white sky at either side (which also eliminates the need to give it a transparent background layer in Photoshop).

general background now appears to have a box round it, that is because it has a background that is the same colour as the general background of the page, not a transparent background.

Just because you don't have access to a layer based image editor or media server doesn't mean you can't create some of the effects that VJ software and media servers are rightly famous for. You will need to think creatively, and spend some time trying things out. One trick is to cut images into 4x3 rectangular shapes (or 16x9 if you are using wide screen) eliminating the need for transparent and background layers.

In the castle scene mentioned earlier in this section, managing the transition between day time and night time will be a little more time consuming without layers, but it is possible through creative use of pre-set effects in non-layer based off-line editing software such as Picasa or Lightroom.

Layers and Image Control on Media Servers

On most media servers, changing the transparency of layers is the main way to move from one video clip or source to another. For example, to perform a simple transition on a layers-based media server, such as fading between one video clip and another, you might use the transparency of each layer. To begin, content for the first video cue state could be on layer 1 and for next video cue state on layer 2. Layer 1 would be set to no transparency and layer 2 to fully transparent. The output would be the first video cue state. At the cue point for the second video cue state, the transparency of layer 1 would increase and that of layer 2 would decrease. As this happened, more and more of the content on layer 2 would be visible while at the same time the content on layer 1 would be vanishing. By the end of the transition, the output would only be content from layer 2 (video cue state 2). Layer 1 would be completely transparent and layer 2 would have no transparency.

Media Servers and Object Tracking

Media servers can do a great deal more that this however. The Headlong Theatre / Almeida production of the play *Chimerica* used a media server to project content onto the two-storey high cube at the centre of their set. Content from the server was mapped onto the faces of the cube so that it looked as if the cube was a building. Content included backgrounds of different styles of brickwork that turned the flat faces into building walls, and frames for the holes cut in each face that turned them into windows and doors. The technically impressive thing was that the content stayed ‘stuck’ to the cube, even as it rotated. This very ambitious production design could not have been achieved without a sophisticated media server. (Set design was by Es Devlin with Video Design by Finn Ross. You may still find video clips of highlights from this show on line.)

However, this level of complexity takes real expertise to manage. There is so much else to think about in all but the simplest video designs that adding the stress of learning how a media server (and its lighting console controller) works, is probably best avoided. If you do have to work with a media server for your first video design, make sure you get plenty of time to thoroughly familiarise yourself with what it can do and how it can do it. If at all possible, get someone else to do the programming too – someone you trust to understand how to make what you need to happen. Failing that, make sure you have the phone number of someone likely to be able to suggest ways of getting out of trouble – who won’t mind you calling late at night! Failing that, seriously consider using presentation software instead. Seriously, without experienced help on hand, or at least nearby, using a professional media server for the first time can be an extremely unfulfilling experience, and best avoided.

Isadora

Developed by and for a contemporary dance company, this extremely flexible software has proved to be a fabulously creative tool for performance designers around the world. Like VJ software, Isadora is built with real-time interactivity in mind. It is especially good for system designs that want the actions or movements of performers to change or affect the video content. With Isadora, these performer triggers can be almost anything that generates any kind of signal, including Wii devices and Infra-red security cameras. Yes, that’s right – with this software and a few relatively inexpensive peripherals you can create an interactive “video design for live performance or an art installation”. To quote from the Troikatronix website from where the software can be purchased:

“ Within Isadora, over 250 basic building blocks – called actors – are at your fingertips. Each actor has a unique function, from receiving a MIDI message to warping video imagery. By connecting these actors together, you can accomplish nearly any goal, from simply playing a video to creating a unique interactive system that responds to a live performer.”

One of the great things about Isadora is that the user decides how complex the system is going to be. If you simply want to use it to play a set of clips triggered by pressing the space bar on the playback machine, you can do that. If you want to have a clip of a spinning world track a disc across stage, you can do that too – it's just going to take a bit of experiment and programming to make it work right every time.

One way to work with Isadora is to break the requirements of the design into a series of tasks, and then work out how each task can be accomplished. Say we want to project a video clip onto an object that moves across stage:

- Define how you can let the software *know* where the object is. If the object is moved by part of an automated system, this might be by getting the automation system to feed position data directly to the computer. If the object moves independently, it might be by tying the output of a Wii sensor into the software. Alternatively it might be by pointing a video camera at it the stage and somehow getting information about the position of the object from the resulting video image. If the object stands out from the background in the camera shot, this will not be too much of a problem. If the object is a person – the only person on stage, then by using an infra-red camera form a security system the person can be tracked by the heat image they emit.
- The next problems to solve are to do with making the data mean something to the software – finding an Isadora *actor* or set of *actors* to read the data (from the automation system or from the video camera) and turn it into a set of instructions.
- That set of instructions is then used to define where in the projection field the clip needs to be at any given time. Another set of Isadora *actors* make sure the right video signal is then sent to the projector, and the video clip *sticks* to the object, where ever it (or he/she) moves.

Of course there are probably going to be any number of additional problems to be encountered and solved along the way. However, my experience is that once users have got the concept, solving these problems becomes a fun challenge – providing everyone knows it's probably not going to work perfectly first time!

Video systems built using Isadora generally render images in real time. As with other software packages that do this, the quality of the resulting image is highly dependant on the processing power and on-board memory capacity of the playback machine, and its video cards. Isadora will run on Mac or Windows, however most users I have spoken to prefer the Mac environment for their more complex projects.

Isadora has great flexibility built in, but this means that to use it well requires planning. To build in significant interactivity often needs time for experimentation too. As intuitive as this software is, it takes time to learn how to make things happen and to implement changes quickly. Make sure you give yourself enough time to play with a system and for it to become intuitive to you.

If interactivity is at the heart of the video design, using the actions of performers to trigger clips and effects or mapping video onto or around bodies on stage, Isadora is very useful software. With any software, to do this well will take time. If instead what you want is to create a repeatable 'called show' in the North American/UK tradition, with every cue and effect triggered by an operator, or if you have very little time to play with the system to get it right, Isadora may not be the best choice.

Vision Mixers and Cameras

Time was, and it's not that long ago, when a vision mixer was at the heart of almost every stage video system. Pre-prepared content was stored on tapes or discs, and transitions between clips involved an operator moving a lever to fade between one input and another. While it is still possible to do this, it is usually far more cost effective, and reliable, to do this kind of show on a computer using the software mentioned above. Even video systems incorporating multiple live cameras can now be managed without the need for a vision mixer. Full screen, focusable web cameras plug straight into USB or Firewire ports, providing live camera input to the video design at a manageable cost. Inexpensive video capture kit can let you take the output of most domestic or semi-professional video cameras and use it with one of the software packages mentioned above.

(This kind of video capture is usually relatively low resolution, typically around 700 pixels wide. If you need to capture higher resolution images will generally involve Firewire or the faster USB 3, and more expense.)

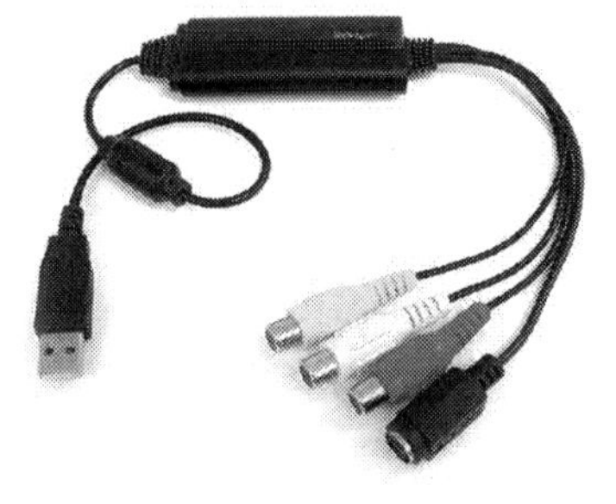

This inexpensive USB adaptor enables S-Video or Composite Video signals to be processed by a computer.

If it sounds as if I'm trying to steer you away from using a vision mixer, it's because I am, especially if it's an older analogue only one. If you already have an older analogue vision mixer, and its output is compatible with the projector(s). and/or display screens, and with any the cameras, video tape players or other input devices you want to use (i.e. the vision mixer uses the same connectors and cable system that

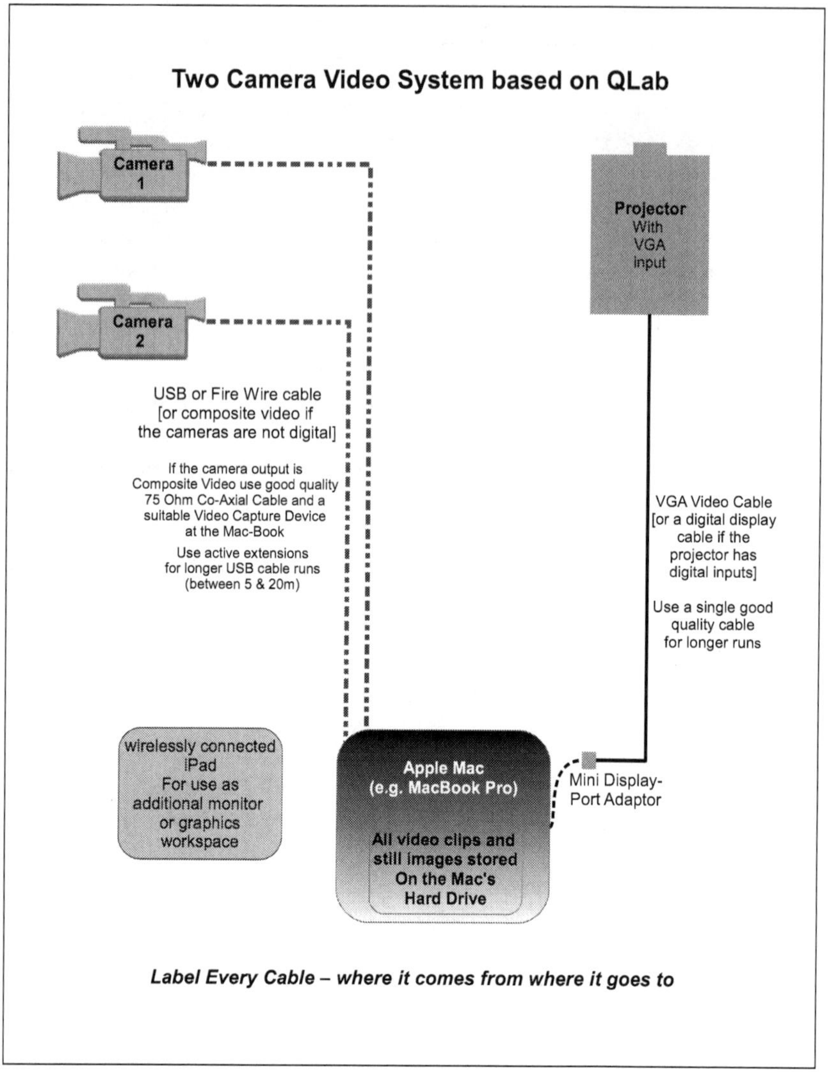

the other equipment does) the project may be worth perusing. Check out the technical appendix for more on connectors, cables and compatibility.

Even if the core of your system is all compatible, you can still expect to run into difficulties, ageing equipment and manufacturer to manufacturer inter compatibility issues among them. Most of this stuff was not made with domestic user in mind. Manuals tend to be full of apparently meaningless

Two Camera Video System based on an Analogue Vision Mixer

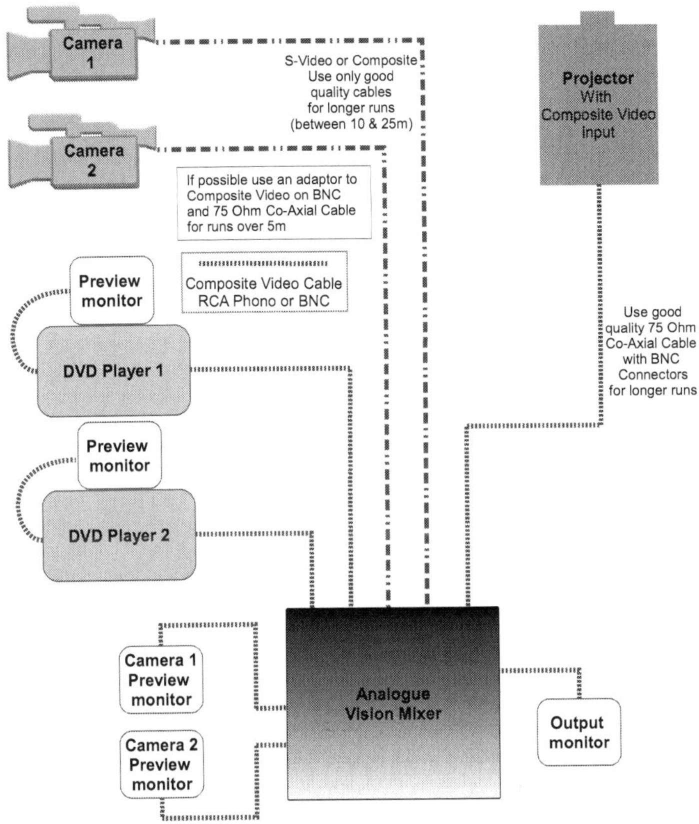

For more information
Turn to the Technical Appendix

Label Every Cable – where it comes from where it goes to

abbreviations and systems can be very difficult to troubleshoot. If at all possible, try to find an experienced video technician/engineer to join your team. As you might gather from figure 3, I have found digital systems far less cumbersome and easier to use than an analogue vision mixer system, especially when the equipment for the vision mixer based system has come from a number of different sources.

One final tip: do remember that in general vision mixers don't have built-in monitors. For your operator to see what is coming from the cameras, DVD players etc. and what is about to get on stage, you will need to provide some.

Working in the Tech

The usual way that a tech rehearsal works is that the technical team put together everything required for each section of the piece. This will include putting the right bits of set in the right places, setting the right lighting, playing the right sound, and of course displaying the right video content. Much of the time is taken up deciding exactly what is *right* of course – as this is very often the first time all the elements have come together. Usually the performers are involved too – though they will be 'walking through' their part rather than full out performing. (If the performers are not involved, the rehearsal is often referred to as a *dry tech*.)

Tech can be a very stressful time for everyone involved. Generally the better prepared you are, the less stress you will generate – for yourself and for others. As discussed elsewhere, a scene by scene or cue by cue storyboard can be very useful, to help keep the focus on what has been planned. However, it's also good to be open to the unplanned happy accident and to trying out alternatives. Unless you really are pushed for time in the tech, it is a good plan to have alternative versions of all your content ready to try out. This is where a well organised file structure really comes into its own, helping you to find alternative content quickly.

So generally speaking for the video designer, during the tech the content for each section of the show with video in it will be decided, and put in order ready for the playback machine to send to the projector(s) or screen(s) *on cue*. As the video designer, you will be building a set of video *cue states*. Any live manipulations or other non-automatic actions will also be noted, and whoever is to perform these will get a chance to try them out. I'm thinking here of manipulations using VJ software for example, performer triggers, or anything that involves a live camera, but there are bound to be certain other things from time-to-time.

What will also be decided is where in the piece each cue state will begin and/or end, and where each manipulation etc, will occur. That is, the cue points will be agreed and noted. Cue timings will be agreed and noted too, and tried out to make sure they work.

Cue No	Placement	Description	File	In time	Duration	Out time
0.5	House opens	waves	preset_waves1	0	20min	NA
1	With house lights	Fade to blackout	NA	6		
2	Page 8 Scene Change	Waves – approaching storm	Act1_waves12	3	3mins	6
3	End of Scene Change (Lx 12)	Fade to Blackout	NA	6		
4	Top of page 14 with sound cue	Waves return, storm nearer	Act1_waves21	8	6mins	

This short example for a video cue list gives a reference for the cue point (placement) and brief description of what the cue should be doing (description) the name of the content file, and some cue time information. This is really the minimum you should be recording during the tech.

Once all the elements of each section have been agreed, and plotted, noted or recorded, the whole section is *run*. That is, starting from a specific point in the piece, everyone does their planned cues at the planned cue points. This is usually to see if all the elements will work together through key transitions. If the director (or someone else with enough influence, which might be you as video designer) is not happy with a section, adjustments are called for and made, and the section is run again.

It is important that who ever is running the video is aware of what is going on at all times during the tech. If a particular cue state is requested on stage, the video operator(s) should know if it's just to have a look at that content or it is in preparation for a section to be *run* for example. Generally it is better to ask if you are unsure. Although this may cause a moments irritation, it's usually better than discovering the wrong content is playing when a *run* is called.

There may well be times during the tech when the changes you would like to make, or that the director asks you to make, cannot be made there and then. For example if a video clip needs to be re-shot, that will have to wait. It's usually not worth holding up the whole tech to to re-make a complex piece of animation or perform some tricky edits in

Photoshop either. This can cause tension, especially if some people on the team don't really understand what is involved in creating what they want. In a situation like this the video designer (or video design team) will sometimes need all their diplomacy skills to avoid a major row. I have found that honesty is usually the best policy. Try to explain carefully and with as little technical language as possible, what needs to happen and how long it will take. Along side this strategy, offer an alternative. Try to understand the 'why' behind what is being asked for and see if you can produce something that is closer to satisfying that 'why' than the first offering. Sometimes the idea of a place-holder can be useful – suggest that the present content be used for now, on the understanding that as soon as possible it will be changed for something closer to everyone's liking.

Throughout the technical period, try to keep your notes up to date. It's important to record what content has been agreed for each cue state, all the cue points for that cue state, and all the cue times too. Usually it will be easy to get this information from the playback machine, but I like to have a separate note too. There is a lot of other information it's good to take note of beside the cue information. For example, if you edit a content file, make a note of where the original and the new version are stored, and try to maintain a logical approach to file naming. Again, if you perform a particular edit on a piece of content, note all the changes so that you can do the same again if required. Don't rely on your memory, or on scraps of paper or Post It Notes. Try to be logical and consistent. Keep all your notes in a single book or a single computer document – and guard that carefully. I used to have a large notebook for every show. Although I still use notebooks for other things, these days I tend to have a master document on my laptop computer, backed up regularly using a cloud service such as Dropbox or Google Docs.

Usually a well planned tech will start at the beginning of the piece and slowly work through to the end. This gives everyone a chance to do things in the order that they will happen in the show. Sometimes however, it is agreed to tech a particularly challenging or potentially dangerous section first, just to make sure hat it will work, and then go back to the beginning. If you do find yourself making show cues out of order, you (and your team) will need to be especially alert. Programming and other changes made early in a show may affect the look of cues already recorded for later in the show. Of course this warning stands when you are making changes and updates at any time, but often the tech is the first time that you become aware that this might happen.

First Dress Run – Preparing

As the tech draws to a close, the next thing everyone will usually be aiming for is the first dress rehearsal or dress run (dress because the performers wear their full costume and make-up – they are *dressed).* This will be the first attempt to run the show all the way through without having to stop for missed cues or anything else. It might well be the only time you all get to see the show as close to the way it will be in front of an audience but without an audience present. If you are really unlucky, this first dress run will be in front of an audience, but that is usually something everyone will want to avoid.

Try to assess how much work you (and your team) will need to do before you will be ready to do this first dress run. If new content has to be made, how long will that take? What equipment and which people and/or space will be needed? If adjustments need to be made to the projector(s),screen(s) or playback systems, how long will that take and who will be needed? Does anything need to be bought or hired? Where will it come from, how much will it cost and who will fetch it? Once the tech is complete, it is likely that the production manager (or whoever has taken on responsibility for making sure everything is ready in time for opening night) will need to get all this information from you, to help him or her plan the next hours' or days' activity. If you have written it all down, you can hand over your list and get straight on with your most important jobs.

This can be a good time to make back-up copies of show content and cue files too. As with all computer related things, try to be logical. Decide on a system and stick to it. I like to use USB drives for smaller shows and hard drives for larger ones, kept somewhere safe away from the operating position. This can help minimise the impact of little accidents such as coffee or soft drinks in the computer, or even more serious occurrences such as theft of show computers, large scale electrical disturbances or fire.

Throughout this time try to stay in communication with the director, the production manager and others in the team. Even if you seem to be welded to the seat in front of your computers, making and editing images like a demon, try to let others know how you are progressing, and keep abreast of what else is going on. For example, there may be little to be gained from working late into the night if others have decided to delay the dress run by a day. Get some food and some sleep and be in better physical shape for the days ahead.

Once the date and time for the a dress run has been agreed, you will need to make sure all your team know that. You will also need to keep the director and production manager up-to-date with the status of your department. If you have problems, let others know, and share the responsibility for solving them.

If your show has a show caller, make sure that he or she has up-to-date cue information. It's not a great idea to assume the show caller took complete notes, though of course many will have done. However, yours is usually just one department that needs to be cued and who knows how much trouble the other departments were causing while you were sailing through the tech, all calm and well organised.

Dress Runs

If at all possible have someone else take over operating the video cues for the dress run or runs. As a designer, you will want to see what your work looks like on stage through every moment of the show, and it's not usually possible to do that if you have your head in computer screens waiting for the GO for the stage manager or show caller. If it's not possible, the next best thing is to get someone whose visual judgement you trust to take accurate note for you during all the dress runs. You'll need to brief this person, let them know what it is your design is trying to do, and perhaps give them a copy of the cue list so they know what is supposed to happen when.

Don't be afraid to continue to suggest changes to content, cue placement and timing through the whole of this period. It's usually a good idea to consult with others before you make any major changes. Beside the aesthetic and other concerns of the director and your fellow designers, it is possible that performers or even stage hands have started to take cues from the content, and they may get confused if you change it.

Notes

In an ideal world, everyone would know exactly what to do throughout the whole show and do it right from the first dress run onwards. Also in this ideal world, all the content (and all the lighting and sound cues too for that matter) would prove themselves to be *right* on the first dress run and never need to be altered again. Of course it's not like that in our world. Each run is an opportunity to take notes – for the director, and for you and other designers. Where possible you can then feed back: to your operators and/or the show caller about cue placement, to your programmer (or to yourself) about cue time, or content. It is also an opportunity for the director and other designers to feed back to you

– perhaps they don't like this or that piece of content or they feel a cue position should change. There is a good deal of skill involved in giving effective notes, and in deciding what vague or unclear notes might mean too for that matter. Try to make your notes as clear as possible and be open to negotiations, at least some of the time. Try to be clear about the difference between suggestions and commands – in the notes you give and in interpreting the notes you receive. It can be a tricky business but it's an important part of refining a production and making it as good as it can be.

Celebrate, Relax and Reflect

Once the audience come in, things will change again. Sometimes you will be expected to make changes based on how the audience react or how the performers alter their performance in reaction to the audience. Sometimes those in charge will insist that once the audience is in the show is 'locked down' and cannot be changed. Whatever the situation on your show, it is to be hoped that sooner or later all the designers will have a chance to be a bit less frantic and reflect on what they have achieved. Like many theatre makers, I'm a great believer in learning from my mistakes – and naturally I advise you to do the same. But don't forget to celebrate your triumphs too. For anyone, completing a first video design is a major achievement. Remember all the qualities and skills I said a video designer had to have in the first chapter? Well achieving a video design means you have at least most of those qualities. So, if it hasn't put you off for life, where do you go from here?

There is no single answer. So much depends on the style or styles you want to work in and the type of performance you want to be involved in. However it seems to me there are a few things we can all reflect on and use to build our practice.

1. Was there anything I wanted to do that I didn't manage to do?
    - If that was through lack of the right technology, what technology do I need and how do I get hold of it?
    - If it was through my lack of knowledge of how to make my technology do it, where can I get a bit more training or confidence? Where can I practice?
    - If it was because someone wouldn't let me try it – how do I get better at negotiating, at getting my own way?
2. Can I use my work on this show to get more opportunities?

- Can I invite people to see my work? Did I?
- Can I make a video show-real of my best work on the production? Who can I show it to and how?

3. Who really helped me get this one to work?
   - How do I say "thanks" in a practical way?
   - How do I make sure I do more work with them?
   - What else can I learn from this person and others like them?
   - How do I go about making that happen?

And that's probably enough to be going on with. I hope that many readers of this book will go on to be confident and creative video designers, and in that, I wish you all the best.

Copyright Appendix
COPYRIGHT AND THE PROJECTED IMAGE

Copyright is the legally established right of ownership of a work. In most legal territories, it was set up to protect writers of books (and sometimes plays) from those wishing to make money from copying work without the permission of the author, and without paying anything to the author. Copyright now extends over a great many types of works, including still and moving images, and many kinds of design. As a creative video designer, this protection is as valuable to you as it is to the creators of any original artwork or images you use in your design.

To quote the US based website clickandcopyright.com: "Copyright infringement occurs when someone other than the copyright holder copies the "expression" of a work. This means that the idea or information behind the work is not protected, but how the idea is expressed is protected. For example, there have been many movies about pirates, but only one "Jack Sparrow". Copyright infringement is a civil offence, and can lead to expensive legal action and damages.

Copyright is there to try to ensure that creative people are acknowledged as the creators of the work they do, *and* so they can receive some share in any profit made out of their work. In more formal language, that they benefit from its exploitation.

So copyright has two main elements:

1. The Moral Right of the person or persons who originally created the work to be acknowledged. For example, I can't claim to have painted the Mona Lisa or written Hamlet without infringing the moral rights of Leonardo da Vinci (who did paint the Mona Lisa) or Shakespeare (who most people agree did write Hamlet). The moral right to be credited as the author of a work exists from the creation of the work, and remains throughout its life. Clearly though, in order to assert the moral rights of an author, painter or other creative person, it will be necessary to be able to prove that they actually were the original creator of the work.
2. The Exploitation Rights of the creators to benefit from sales and other uses of the work. By agreement, these rights can be sold on, in whole or in part, or waived. This is often referred to as a "rights agreement" or "royalty agreement". For example, a small percentage of the original sale price of every copy of a Harry Potter book goes to its author JK Rowling. In addition, she will also benefit from profits made on the films, as they are clearly a "expression" of the work. The details of exactly how JK Rowling benefits from the expression of her work will be contained in rights agreements.

While moral rights last for ever, exploitation rights are limited in time; the right of the creator's estate to benefit from exploitation of their work usually ends some years after the death of the author. This means that for example, while we still need to credit Sir Arthur Conan Doyle as the creator of Sherlock Holmes (this is his moral right), there is no longer any benefit to the Conan Doyle estate from profits made on sales of the books, or films and TV programmes for that matter, because his exploitation rights have expired.

The time period for exploitation rights varies for different types of work and from place to place. For most written work exploitation rights last for between 50 and 70 years after the author's death. For works with multiple creators (such as feature films) the term is usually 70 years from the first publication (showing). For photographs, the limit internationally is not less than 25 years from the date of creation, though it is longer in most territories, especially if the photograph was published in a book.

In the UK, the current duration of copyright in artistic work, including photographs, is life of the author plus another 70 years. The situation for photographs of artworks that are themselves out of copyright (e.g. a recent photograph of an old painting) is that copyright lies with the photographer (or more likely his or her employer since most of these images are taken by museum staff). So you can't just use an image of a painting by Rembrandt for free just because he has been dead a long time!

Exploitation rights cover issues such as the ways in which a work may or may not be used. For example a song writer (or the song's publisher if the writer has sold his or her exploitation rights) can refuse to give permission for their song to be used to advertise a particular product, or to be re-recorded and released by a particular artist.

In the case of photographs and other artwork then, the moral right of the photographer or artist to be credited as the original creator remains even if you edit the photograph or artwork. (The urban myth that after a set number of Photoshop type manipulations the image becomes yours is just that, a myth.) The right of the originator to limit or restrict the use of the work exists too. Some photographers and artists are very active in stopping "adulterated" versions of their work appearing, but most are too busy taking care of their day-to-day practice to get involved. However, you should not exploit this, always ask for permission and cite the original artist.

Professional photographers, especially well-known ones, often control how their iconic images are used through agencies such as the Magnum agency.

So permission to use a particular image or set of images as a substantial part of a video design might come from the original photographer/artist, or their agent or publisher. It will almost always come with a demand that the original photographer or artist is credited. It may include a fee for use, a royalty, and evading payment of a royalty may result in a legal action against the individual designers and the production!

The rights surrounding moving images are more complex, partly because usually no single person can be asserted as the creator. In the world of commercial film, most of the people involved will have signed their exploitation rights over to the producers, the studio or the distributors. For video art produced by a solo artist however, rights are most likely to remain with the solo artist, though may be transferred to a gallery or a funder.

The Berne Convention for the Protection of Literary and Artistic Works

Most territories base their copyright law on the Berne Convention, which dates back to the 19th century. In recent times this has been updated frequently to meet the developing needs of our super-connected digital world. It is relatively easy to find an up-to-date information on the details of the convention on the internet. It may be worth looking this up as a starting point, but its worth baring in mind that the main concern of the original signatories of the convention was the protection of literary works – books. It can be quite hard to find definitive information on the exploitation of images in general, and I found it almost impossible to find definitive information on the use of copyright material in live performance design! What I am writing here is general guidance only; if you want to get definitive advice for your production, you may need to go to a local professional body or specialist advisor.

Here are some general points to consider:

- Almost all images have an originator, and that person (or persons has moral rights for ever.
- You have a duty to acknowledge the creator of original work you use in your design, just as a theatre company acknowledges the writers of the plays it produces. This is the creator's moral right, and it exists from the moment of creation onwards.
- As a video designer, you have a moral right to be acknowledged as the creator of your video designs. You do not need to do anything to gain this moral right, though it may be a good idea to make sure you can prove you were the originator just in case. (Get a written contract)

- Exploitation rights are concerned with permissions and payments for a use. They may be held by the creator of the original work, his or her employer or publisher, or an agency, or a commercial organisation.
- Exploitation rights expire, usually 70 years after the death of the original creator.
- Exploitation rights include the right to be paid a royalty for the use of your work and to have some say in where and how your work can and cannot be used – but all exploitation rights need to be negotiated.
- Expect to pay a royalty – to the originator or their agent – on almost any high quality images[1] you do not originate yourself.
- This is still true no mater how many changes you make to the original image in programmes such as Photoshop or After Effects.
- Always acknowledge the sources of key images originated outside the production, even if the originator or their representatives have agreed to waive the royalty. You can do this with a short note in your production's programme, through a slide shown right at the end of the piece, or maybe notes on the production's website.
- Even when exploitation rights have expired, the moral right remains – so if you use the work of long dead artists, acknowledge the original artist.
- While you are working at a small or local scale, look at making use of agreements such as Creative Commons licences. You can find out more about Creative Commons agreements for the territory you are working in the internet. For the UK try www.creativecommons.org.uk

Multinational Corporations

Some large corporations are particularly aggressive when it comes to protecting their rights to any images that are part of their branding. This includes most major car manufacturers, international fast food corporations, international film and theme park corporations, and the International Olympic Committee's guardianship of the five rings. These companies and organisations have usually spent a great deal of money developing and protecting their visual brand, and will not allow that to be undermined by anyone. Do not use these companies images without explicit permission.

Even if the corporation does not pursue you itself, such is the influence of some of these organisations that local authorities may prosecute on their behalf. Remember, if you do get caught using images the law

1 Most images you can download for free from the internet are not of sufficient quality to successfully project. See "resolution".

deems to belong to someone else, you as designer, the production, the producers, and venue could all be liable for damages in a civil court. In English law, if the production is deemed to be attempting to pass itself off as something it is not – say as officially authorised by a corporation whose logos you have been using in the video design – you could be breaking the criminal law, and that could lead to fines and imprisonment!

So the message is – Don't mess with these guys, they play tough!

Fair Use

On the positive side however, there is material that falls under Creative Commons licences, and Fair Use. Though it is worth remembering that Fair Use does not necessarily have legal standing in all territories, it is part of the Berne Convention. Basically the idea of Fair Use protects casual use of copyrighted material in the creation of another work – providing certain criteria are met. When deciding upon whether a particular use of copyright material counts as Fair Use or not, most copyright law takes into account the following factors:

- Is the use acknowledged? (cited?) The concept of Fair Use comes primarily from the needs of the academic world where it is common to include quotations from the work of others in text books and dissertations, etc. For a video designer, the casual use of a visual 'quotation' might be acknowledged in a number of ways as previously discussed.
- The purpose and character of the use – e.g. is it part of an educational or community project or a large scale commercial spectacular? (The former is more likely to be considered fair use than the latter.)
- The nature of the copyrighted material – including such things as how well protected it has been in the past. If an image has been freely available for some time, it is unlikely to be protected against Fair Use. However including in your design something like the Olympic Rings, which only ever appear commercially under licence to the International Olympic Committee, is unlikely to be considered Fair Use (see also the final point).
- The proportion of the copyrighted work used – e.g. just one or two rings is more likely to be Fair Use than all five. This is sort of self defeating in most cases – if you include enough of the copyrighted material for it to be recognised, it's likely that it's not Fair Use.
- The likely impact on the potential market value of the copyrighted work – the argument goes: if you are allowed to use the five rings free of charge, why should Coca Cola have to pay such huge amounts to

put the rings on their canned drink? Also if you use the copyrighted image in an attempt to make it less likely that people will buy their products, its not likely to be considered Fair Use.

So Fair Use can be a defence for using copyright material in certain circumstances. It could be a defence for using a few images from a website of generic symbols as part of a design for a community play. The symbols are widely available, no previous attempt has been made to assert exploitation rights over them, the community play is not primarily a commercial production, and its unlikely to reach a mass audience. It's *not* going to be a defence against using the Ford Motor Corporation's logo as a key design motif in a large scale national tour of a production highlighting the evils of the motor car, however.

And if I take all my own pictures / shoot all my own video?

Well if you do that then you are the originator, and you own the copyright; unless you are employed by the production and explicitly enter into an agreement giving them copyright of all the material you produce. This is not unusual, as such an agreement protects the production against being blackmailed at a later date by an unscrupulous video designer wanting extra payment for use of his or her copyright material. However, even in that case, you would retain the moral right to be credited as photographer or videographer.

However, that is not quite the end of the story. If your photographs or video contains a "substantial part" of someone else's copyright material, you should be getting permission to "commercially exploit" it from the copyright holder. Copyright material might include a building (copyright holder likely to be the architect or the building's owner), an art work such as a painting or sculpture (copyright holder likely to be the artist, or the gallery or space that houses the work) or an iconic store front design or logo (copyright likely to be held by the corporation that owns the store – see section on Multinational Corporations above). Of course Fair Use will usually come into play here, but if your design shows a substantial part of the copyrighted work, or the copyrighted work forms a substantial part of your design, it is unlikely to be deemed Fair Use.

For example, say you shoot a video of two of your actors performing a scene in front of a chain coffee bar. If the signage and store-front appear only briefly, or maybe out of focus this would probably be considered Fair Use. If however, you shoot the scene in wide angle, with the coffee bar's logo in shot throughout, crisply focused, that's probably not Fair

Use, and you should be seeking permission, preferably in writing. The point is that in the first instance, the copyrighted store-front and signage are incidental to the images that end up in your design, but in the second instance they could be considered to form a substantial part of your design for that scene.

Release forms – as used by professional photographers or reality TV makers, for example – are a formal way of recording that you have got permission to use images of buildings or artworks, just as they are for people. The form need not be complicated. Examples appropriate to the location you are working in can be easily be found on the internet.

Of course, the exact nature of "incidental to", "substantial part" and "main subject" is the kind of thing many lawyers earn their living arguing about – and I doubt very much that you will want to be paying them to do that. If you are not sure you meet the criteria for Fair Use, try asking someone who you believe to be a representative of the copyright holder, but be prepared to pay for using the image, even if you shot it yourself!

And this brings us to a reality check:

The employees of large corporations are unlikely to grant permission for anything. Excuses I've heard range from: "I don't think head office would like that," to "sorry, too many forms to fill in and I just don't have the time," to "if I let you then everyone will want to"!

Meanwhile the owner-operator of your local café, coffee shop or even cinema (if you are lucky enough to have one) is much more likely to be sympathetic, especially if you offer a "free advertisement" in your programme.

Images of People

Some territories have granted people the explicit right to have a say in how any recognisable image of them is used. While not strictly speaking copyright, this may be an issue for some productions. For example, if you make use of live camera images of your audience you will probably need to tell the audience you are going to do that before the show begins. This might be through a notice in the foyer or an announcement before the show begins or a notice in the publicity for the show. You might also think about how the production might give individuals the opportunity to not take part, for example by sitting in a section of the audience that is not filmed.

Most territories have restrictions on the use of all CCTV and surveillance footage. Although the regulations and codes of practice will usually be

Example of a simple model release form

Shoot Date:
Shoot Location:
Model's Name:
Model's Contact Details:
Photographer's Name:
Photographer's Contact Details:
Production Company Name:
Production Company Contact Details:
I, the model, grant you, the Photographer / the Production Company*, usage of the photographs subject to the following conditions:
I understand that the photographs taken of me during this sessions can be used wholly or in part in the video design for Production XXXX, and in the portfolio of the photographer and video designer and production company*.
The photographs may be used to represent an imaginary person and any wording associated will not be attributed to me unless my name is specifically mentioned.
Any special conditions outlined below:

Model: ____________________________

Photographer: ______________________________

both parties to sign here to agree these special conditions.
I acknowledge that by signing this form, subject to the usage restrictions above, I give up all claim of ownership of the photographs, and assign copyright to the photographer / the Production Company* named above. No further payment will be due. Use of the photographs may be granted to third parties, however the photographs will remain the property of the Photographer / Production Company*.
I have read this form carefully and fully understand the implications. I am 18 years old or over.

Signed: _________________________(model) Date: _____________________

*(delete which ever is not applicable)
Adapted from www.creativephotobook.co.uk

designed to ensure private security contractors don't exploit the public, by using images from CCTV to blackmail or make fun of members of the public for example, theatre makers will usually need to pay attention to these regulations too. For example in the UK, in most circumstances, videoing people without their knowledge is illegal.

It is generally a good idea to try to get explicit permission in writing to use identifiable images of particular people, especially if these images form a significant or substantial part of the video design. This can be especially problematic if the production implies that the person whose image you are using holds particular opinions or has done something illegal or morally repugnant. (I'm thinking here of a production that might use a picture of an amateur model on a "wanted" poster for example, rather than something documentary where a "real person" is accused on stage – that potentially opens the production up to a completely different set of legal risks.) Again, a simple model release form, appropriate to the laws and customs of the country you are working in, can usually be downloaded from the internet. Below is an example adapted from a form for UK photographers.

More generally, people have the right to object to their image being used in a negative or derogatory way. It is not a good idea to do this, and it is probably the quickest way to get yourself an angry (and potentially expensive) letter from a lawyer!

Copyright can work *for* you too

Remember that copyright is there to protect your original work too. While you might see it as a pain at times, if someone 'steals' your work, using it without acknowledgement or without compensating you for the time and skill involved in producing the work, the law is there to protect you too.

As the creator of a piece of copyright work, you need do nothing special to initiate the copyrighted status. You have the right to assert that you are the author of the work, and in the first instance, the right to be consulted about how the work is used, and the right to share in any profits gained from exploitation of the work. Of course, in a professional situation, if your contract includes clauses that assign your exploitation rights to someone else, then you lose them. With this in mind, you may want to get some advice from a professional body such as the Association of Lighting Design (www.ald.org.uk) who also represent video designers in the UK, before signing such a contract.

If challenged, you will need to be able to give some sort of proof that you are indeed the originator of the work in question. With this in mind, it is a good idea to tag any digital photographs or videos you produce with your name as author. This is relatively easy to do on any MAC or PC running Windows 7 or later, or through most picture editing programs such as Photoshop or Picasa. (Any decent photo editing package will also help you to catalogue your images – something that becomes more and more useful the more work you do in this area – and archive the content from completed designs.)

You will want to make sure your name appears in the programme, and probably in any publicity material, usually as Video Designer. This is called a credit. You should also keep a record of all the productions you design for including the name of the show, dates and places of performances, and the names (and contact details) of all the members of the creative team. All of this will help you assert your right to be credited as the originator of your individual work, and a co-originator of the production design.

The expense of going to law

In England and Wales, and many other countries, the application of copyright law is based on what is known as case law or precedent, and is handled by the Civil Courts. Generally speaking, this means that taking a case to the courts is expensive – potentially very expensive – in terms of costs as well as any damages awarded. It is a good idea to try to resolve copyright matters without recourse to lawyers and the courts. Better yet, try to establish copyright ownership and negotiate acknowledgement, and if necessary payment, before using material as part of a video design.

Regarding copyright on your own work, the best advice I can give here is to negotiate an agreement in advance, and write down the details of that agreement. Bear in mind that few theatre productions make large sums of money for anyone, and that most people involved in making theatre are doing it for other reasons (which is not a reason for them to be exploited – but that is a discussion for another time and place). I imagine readers of this book are likely to be building a reputation rather than be established practitioners; flexibility and understanding should be expected on both sides, and a flexible approach is more likely to get you more work than a rigid application of rights.

Technical Appendix
CABLES AND CONNECTORS

with thanks to James Valpy who wrote the original version of these notes

Video Signals

In any video signal, there are a number of different types of information. This will include information about each line or pixel in the image and information the display machines (televisions, projectors, computer screens, etc.) need in order to display the images correctly. There are many ways of getting video information from one point to another; the way that the information is sent conforms to a **video standard**. At some point a group of people will have sat down to get some level of conformity so that manufacturers can make equipment that is compatible with other manufacturers' equipment. The keys to conformity are agreement on how picture information is coded for transmission (by cable, or by wireless) and which connectors are used in what ways.

Analogue and Digital

Until recently, almost all video signals were analogue. Even when video information is stored digitally, as it is on a DVD or in a computer file, to transmit it from source to display it is coded into an analogue signal. Even our digital computers generally use analogue video formats to send images to their screens or to a projector.

Remember that this section is about getting video images from one place to another as images, not as stored data files – video data files are stored as digital information. Nor are we talking about display technology (yet). Video displays are inherently digital since they break the image down into discrete pixels, each with a number of digital values associated with it. (This in contrast to analogue film, which records information in a continuous way, rather than in a stepped digital way. The fact that at the highest digital resolutions we can now make the steps so small as to be indistinguishable from the continuous nature of analogue is not the issue here.)

Digital coding happens for domestic cable formats such as HDMI and domestic Optical and the newer computer display format DVI.

TV Standards

Television pictures are generally coded to either NTSC (in most of the Americas, Japan and a few other countries), PAL (in Europe, much of

Asia and Africa, and Australia) or SECAM (in the countries of the old Soviet Union and some African countries). Without a converter of some sort, most analogue video equipment will accept only one of these TV standards. To keep things manageable, make sure all your analogue video equipment and all your video content uses the same TV standard.

Composite Video

Composite video is an analogue picture only signal. Composite video tends to be used for digital cameras, CCTV cameras and video capture cards in computers. It is an easy way of getting video from A to B in one cable.

The most common domestic connector used for composite video is the RCA phono (like the kind used in home hi-fi). This cable has one pin that all of the information gets sent through, plus the grounded casing. This is a handy standard as it only uses one cable. However that's a lot of information to try to get down the one cable, and composite video has quality limits.

RCA connectors are fine for short cables, say between equipment in a rack or on the same table. However, when you do need longer cables, generally the RCA connector is replaced with a BNC (Bayonet Neill-Concelman) and the standard audio signal cable is replaced by 75 ohm coaxial cable.

BNC connectors on coaxial cables are generally referred to as BNC cables. BNC cables are use in professional video applications as a replacement for RCA connectors and audio quality cables.

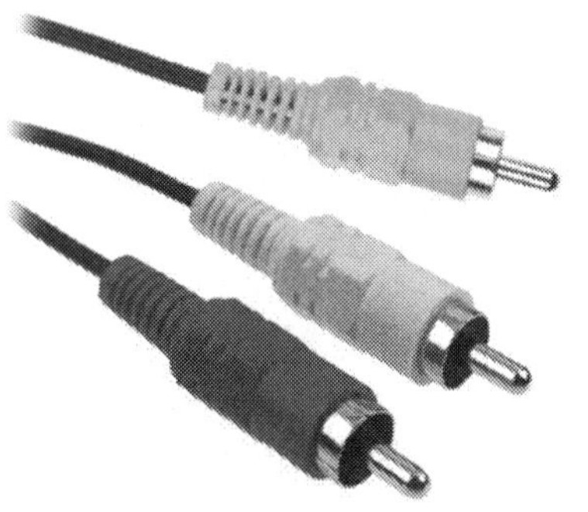

RCA phono domestic video cable. Yellow for the composite video signal, red and white for the stereo sound signal.

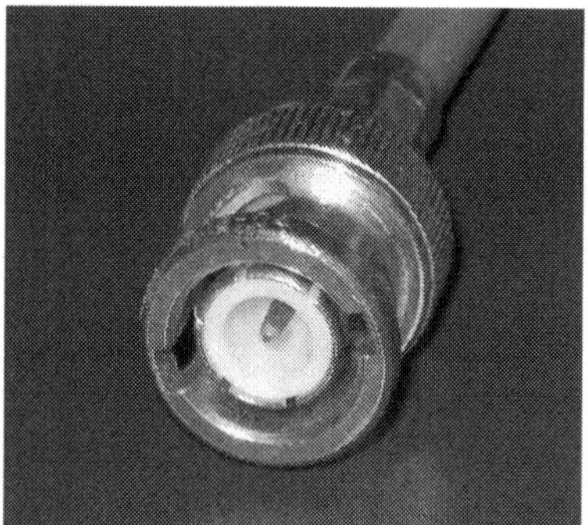

A professional BNC connector, with a locking ring.

It is quite common to see three RCA phono cables bound together in domestic video systems. The other two cables are for stereo sound – red for right and white for left. Generally, in video systems for the stage, if sound does come from the video playback machine, it does not go to the projector or display screen, but instead to a separate sound system.

Analogue Component Video

When higher quality is required than composite can provide (and when there are long cable runs) it's time to consider component video. This requires five cables to carry the five components – red, green, blue, horizontal sync and vertical sync. This standard is common in professional systems. BNC on 75 Ohm coaxial cable are the usual accepted connector standard here.

VGA – Video Graphics Array

VGA connectors are still a common sight on most projectors, desktop computers and computer monitors. VGA is a manipulated form of component video. It has more connecting pins and it is possible to send higher quality signals in this form as there has not been as much compression and manipulation of information that will cause loss of quality. VGA cables carry analogue component RGBHV (red, green, blue, horizontal sync, vertical sync) video signals, and data.

The data is an important feature of VGA technology; it is useful, most of the time. It tells a computer what is connected to the display port. If you are using a projector or other device that does not output this data information, or a cable system that does not pass this data back, the computer that is driving the graphics card will not let it output video.

One simple solution to this is to use a device that mimics the EDID output and 'fools' the video card, such as a Parrot. (It sends out its own customisable EDID and allows you to be more flexibility with your resolutions.) www.DVIPARROT.com

The main benefit with VGA over the five cable component on BNC is that if you are using a computer, you can customise resolutions and you generally have more control over the signal, therefore it is flexible enough to fit the specifications of your project.

With good cables and a VDA (video distribution amplifier) you can have VGA cable runs of up to 40m before the signal starts to drop out. When the signal drops out, you see missing colour information (either red, green or blue missing from the output image) or you may lose vertical/ horizontal scan information (which will cause the image to flicker). None

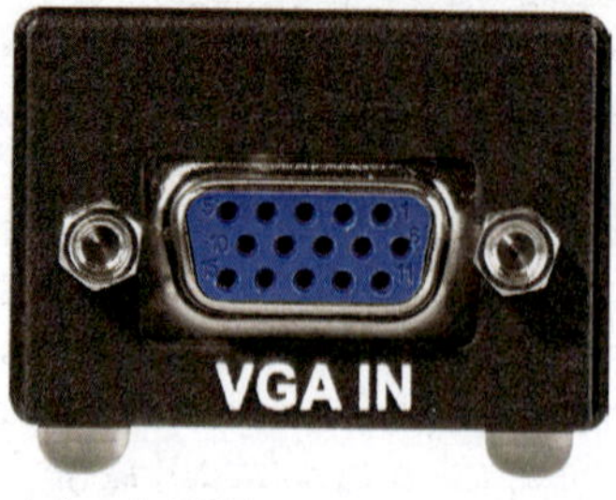

A female VGA connector

of these situations is ideal. If you want to send VGA longer, you need to boost the signal every 30-40m with another VDA. Good quality VGA cables are expensive and can be vulnerable to breaks inside. This is one reason why many professional systems do without the EIDI pins and use five BNC cable systems instead.

The VGA connector comes in two forms, commonly referred to as male with pins, and female with sockets (see illustration) Equipment usually has female connectors and cables usually have male connectors on both ends, but check before you go off an buy an expensive cable.

Most, if not all cables that carry power (as opposed to signals) are male at one end and female at the other. This is so that you can't touch pins with power and get electrocuted. Many signal cable systems however, use cables with a male connector on both ends, with female connectors on the equipment. This is often due to the bi-directional nature of signal traffic, and the fragility of the pins of many multi-pin connectors. It also means that without an adaptor you can't plug two such cables together!

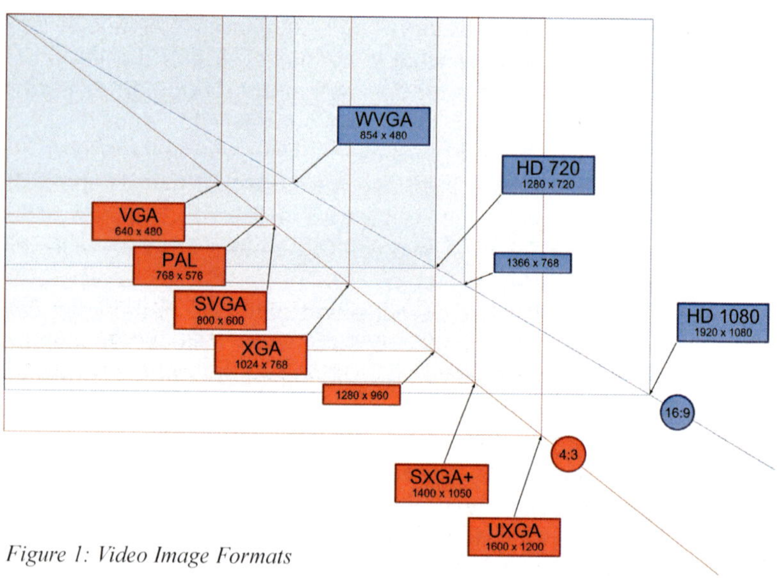

Figure 1: Video Image Formats

Digital Video Cables, Links and Expansion Modules

The digital visual interface (DVI) is a video standard designed to provide very high quality on digital displays. It is found on high-end graphics cards, and Apple MAC computers.

It was developed by an industry group, the Digital Display Working Group (DDWG) to replace VGA technology. It is designed for carrying uncompressed digital video data to a display. The DVI interface uses a digital protocol in which the desired illumination of pixels is transmitted as binary data. When the display is driven at its native resolution, anything up to 1920x1200 for a single link, it will read each number and apply that brightness to the appropriate pixel.

There are at least five different types of DVI cable.

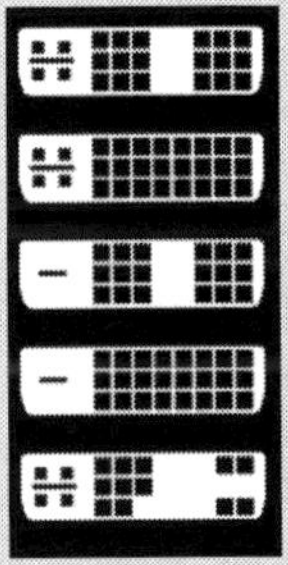

1 DVI-I single link which has digital and analogue pins

2 DVI-I dual link which also has digital and analogue pins

3 DVI-D single link has only digital pins

4 DVI-D dual link again with only digital pins

5 DVI-A analogue which has only analogue pins + DDC pins. It's a VGA cable using a DVI connector, but not necessarily with the data (see above). This lack of data can be a problem.

DVI cables are not generally suitable for long runs. At HD1080 resolution, a 5m length limit is recommended. However, according to at least one source, provided good quality cable is used a 15m cable can support resolutions up to HD720. For longer distances, a DVI booster may be required.

Increasingly, as professional video systems move away from analogue video communication, digital video signals are distributed from playback machine to projector using fibre optic links. (See the system diagram of Kinghoffer at the end of this appendix.)

Where this is not possible, digital video signals are converted to analogue component signals using a scan converter (see later) and distributed using bundles of five BNC cables.

In the DVI types above, single and dual link refers to the potential bandwidth of the digital signal, which in turn relates to the maximum possible resolution that can be transmitted. As already stated, for a single link cable, the maximum resolution is 1920x1200 pixels, more than double the resolution of standard VGA. Dual link expands the possible resolution even further, effectively to the limit of the copper cable.

Graphics Expansion Modules are designed to give greater flexibility to home and commercial computer users. A module such as the DualHead2Go from www.Matrox.com expands the display output of any computer into two screens. This is different from running the same output of two screens. As the sales literature says, you can run separate applications on each screen. Or, if you were running drawing or editing software, you could have the tools on one screen and the images on another.

They can be very useful for video system designers too. Even if you are simply using a desktop computer running Powerpoint for your show, the two outputs of the DualHead2G can be used to give the operator a preview screen that is different to the slide output sent to the projector. (Of course it you run the program on a laptop, you will already have a screen for the operator – the laptop screen.) A graphics expansion module can give you two different video images feeding two projectors, all from the same laptop computer.

Matrox also do a TripleHead2Go, expanding graphics output to three screens, though this usually works best with a Dual Link DVI output. With this in your video system you could feed a single image to three projectors, making use of over 3000 pixels width, or feed the projectors with three different images (though controlling all that is likely to be challenging).

The current models of Dual- and TripleHead2Go have options for VGA output (as well as DVI). This means the standard set up sees a short DVI cable from the playback computer going to the graphics expansion module and longer VGA cables going from there to the projectors/display screens (via video distribution amplifiers if required).

SCART and HDMI

SCART – Radio and Television Receiver Manufacturers' Association – (in French) was the standard cable for connecting up analogue home video equipment. HDMI (high definition multimedia interface) is fast replacing SCART as home video goes digital. Both standards allow automatic communication between devices and screens, selecting which input the screen displays and setting aspect ratio for example. They are also both standards designed for short cable lengths: no more than four to five metres in normal situations.

The fact that they make things happen automatically, and the limit on their length, generally make them unsuitable for stage video systems. If the only way to get video signals out of a device is via SCART, buy an adaptor to access the composite video signal and use that rather than trying to extend a SCART cable.

If you need to use equipment that only outputs HDMI, my first advice would be to transfer the content to something else, say a computer hard-drive. Alternatively, HDMI should be directly convertible to DVI – if all the manufacturers have implemented the standards correctly – so you could simply buy a suitable adaptor here too. But don't assume it will work. Try it out before you get to the theatre or concert hall.

Conversion – from one Video Standard to Another

If at all possible, try to design your video system using one video standard throughout.

Sometimes that is not possible however, and you have to change the standard. If the signal format is the same, and it is only the connector format that is not compatible this can be done with a passive adaptor such as a SCART to composite video adaptor or a DVI-A to VGA for example. In both these cases, some information is being lost, and this may be a good thing, or it may have negative consequences, as with the loss of display control data in going from VGA to component video above.

Sometimes you need to change the signal format as well as the connector type. A common example of this is when the VGA output of a computer needs to be displayed on an older screen or projector that only accepts composite video signals. VGA is a form of component video, and the signal format needs to be actively processed to turn it into composite video signals. To do this processing you will need a scan converter.

Scan conversion or scan rate converting is a technique for changing the vertical and horizontal scan frequency of video signal for different purposes and applications. When scan converting, it is possible to get distortion of the image or you may see that the image will not fill the entire output device. Most scan converters try to sort this out automatically. If you use one that does not, however, you may need to access parameters within the scan converter, using external switches or by connecting it to a computer.

Perhaps you are wondering "what is this scan rate?" Read on...

Interlaced Scanning vs Progressive Scanning

When we refer to scanning method of video signals and hardware, we are describing how the information in the video signal is being processed into an image. There are two types of scanning: progressive and interlaced.

Modern pixel-based displays (LCD, DLP, LCOS, plasma, etc) are progressive scan and require progressively scanned video sources. Older televisions and video devices use the older interlaced scan technology. Most pre-digital video was made using interlaced scan technology. As we will see, this material will need to be re-coded before it can be used with progressive scan display equipment.

Interlaced Scanning (i)

In this system a complete image frame is encoded in two fields, one containing all the odd lines, and the next containing all the even lines. When displayed, the image is drawn with all the odd lines being scanned from top to bottom, followed by all the even lines top to bottom. Fifty or 60 separate fields are shown every second. (That's 25 or 30 fully formed frames per second or FPS, depending on the video format).

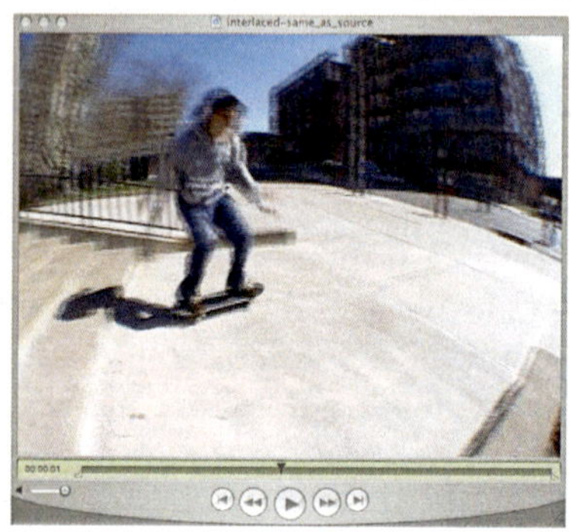

This is what happens when you play an interlaced source video on progressive screen technology, without doing a scan conversion first.

When you play an interlaced movie on a progressive monitor, such as a computer monitor, you end up seeing both odd and even fields blended into one frame. The result often looks terrible, especially on shots with a lot of motion. It is possible to 'De-interlace' an interlacedi video source by using video editing software such as Final Cut Pro or After Effects.

Progressive Scanning (p)

This is for newer digital screens. Computer monitors and HDTV sets use progressive scans. The image is displayed one line after the other, and does not skip lines to return and display the rest. This also happens rather quickly at 60+ frames per second, which produces less flicker from the screen.

And this explains what the (i) and the (p) stand for in the shorthand names for HD Video Formats.

720p	pixel dimensions of 1280 x 720, progressive scan
720i	the same 1280 x 720 pixels, but interlaced
1080p	pixel dimensions of 1920 x 1080, progressive scan
1080i	the same 1920 x 1080 pixels, but interlaced

1080p is the highest quality video as a standard, but that's only good if your screen or projector can handle it. When you are designing a system, look at the maximum resolution capability that the hardware can handle and design the content to reach that maximum. Don't go overboard. You can always zoom or scale clips depending on what you are using to play them back.

Projector Types

DLP

In DLP (digital light processor or processing) projectors, the image is created by microscopically small mirrors laid out in a matrix on a semiconductor chip, known as a digital micromirror device (DMD). Each mirror represents one or more pixels in the projected image. The number of mirrors corresponds to the resolution of the projected image, often half as many mirrors as the advertised resolution due to wobulation. (Yes, it's an actual term created by HP!) These mirrors can be repositioned rapidly to reflect light either through the lens or on to a heat sink (called a light dump in Barco terminology).

Rapidly toggling the mirror between these two orientations (essentially on and off) produces greyscales, controlled by the ratio of on-time to off-time.

The Colour Wheel Rainbow Effect

A single-chip projector alternates between colours and produces separate red, green, and blue images. DLP projectors that utilise a mechanical spinning colour wheel may exhibit an anomaly known as the 'rainbow effect.' This is best described as brief flashes of perceived red, blue, and green 'shadows' observed most often when the projected content features high contrast areas of moving bright or white objects on a mostly dark or black background. The scrolling end credits of many movies are a common example, and also in animations where moving objects are surrounded by a thick black outline. Brief visible separation of the colours can also be apparent when the viewer moves their eyes quickly across the projected image. Some people perceive these rainbow artefacts frequently, while others may never see them at all.

LCD

To display images, LCD (liquid crystal display) projectors typically send light from a metal halide lamp through a prism to three polysilicon panels, one each for the red, green and blue components of the video signal. As polarised light passes through the panels, individual pixels can be opened to allow light to pass or closed to block the light. The combination of open and closed pixels can produce a wide range of colours and shades in the projected image.

Fill Factor

One aspect of image quality rarely mentioned on projector sales websites is fill factor. This can be thought of as how much of the screen is filled with image. Each type of projector technology has an inherent gap between pixels, or between mirror cells if it's a DLP. (As already noted due to things like wobulation, a mirror cell may be more than one pixel). The higher the fill factor, the less of the image is in these gaps between pixels, and more of it is pixels of content. The gaps between pixels or cells create a grid of fine lines. This can become quite visible, especially if your audience is close to the screens – as happens very often in studio productions, or when we use projected images to light people. At the moment, DLP projectors seem to have a higher fill factor than LCDs, so the lines are less obvious with a DLP projector.

If you think this might be a factor, try to find out more about the projector(s) you are using, and experiment. It can be possible to lose almost all the effect of the lines by slightly defocusing the projectors. You may need to decide if losing the lines is more or less important than the sharpness of the content.

Green Flash

Occasionally, when LCD projector light hits the screen at a shallow angle, some observers will see a distracting green light in the reflection of image. This first happened to me in a studio production set in the round with a projector in each corner. The projectors lit performers and the floor at around 35 degrees. The audience opposite each projector saw a strong green component in the light reflected from the floor, even when very little green light appeared to be present in the projected image.

The effect is a biproduct of the polarisation that is part of the way an LCD projector makes its images, and there is no obvious way round it. Again, try to experiment with different set-ups and see if you can achieve what the production design needs in other ways.

Rigging

Getting the projector into the right place, safely, and then being able to make adjustments can raise a whole new set of problems. Remember that whenever something is suspended over the heads of other people, there is usually a legal (as well as a moral and financial) responsibility on the person in charge to make sure that it's done as safely as possible. If the worst was to happen and a projector fell and hurt someone, a court might well decide that the video designer was in charge of the suspension of the projector, even if he or she did not actually rig it. If you are at all unsure about any aspect of getting a projector to where it needs to be, and keeping it there safely, take advice from people with the appropriate skills and knowledge that you trust. If the situation is unusual, it is often a requirement to write down the way you are going to do things (a method statement) and the way you have gone about making the whole process as safe "as is reasonably possible" (a written risk assessment).

If you hire from a company familiar with the needs of live performance design, they should supply you with all the necessary equipment to hang your projector safely, and be able to give you good advice on how to use it all. If you are using a projector in a fixed position provided by the venue (may be you are using the projector usually used for lectures, etc.) then you don't really need to worry either.

If you have to sort out how to get a projector in place, read on.

In most performance spaces there are bars or pipes used to hang lighting, scenery and drapes, usually 48 or 50mm (or two inches) in diameter. These hanging positions can be used for suspending projectors too. If there is not a suitable hanging position where you need to put a projector, it may be possible to create one. This might be by simply extending an existing hanging position with scaffolding pipe and clamps, or there may be a need to do something more permanent, say bolting fastenings to a wall to make a new hanging position. It may also be possible to extend up or down from a suitable existing hanging position. Always check with the person in charge of the technical infrastructure of the venue before you plan to do any of these things. She or he is likely to have more experience in these matters and may see an alternative simple solution that will work equally well.

When planning where the projector(s) will go, don't forget the audience. It's not usually a good idea to block the view of audience members with a projector, and you should never restrict an exit or entrance by anything you do. Also, projectors have fans which can be distracting. Try to keep this in mind too when deciding where the projector(s) will go.

There are two approaches to mounting small- and medium-sized projectors. Either using a mounting plate screwed or bolted directly to the projector, or using a cradle to sit the projector in. Most lecture system projectors are rigged using mounting plates. Most show projectors use some kind of cradle. This is mainly because cradles tend to be more flexible, both in terms of accommodating different sizes of projector and accessories, and in being able to cope with the more extreme angles we often need in video for stage.

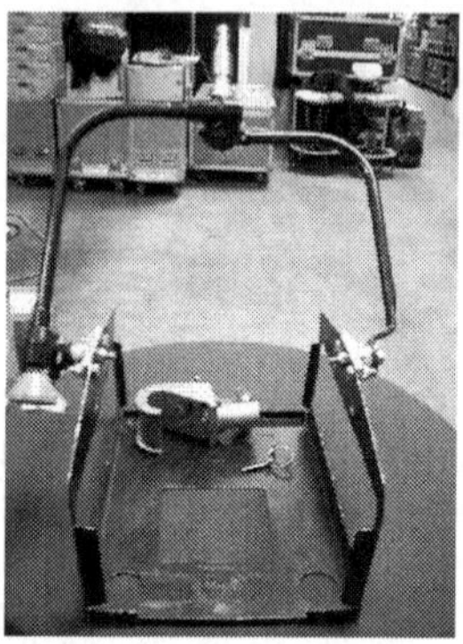

A projector cradle incorporating the yoke of a old TV lantern. The pan and tilt of this cradle can be adjusted from below using the blue and white knobs on the side and a special pole.

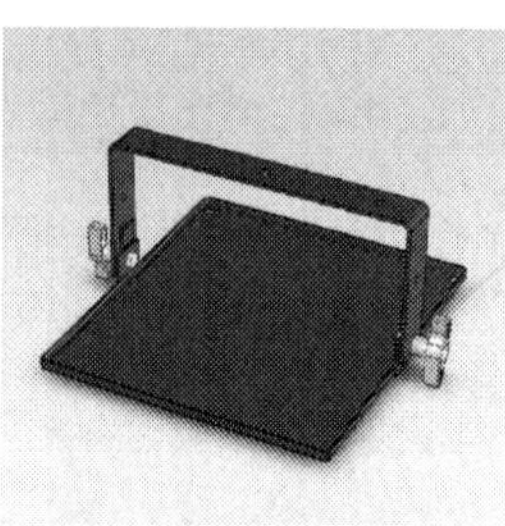

A projector cradle from UK stage engineering firm Doughty Engineering.

If you don't need to tilt your projector(s) steeply, a mounting plate solution could be the best choice. Mounting plate systems are offered by several engineering companies. In the UK, Unicol have been the market leader for some time, and have a relatively comprehensive selection of solutions. Other manufacturers and importers are worth checking out too. Mounting plates usually need additional components in order to attach the projector to the lighting bar (or other fixed hanging position). They tend to be made for permanent installation, with a ceiling plate at the top designed to be bolted in place. What you are unlikely to find is anything from the catalogues that takes the mounting system directly onto a lighting bar or pipe. If you talk to a friendly lighting person, he or she may well be able to help here, by drilling a hole in a ceiling mounting plate and attaching a suitable lighting fixture clamp. You will both need to make sure you have not compromised the strength of the ceiling plate and the rest of the system by doing this of course. You will also need to check that you can tilt the projector to the angle required by the video design.

Projector cradles are likely to be available from anywhere that hires projectors for use on stage. However, if you are not hiring your projector, the hire company may not wish to hire just the cradle. Many people improvise projector cradles, some to great effect. The one pictured top (opposite page) has pole operated adjustment using parts from lantern originally designed for a TV studio.

When using cradles such at these, it is usual to secure the projector in the cradle. For a small light projector, several cable ties might be suitable. For larger projectors, an adjustable luggage or cargo strap might be best. What ever you use, make sure you don't cover any ventilation grills or control panels, or crush the projector.

Projector Control Options

Once the projectors are rigged, you will usually still need to access the projector menu to make adjustments or simply to switch them on and off (most projectors like to run their fans for a period once the lamp has been switched off to keep everything nice and cool and ready to work properly for next time). You may need to adjust the keystone correction or the lens shift, or the colour balance. You might even need to adjust the focus and zoom of the lens (generally you will need to stick to the projector maker's lenses if you want to be able to do this however.) However, very often your projector(s) will be rigged in some place that is difficult to access easily and you will want to control them remotely. Here are the main options:

Remote control – Similar to a TV remote control, uses infrared binary technology to send control information to a projector; these can be temperamental.

Web remote – You can use a browser on a computer to view status of projectors, and take control of some functions. Projectors with this enabled are very useful as it is possible to see exactly what the projector is doing from the control position and take control. This uses the same technology as browsing to your router at home. No Software required.

Barco Projector Toolset – A piece of software by Barco for controlling and interfacing with Barco projectors. Similar software is available for some other makes of projector. This is usually a more complex operation than web remote, and you need to install software on your controlling computer.

Wired remote control – These are the same controllers as the infra-

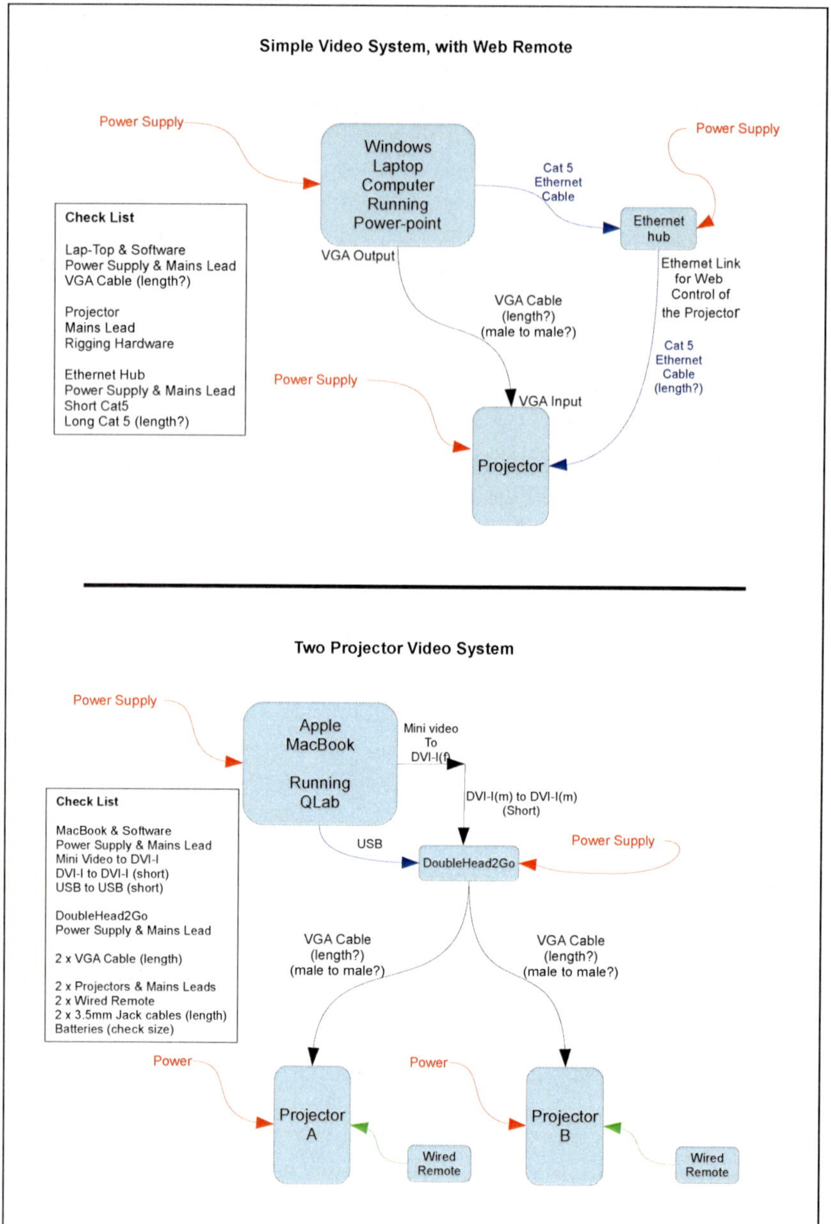

Figure 2 System Drawings

red remote controllers but have a 3.5mm stereo socket on them. The situation that you would use these for is if you have two projectors in proximity to one another as a standard wireless control would make it difficult to control each one separately. Watch out for voltage drop on long cable runs.

Planning Prevents Poor Performance

Finally in this section a word on planning. Even if you have the simplest of video systems, it's worth drawing out a diagram that includes all the equipment and all the cables you need to connect it and make it all work. From this you can make a checklist that will help you make sure everything you need is there. This drawing is likely to be helpful too if/ when it comes to fault finding.

Master & Margareta System Drawing

The Master & Margareta system diagram (overleaf) is for a very large stage video design. It was conceived and realised by Finn Ross and Adam Young of the video design collective Mesmer, for the theatre company Complicite. As you can see the system includes six projectors and four digital video cameras (one operated remotely), two Catalyst media servers and a great deal of processing and data routing equipment – not to mention lots of cables and converters.

This is a very high end video system. The skills and knowledge required to put this all together are way beyond the scope of this book. Rather depressingly, because of the unstoppable advance of technology in this field, especially at the high end, to put a system like this together in five years time will probably need new knowledge and perhaps an entirely new approach. At this level of practice, you need to be constantly updating yourself.

Some things remain the same however. Images need to be created or accessed from a store, manipulated or prepared in other ways, and sent to machines that will display them. The more you know about how that happens, the more technically ambitious you can be. But this is not video design, this is video system design. Without creative content that enhances the overall production design, this stuff is just so much expensive equipment sitting doing nothing.

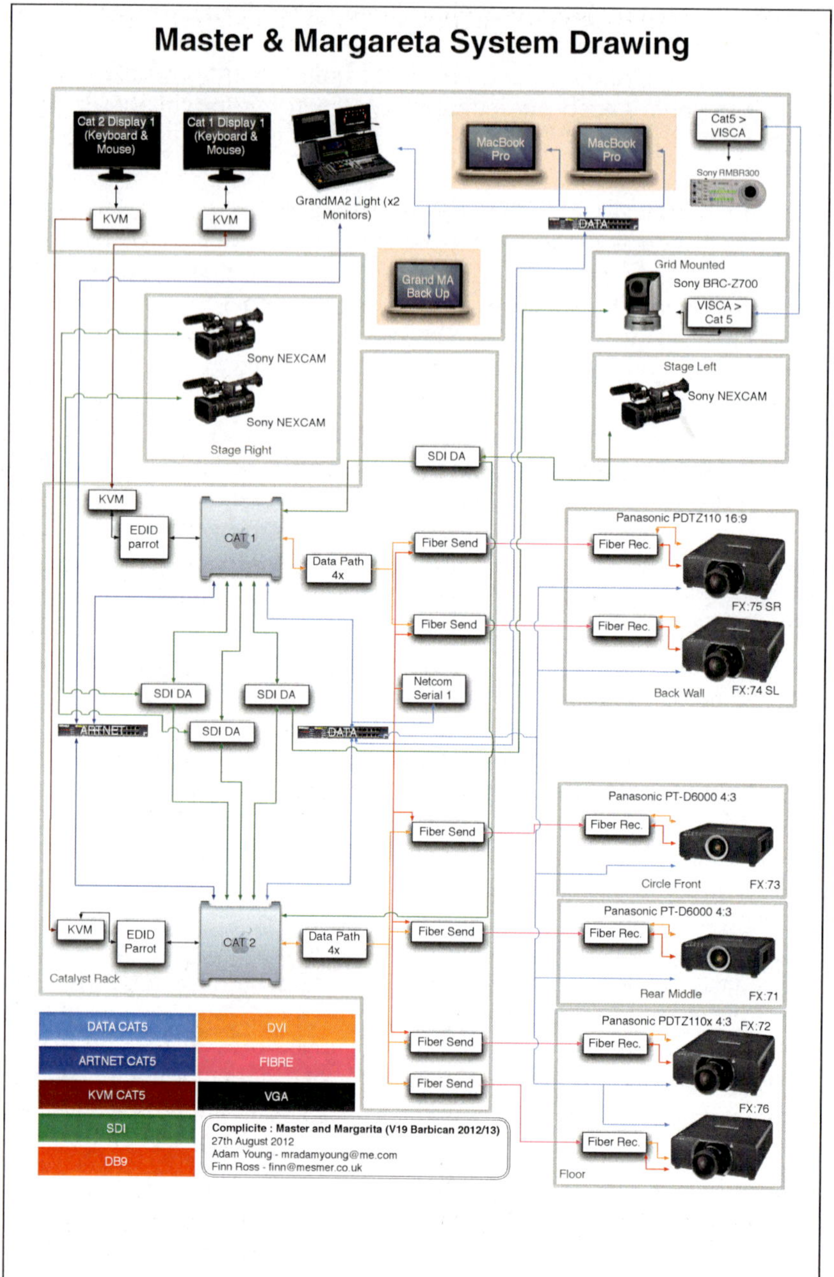
Master & Margareta System Drawing
Cat 2 Display 1 (Keyboard & Mouse)
Cat 1 Display 1 (Keyboard & Mouse)
GrandMA2 Light (x2 Monitors)
MacBook Pro
MacBook Pro
Cat5 > VISCA
Sony RMBR300
KVM
KVM
DATA
Grand MA Back Up
Grid Mounted
Sony BRC-Z700
VISCA > Cat 5
Sony NEXCAM
Sony NEXCAM
Stage Right
Stage Left
Sony NEXCAM
SDI DA
KVM
EDID parrot
CAT 1
Data Path 4x
Fiber Send
Fiber Send
Panasonic PDTZ110 16:9
Fiber Rec.
FX:75 SR
Fiber Rec.
Back Wall
FX:74 SL
SDI DA
SDI DA
Netcom Serial 1
ARTNET
SDI DA
DATA
Panasonic PT-D6000 4:3
Fiber Send
Fiber Rec.
Circle Front
FX:73
KVM
EDID Parrot
CAT 2
Data Path 4x
Fiber Send
Panasonic PT-D6000 4:3
Fiber Rec.
Rear Middle
FX:71
Catalyst Rack
Panasonic PDTZ110x 4:3
FX:72
Fiber Send
Fiber Rec.
Fiber Send
FX:76
Fiber Rec.
Floor
DATA CAT5
DVI
ARTNET CAT5
FIBRE
KVM CAT5
VGA
SDI
DB9
Complicite : Master and Margarita (V19 Barbican 2012/13)
27th August 2012
Adam Young - mradamyoung@me.com
Finn Ross - finn@mesmer.co.uk

Professional Production Credits Appendix

Bad Girls - Photos by Nick Moran
Book by Maureen Chadwick & Ann McManus
Music & Lyrics by Kath Gotts
Directed by Maggie Norris
Set & Costume Design by Colin Richmond
Lighting Design by Tim Mitchell
Sound FX & Video Design by Mic Pool
Sound Design by Paul Groothius
Choreography by Ann Yee Music Direction by Dane Preece
Orchestration by Martin Koch
Orchestral Management by Sylvia Addison
Casting Director, Jill Green
Production Manager, Richard Bullimore

Death of Klinghoffer - Photos by Nick Moran
Conductor Baldur Brönnimann
Director Tom Morris
Set Designer Tom Pye
Costume Designer Laura Hopkins
Lighting Designer Jean Kalman
Choreographer Arthur Pita
Video Designer Finn Ross
Librettist Alice Goodman
Sound Designers Mark Grey and David Sheppard

Orientations - Photos by Nick Moran
Written & Directed by Michael Walling
Costume Design by Seema Iqbal
Lighting Design by Nick Moran
Video Design by Billy Hiscock

Consumed - Photos by Nick Moran
Theatre Company: Border Crossings
Conceived and Directed by : Michael Walling
Devised and Performed by: Song Ru Hi, Serge Soric, Ning Li Tong
Set and Lighting Design by: Nick Moran
Digital Video Design by: Dori Dong
Costume Design by: Sten Volmuller
Music By: Dave Carey
Devised in Shanghai Dramatic Arts Centre and Tara Arts London
Premier at Tara Arts London February 2013, prior to UK and Chinese Tour

ENTERTAINMENT TECHNOLOGY PRESS

FREE SUBSCRIPTION SERVICE

Keeping Up To Date with

Electric Shadows

Entertainment Technology titles are continually up-dated, and all major changes and additions are listed in date order in the relevant dedicated area of the publisher's website. Simply go to the front page of www.etnow.com and click on the BOOKS button. From there you can locate the title and be connected through to the latest information and services related to the publication.

The content of this book is correct at the time of publishing, to the best of the authors' knowledge. We welcome suggestions and comments for future editions of the book, which should be addressed to n.moran@talktalk.net

Titles Published by Entertainment Technology Press

50 Rigging Calls *Chris Higgs, Cristiano Giavedoni 246pp* **£16.95**
ISBN: 9781904031758
Chris Higgs, author of ETP's two leading titles on rigging, An Introduction to Rigging in the Entertainment Industry and Rigging for Entertainment: Regulations and Practice, has collected together 50 articles he has provided regularly for Lighting + Sound International magazine from 2005 to date. They provide a wealth of information for those practising the craft within the entertainment technology industry. The book is profusely illustrated with caricature drawings by Christiano Giavedoni, featuring the popular rigging expert Mario.

ABC of Theatre Jargon *Francis Reid 106pp* **£9.95** ISBN: 9781904031093
This glossary of theatrical terminology explains the common words and phrases that are used in normal conversation between actors, directors, designers, technicians and managers.

Aluminium Structures in the Entertainment Industry *Peter Hind 234pp* **£24.95**
ISBN: 9781904031062
Aluminium Structures in the Entertainment Industry aims to educate the reader in all aspects of the design and safe usage of temporary and permanent aluminium structures specific to the entertainment industry – such as roof structures, PA towers, temporary staging, etc.

AutoCAD – A Handbook for Theatre Users *David Ripley 340pp* **£29.95**
ISBN: 9781904031741
From 'Setting Up' to 'Drawing in Three Dimensions' via 'Drawings Within Drawings', this compact and fully illustrated guide to AutoCAD covers everything from the basics to full colour rendering and remote 3D plotting. Third, completely revised edition, June 2014.

Automation in the Entertainment Industry – A User's Guide *Mark Ager and John Hastie 382pp* **£29.95** ISBN: 9781904031581
In the last 15 years, there has been a massive growth in the use of automation in entertainment, especially in theatres, and it is now recognised as its own discipline. However, it is still only used in around 5% of theatres worldwide. In the next 25 years, given current growth patterns, that figure will rise to 30%. This will mean that the majority of theatre personnel, including directors, designers, technical staff, actors and theatre management, will come into contact with automation for the first time at some point in their careers. This book is intended to provide insights and practical advice from those who use automation, to help the first-time user understand the issues and avoid the pitfalls in its implementation.

Basics – A Beginner's Guide to Lighting Design *Peter Coleman 92pp* **£9.95**
ISBN: 9781904031413
The fourth in the author's 'Basics' series, this title covers the subject area in four main sections: The Concept, Practical Matters, Related Issues and The Design Into Practice. In an

area that is difficult to be definitive, there are several things that cross all the boundaries of all lighting design and it's these areas that the author seeks to help with.

Basics – A Beginner's Guide to Special Effects *Peter Coleman 82pp* **£9.95**
ISBN: 9781904031338
This title introduces newcomers to the world of special effects. It describes all types of special effects including pyrotechnic, smoke and lighting effects, projections, noise machines, etc. It places emphasis on the safe storage, handling and use of pyrotechnics.

Basics – A Beginner's Guide to Stage Lighting *Peter Coleman 86pp* **£9.95**
ISBN: 9781904031208
This title does what it says: it introduces newcomers to the world of stage lighting. It will not teach the reader the art of lighting design, but will teach beginners much about the 'nuts and bolts' of stage lighting.

Basics – A Beginner's Guide to Stage Sound *Peter Coleman 86pp* **£9.95**
ISBN: 9781904031277
This title does what it says: it introduces newcomers to the world of stage sound. It will not teach the reader the art of sound design, but will teach beginners much about the background to sound reproduction in a theatrical environment.

Basics: A Beginner's Guide to Stage Management *Peter Coleman 64pp* **£7.95**
ISBN: 9781904031475
The fifth in Peter Coleman's popular 'Basics' series, this title provides a practical insight into, and the definition of, the role of stage management. Further chapters describe Cueing or 'Calling' the Show (the Prompt Book), and the Hardware and Training for Stage Management. This is a book about people and systems, without which most of the technical equipment used by others in the performance workplace couldn't function.

Building Better Theaters *Michael Mell 180pp* **£16.95** ISBN: 9781904031406
A title within our Consultancy Series, this book describes the process of designing a theatre, from the initial decision to build through to opening night. Michael Mell's book provides a step-by-step guide to the design and construction of performing arts facilities. Chapters discuss: assembling your team, selecting an architect, different construction methods, the architectural design process, construction of the theatre, theatrical systems and equipment, the stage, backstage, the auditorium, ADA requirements and the lobby. Each chapter clearly describes what to expect and how to avoid surprises. It is a must-read for architects, planners, performing arts groups, educators and anyone who may be considering building or renovating a theatre.

Carry on Fading *Francis Reid 216pp* **£20.00** ISBN: 9781904031642
This is a record of five of the best years of the author's life. Years so good that the only downside is the pangs of guilt at enjoying such contentment in a world full of misery induced by greed, envy and imposed ideologies. Fortunately Francis' DNA is high on luck, optimism and blessing counting.

Case Studies in Crowd Management
Chris Kemp, Iain Hill, Mick Upton, Mark Hamilton 206pp **£16.95**
ISBN: 9781904031482
This important work has been compiled from a series of research projects carried out by the staff of the Centre for Crowd Management and Security Studies at Buckinghamshire Chilterns University College (now Bucks New University), and seminar work carried out in Berlin and Groningen with partner Yourope. It includes case studies, reports and a crowd management safety plan for a major outdoor rock concert, safe management of rock concerts utilising a triple barrier safety system and pan-European Health & Safety Issues.

Case Studies in Crowd Management, Security and Business Continuity
Chris Kemp, Patrick Smith 274pp **£24.95** ISBN: 9781904031635
The creation of good case studies to support work in progress and to give answers to those seeking guidance in their quest to come to terms with perennial questions is no easy task. The first Case Studies in Crowd Management book focused mainly on a series of festivals and events that had a number of issues which required solving. This book focuses on a series of events that had major issues that impacted on the every day delivery of the events researched.

Close Protection – The Softer Skills *Geoffrey Padgham 132pp* **£11.95**
ISBN: 9781904031390
This is the first educational book in a new 'Security Series' for Entertainment Technology Press, and it coincides with the launch of the new 'Protective Security Management' Foundation Degree at Buckinghamshire Chilterns University College (now Bucks New University). The author is a former full-career Metropolitan Police Inspector from New Scotland Yard with 27 years' experience of close protection (CP). For 22 of those years he specialised in operations and senior management duties with the Royalty Protection Department at Buckingham Palace, followed by five years in the private security industry specialising in CP training design and delivery. His wealth of protection experience comes across throughout the text, which incorporates sound advice and exceptional practical guidance, subtly separating fact from fiction. This publication is an excellent form of reference material for experienced operatives, students and trainees.

A Comparative Study of Crowd Behaviour at Two Major Music Events
Chris Kemp, Iain Hill, Mick Upton 78pp **£7.95** ISBN: 9781904031253
A compilation of the findings of reports made at two major live music concerts, and in particular crowd behaviour, which is followed from ingress to egress.

Control Freak *Wayne Howell 270pp* **£28.95** ISBN: 9781904031550
Control Freak is the second book by Wayne Howell. It provides an in depth study of DMX512 and the new RDM (Remote Device Management) standards. The book is aimed at both users and developers and provides a wealth of real world information based on the author's twenty year experience of lighting control.

Copenhagen Opera House *Richard Brett and John Offord 272pp* **£32.00**
ISBN: 9781904031420
Completed in a little over three years, the Copenhagen Opera House opened with a royal gala performance on 15th January 2005. Built on a spacious brown-field site, the building is a landmark venue and this book provides the complete technical background story to an opera house set to become a benchmark for future design and planning. Sixteen chapters by relevant experts involved with the project cover everything from the planning of the auditorium and studio stage, the stage engineering, stage lighting and control and architectural lighting through to acoustic design and sound technology plus technical summaries.

Cue 80 *Francis Reid 310pp* **£17.95** ISBN: 9781904031659
Although Francis Reid's work in theatre has been visual rather than verbal, writing has provided crucial support. Putting words on paper has been the way in which he organised and clarified his thoughts. And in his self-confessed absence of drawing skills, writing has helped him find words to communicate his visual thinking in discussions with the rest of the creative team. As a by-product, this process of searching for the right words to help formulate and analyse ideas has resulted in half-a-century of articles in theatre journals. Cue 80 is an anthology of these articles and is released in celebration of Francis' 80th birthday.

The DMX 512-A Handbook – Design and Implementation of DMX Enabled Products and Networks *James Eade 150pp* **£13.95** ISBN: 9781904031727
This guidebook was originally conceived as a guide to the new DMX512-A standard on behalf of the ESTA Controls Protocols Working Group (CPWG). It has subsequently been updated and is aimed at all levels of reader from technicians working with or servicing equipment in the field as well as manufacturers looking to build in DMX control to their lighting products. It also gives thorough guidance to consultants and designers looking to design DMX networks.

Electric Shadows: an Introduction to Video and Projection on Stage *Nick Moran 234pp* **£23.95** ISBN: 9781904031734
Electric Shadows aims to guide the emerging video designer through the many simple and difficult technical and aesthetic choices and decisions he or she has to make in taking their design from outline idea through to realisation. The main body of the book takes the reader through the process of deciding what content will be projected onto what screen or screens to make the best overall production design. The book will help you make electric shadows that capture the attention of your audience, to help you tell your stories in just the way you want.

Electrical Safety for Live Events *Marco van Beek 98pp* **£16.95** ISBN: 9781904031284
This title covers electrical safety regulations and good practise pertinent to the entertainment industries and includes some basic electrical theory as well as clarifying the "do's and don't's" of working with electricity.

Entertainment in Production Volume 1: 1994-1999 *Rob Halliday 254pp* **£24.95**
ISBN: 9781904031512

Entertainment in Production Volume 2: 2000-2006 *Rob Halliday 242poo* £24.95
ISBN: 9781904031529
Rob Halliday has a dual career as a lighting designer/programmer and author and in these two volumes he provides the intriguing but comprehensive technical background stories behind the major musical productions and other notable projects spanning the period 1994 to 2005. Having been closely involved with the majority of the events described, the author is able to present a first-hand and all-encompassing portrayal of how many of the major shows across the past decade came into being. From *Oliver!* and *Miss Saigon* to *Mamma Mia!* and *Mary Poppins*, here the complete technical story unfolds. The books, which are profusely illustrated, are in large part an adapted selection of articles that first appeared in the magazine *Lighting&Sound International.*

Entertainment Technology Yearbook 2008 *John Offord 220pp* **£14.95**
ISBN: 9781904031543
The Entertainment Technology Yearbook 2008 covers the year 2007 and includes picture coverage of major industry exhibitions in Europe compiled from the pages of Entertainment Technology magazine and the etnow.com website, plus articles and pictures of production, equipment and project highlights of the year.

The Exeter Theatre Fire *David Anderson 202pp* **£24.95** ISBN: 9781904031130
This title is a fascinating insight into the events that led up to the disaster at the Theatre Royal, Exeter, on the night of September 5th 1887. The book details what went wrong, and the lessons that were learned from the event.

Fading into Retirement *Francis Reid 124pp* **£17.95**
ISBN: 9781904031352
This is the final book in Francis Reid's fading trilogy which, with Fading Light and Carry on Fading, updates the Hearing the Light record of places visited, performances seen, and people met. Never say never, but the author uses the 'final' label because decreasing mobility means that his ability to travel is diminished to the point that his life is now contained within a very few square miles. His memories are triggered by over 600 CDs, half of them Handel and 100 or so DVDs supplemented by a rental subscription to LOVEFiLM.

Fading Light – A Year in Retirement *Francis Reid 136pp* **£14.95**
ISBN: 9781904031352
Francis Reid, the lighting industry's favourite author, describes a full year in retirement. "Old age is much more fun than I expected," he says. Fading Light describes visits and experiences to the author's favourite theatres and opera houses, places of relaxation and re-visits to scholarly institutions.

Focus on Lighting Technology *Richard Cadena 120pp* **£17.95** ISBN: 9781904031147
This concise work unravels the mechanics behind modern performance lighting and appeals to designers and technicians alike. Packed with clear, easy-to-read diagrams, the book provides excellent explanations behind the technology of performance lighting.

The Followspot Guide *Nick Mobsby 450pp* **£28.95** ISBN: 9781904031499
The first in ETP's Equipment Series, Nick Mobsby's Followspot Guide tells you everything you need to know about followspots, from their history through to maintenance and usage. Its pages include a technical specification of 193 followspots from historical to the latest versions from major manufacturers.

From Ancient Rome to Rock 'n' Roll – a Review of the UK Leisure Security Industry *Mick Upton 198pp* **£14.95** ISBN: 9781904031505
From stewarding, close protection and crowd management through to his engagement as a senior consultant Mick Upton has been ever present in the events industry. A founder of ShowSec International in 1982 he was its chairman until 2000. The author has led the way on training within the sector. He set up the ShowSec Training Centre and has acted as a consultant at the Bramshill Police College. He has been prominent in the development of courses at Buckinghamshire New University where he was awarded a Doctorate in 2005. Mick has received numerous industry awards. His book is a personal account of the development and professionalism of the sector across the past 50 years.

Gobos for Image Projection *Michael Hall and Julie Harper 176pp* **£25.95** ISBN: 9781904031628
In this first published book dedicated totally to the gobo, the authors take the reader through from the history of projection to the development of the present day gobo. And there is broad practical advice and ample reference information to back it up. A feature of the work is the inclusion, interspersed throughout the text, of comment and personal experience in the use and application of gobos from over 25 leading lighting designers worldwide.

Health and Safety Aspects in the Live Music Industry *Chris Kemp, Iain Hill 300pp* **£30.00** ISBN: 9781904031222
This major work includes chapters on various safety aspects of live event production and is written by specialists in their particular areas of expertise.

Health and Safety Management in the Live Music and Events Industry *Chris Hannam 480pp* **£25.95** ISBN: 9781904031307
This title covers the health and safety regulations and their application regarding all aspects of staging live entertainment events, and is an invaluable manual for production managers and event organisers.

Hearing the Light – 50 Years Backstage *Francis Reid 280pp* **£24.95** ISBN: 9781904031185
This highly enjoyable memoir delves deeply into the theatricality of the industry. The author's almost fanatical interest in opera, his formative period as lighting designer at

Glyndebourne and his experiences as a theatre administrator, writer and teacher make for a broad and unique background.

An Introduction to Rigging in the Entertainment Industry *Chris Higgs 272pp* **£24.95**
ISBN: 9781904031123
This title is a practical guide to rigging techniques and practices and also thoroughly covers safety issues and discusses the implications of working within recommended guidelines and regulations. Second edition revised September 2008.

Let There be Light – Entertainment Lighting Software Pioneers in Conversation
Robert Bell 390pp **£32.00** ISBN: 9781904031246
Robert Bell interviews a distinguished group of software engineers working on entertainment lighting ideas and products.

Light and Colour Filters *Michael Hall and Eddie Ruffell 286pp* **£23.95**
ISBN: 9781904031598
Written by two acknowledged and respected experts in the field, this book is destined to become the standard reference work on the subject. The title chronicles the development and use of colour filters and also describes how colour is perceived and how filters function. Up-to-date reference tables will help the practitioner make better and more specific choices of colour.

Lighting for Roméo and Juliette *John Offord 172pp* **£26.95** ISBN: 9781904031161
John Offord describes the making of the Vienna State Opera production from the lighting designer's viewpoint – from the point where director Jürgen Flimm made his decision not to use scenery or sets and simply employ the expertise of lighting designer Patrick Woodroffe.

Lighting Systems for TV Studios *Nick Mobsby 570pp* **£45.00** ISBN: 9781904031000
Lighting Systems for TV Studios, now in its second edition, is the first book specifically written on the subject and has become the 'standard' resource work for studio planning and design covering the key elements of system design, luminaires, dimming, control, data networks and suspension systems as well as detailing the infrastructure items such as cyclorama, electrical and ventilation. TV lighting principles are explained and some history on TV broadcasting, camera technology and the equipment is provided to help set the scene! The second edition includes applications for sine wave and distributed dimming, moving lights, Ethernet and new cool lamp technology.

Lighting Techniques for Theatre-in-the-Round *Jackie Staines 188pp* **£24.95**
ISBN: 9781904031017
Lighting Techniques for Theatre-in-the-Round is a unique reference source for those working on lighting design for theatre-in-the-round for the first time. It is the first title to be published specifically on the subject and it also provides some anecdotes and ideas for more challenging shows, and attempts to blow away some of the myths surrounding lighting in this format.

Lighting the Diamond Jubilee Concert *Durham Marenghi 102pp* **£19.95**
ISBN: 9781904031673
In this highly personal landmark document the show's lighting designer Durham Marenghi pays tribute to the team of industry experts who each played an important role in bringing the Diamond Jubilee Concert to fruition, both for television and live audiences. The book contains colour production photography throughout and describes the production processes and the thinking behind them. In his Foreword, BBC Executive Producer Guy Freeman states: "Working with the whole lighting team on such a special project was a real treat for me and a fantastic achievement for them, which the pages of this book give a remarkable insight into."

Lighting the Stage *Francis Reid 120pp* **£14.95** ISBN: 9781904031086
Lighting the Stage discusses the human relationships involved in lighting design – both between people, and between these people and technology. The book is written from a highly personal viewpoint and its 'thinking aloud' approach is one that Francis Reid has used in his writings over the past 30 years.

Miscellany of Lighting and Stagecraft *Michael Hall & Julie Harper 222pp* **£22.95**
ISBN: 9781904031680
This title will help schools, colleges, amateurs, technicians and all those interested in practical theatre and performance to understand, in an entertaining and informative way, the key backstage skills. Within its pages, numerous professionals share their own special knowledge and expertise, interspersed with diversions of historic interest and anecdotes from those practising at the front line of the industry. As a result, much of the advice and skills set out have not previously been set in print. The editors' intention with this book is to provide a Miscellany that is not ordered or categorised in strict fashion, but rather encourages the reader to flick through or dip into it, finding nuggets of information and anecdotes to entertain, inspire and engender curiosity – also to invite further research or exploration and generally encourage people to enter the industry and find out for themselves.

Mr Phipps' Theatre *Mark Jones, John Pick 172pp* £17.95 ISBN: 9781904031383
Mark Jones and John Pick describe "The Sensational Story of Eastbourne's Royal Hippodrome" – formerly Eastbourne Theatre Royal. An intriguing narrative, the book sets the story against a unique social history of the town. Peter Longman, former director of The Theatres Trust, provides the Foreword.

Northen Lights *Michael Northen 256pp* **£17.95** ISBN: 9781904031666
Many books have been written by famous personalities in the theatre about their lives and work. However this is probably one of the first memoirs by someone who has spent his entire career behind scenes, and not in front of the footlights. As a lighting designer and as consultant to designers and directors, Michael Northen worked through an exciting period of fifty years of theatrical history from the late nineteen thirties in theatres in the UK and abroad, and on productions ranging from Shakespeare, opera and ballet to straight plays, pantomimes and cabaret. This is not a complicated technical text book, but is intended to give an insight into some of the 300 productions in which he had been involved and some

of the directors, the designers and backstage staff he have worked with, viewed from a new angle.

Pages From Stages *Anthony Field 204pp* **£17.95** ISBN: 9781904031260
Anthony Field explores the changing style of theatres including interior design, exterior design, ticket and seat prices, and levels of service, while questioning whether the theatre still exists as a place of entertainment for regular theatre-goers.

People, Places, Performances *Remembered by Francis Reid 60pp* **£8.95**
ISBN: 9781904031765
In growing older, the Author has found that memories, rather than featuring the events, increasingly tend to focus on the people who caused them, the places where they happened and the performances that arose. So Francis Reid has used these categories in endeavouring to compile a brief history of the second half of the twentieth century.

Performing Arts Technical Training Handbook 2013/2014 *ed: John Offord 304pp*
£19.95 ISBN: 9781904031710
Published in association with the ABTT (Association of British Theatre Technicians), this important Handbook, now in its third edition, includes fully detailed and indexed entries describing courses on backstage crafts offered by over 100 universities and colleges across the UK. A completely new research project, with accompanying website, the title also includes articles with advice for those considering a career 'behind the scenes', together with contact information and descriptions of the major organisations involved with industry training – plus details of companies offering training within their own premises.

Practical Dimming *Nick Mobsby 364pp* **£22.95** ISBN: 97819040313444
This important and easy to read title covers the history of electrical and electronic dimming, how dimmers work, current dimmer types from around the world, planning of a dimming system, looking at new sine wave dimming technology and distributed dimming. Integration of dimming into different performance venues as well as the necessary supporting electrical systems are fully detailed. Significant levels of information are provided on the many different forms and costs of potential solutions as well as how to plan specific solutions. Architectural dimming for the likes of hotels, museums and shopping centres is included. Practical Dimming is a companion book to Practical DMX and is designed for all involved in the use, operation and design of dimming systems.

Practical DMX *Nick Mobsby 276pp* **£16.95** ISBN: 9781904031369
In this highly topical and important title the author details the principles of DMX, how to plan a network, how to choose equipment and cables, with data on products from around the world, and how to install DMX networks for shows and on a permanently installed basis. The easy style of the book and the helpful fault finding tips, together with a review of different DMX testing devices provide an ideal companion for all lighting technicians and system designers. An introduction to Ethernet and Canbus networks are provided as well as tips on analogue networks and protocol conversion. It also includes a chapter on Remote Device Management.

A Practical Guide to Health and Safety in the Entertainment Industry
Marco van Beek 120pp **£14.95** ISBN: 9781904031048
This book is designed to provide a practical approach to Health and Safety within the Live Entertainment and Event industry. It gives industry-pertinent examples, and seeks to break down the myths surrounding Health and Safety.

Production Management *Joe Aveline 134pp* **£17.95** ISBN: 9781904031109
Joe Aveline's book is an in-depth guide to the role of the Production Manager, and includes real-life practical examples and 'Aveline's Fables' – anecdotes of his experiences with real messages behind them.

Rigging for Entertainment: Regulations and Practice *Chris Higgs 156pp* **£19.95** ISBN: 9781904031215
Continuing where he left off with his highly successful An Introduction to Rigging in the Entertainment Industry, Chris Higgs' second title covers the regulations and use of equipment in greater detail.

Rock Solid Ethernet *Wayne Howell 304pp* **£23.95** ISBN: 9781904031697
Now in its third completely revised and reset edition, Rock Solid Ethernet is aimed specifically at specifiers, installers and users of entertainment industry systems, and will give the reader a thorough grounding in all aspects of computer networks, whatever industry they may work in. The inclusion of historical and technical 'sidebars' make for an enjoyable as well as an informative read.

Sixty Years of Light Work *Fred Bentham 450pp* **£26.95** ISBN: 9781904031079
This title is an autobiography of one of the great names behind the development of modern stage lighting equipment and techniques. It includes a complete facsimile of the famous Strand Electric Catalogue of May 1936 – a reference work in itself.

Sound for the Stage *Patrick Finelli 218pp* **£24.95** ISBN: 9781904031154
Patrick Finelli's thorough manual covering all aspects of live and recorded sound for performance is a complete training course for anyone interested in working in the field of stage sound, and is a must for any student of sound.

Stage Automation *Anton Woodward 128pp* **£12.95** ISBN: 9781904031567
The purpose of this book is to explain the stage automation techniques used in modern theatre to achieve some of the spectacular visual effects seen in recent years. The book is targeted at automation operators, production managers, theatre technicians, stage engineering machinery manufacturers and theatre engineering students. Topics are covered in sufficient detail to provide an insight into the thought processes that the stage automation engineer has to consider when designing a control system to control stage machinery in a modern theatre. The author has worked on many stage automation projects and developed the award-winning Impressario stage automation system.

Stage Lighting Design in Britain: The Emergence of the Lighting Designer, 1881-1950
Nigel Morgan 300pp **£17.95** ISBN: 9781904031345

This title sets out to ascertain the main course of events and the controlling factors that determined the emergence of the theatre lighting designer in Britain, starting with the introduction of incandescent electric light to the stage, and ending at the time of the first public lighting design credits around 1950. The book explores the practitioners, equipment, installations and techniques of lighting design.

Stage Lighting for Theatre Designers *Nigel Morgan 124pp* **£17.95**
ISBN: 9781904031192
This is an updated second edition of Nigel Morgan's popular book for students of theatre design – outlining all the techniques of stage lighting design.
Technical Marketing Techniques *David Brooks, Andy Collier, Steve Norman 160pp*
£24.95 ISBN: 9781904031031
Technical Marketing is a novel concept, defined and elaborated by the authors of this book, with business-to-business companies competing in fast developing technical product sectors.

Technical Standards for Places of Entertainment *ABTT 354pp A4* **£45.00**
ISBN: 9781904031703
Technical Standards for Places of Entertainment details the necessary physical standards required for entertainment venues. Known in the industry as the "Yellow Book" the latest completely revised edition was first published in June 2013.

Theatre Engineering and Stage Machinery *Toshiro Ogawa 332pp* **£30.00**
ISBN: 9781904031024
Theatre Engineering and Stage Machinery is a unique reference work covering every aspect of theatrical machinery and stage technology in global terms, and across the complete historical spectrum. Revised February 2007.

Theatre Lighting in the Age of Gas *Terence Rees 232pp* **£24.95**
ISBN: 9781904031178
Entertainment Technology Press has republished this valuable historic work previously produced by the Society for Theatre Research in 1978. Theatre Lighting in the Age of Gas investigates the technological and artistic achievements of theatre lighting engineers from the 1700s to the late Victorian period.

Theatre Space: A Rediscovery Reported *Francis Reid 238pp* **£19.95**
ISBN: 9781904031437
In the post-war world of the 1950s and 60s, the format of theatre space became a matter for a debate that aroused passions of an intensity unknown before or since. The proscenium arch was clearly identified as the enemy, accused of forming a barrier to disrupt the relations between the actor and audience. An uneasy fellow-traveller at the time, Francis Reid later recorded his impressions whilst enjoying performances or working in theatres old and new and this book is an important collection of his writings in various theatrical journals from 1969-2001 including his contribution to the Cambridge Guide to the Theatre in 1988. It reports some of the flavour of the period when theatre architecture was rediscovering its past in a search to establish its future.

The Theatres and Concert Halls of Fellner and Helmer *Michael Sell 246pp* **£23.95**
ISBN: 9781904031772
This is the first British study of the works of the prolific Fellner and Helmer Atelier which was active from 1871-1914 during which time they produced over 80 theatre designs and are second in quantity only to Frank Matcham, to whom reference is made.
This period is one of great change as a number of serious theatre fires which included Nice and Vienna had the effect of the introduction of safety legislation which affected theatre design. This study seeks to show how Fellner and Helmer and Frank Matcham dealt with this increasing safety legislation, in particular the way in which safety was built into their new three part theatres equipped with iron stages, safety curtains, electricity and appropriate access and egress and, in the Vienna practice, how this was achieved across 13 countries.

Theatres of Achievement *John Higgins 302pp* **£29.95** ISBN: 9781904031376
John Higgins affectionately describes the history of 40 distinguished UK theatres in a personal tribute, each uniquely illustrated by the author. Completing each profile is colour photography by Adrian Eggleston.

Theatric Tourist *Francis Reid 220pp* **£19.95** ISBN: 9781904031468
Theatric Tourist is the delightful story of Francis Reid's visits across more than 50 years to theatres, theatre museums, performances and even movie theme parks. In his inimitable style, the author involves the reader within a personal experience of venues from the Legacy of Rome to theatres of the Renaissance and Eighteenth Century Baroque and the Gustavian Theatres of Stockholm. His performance experiences include Wagner in Beyreuth, the Pleasures of Tivoli and Wayang in Singapore. This is a 'must have' title for those who are as "incurably stagestruck" as the author.

Through the Viewfinder *Jeremy Hoare 276pp* **£21.95** ISBN:: 9781904031574
Do you want to be a top television cameraman? Well this is going to help!
Through the Viewfinder is aimed at media students wanting to be top professional television cameramen – but it will also be of interest to anyone who wants to know what goes on behind the cameras that bring so much into our homes.
The author takes his own opinionated look at how to operate a television camera based on 23 years' experience looking through many viewfinders for a major ITV network company. Based on interviews with people he has worked with, all leaders in the profession, the book is based on their views and opinions and is a highly revealing portrait of what happens behind the scenes in television production from a cameraman's point of view.

Walt Disney Concert Hall – The Backstage Story *Patricia MacKay & Richard Pilbrow 250pp* **£28.95** ISBN: 9781904031239
Spanning the 16-year history of the design and construction of the Walt Disney Concert Hall, this book provides a fresh and detailed behind the scenes story of the design and technology from a variety of viewpoints. This is the first book to reveal the "process" of the design of a concert hall.

Yesterday's Lights – A Revolution Reported *Francis Reid 352pp* **£26.95**
ISBN: 9781904031321
Set to help new generations to be aware of where the art and science of theatre lighting is coming from – and stimulate a nostalgia trip for those who lived through the period, Francis Reid's latest book has over 350 pages dedicated to the task, covering the 'revolution' from the fifties through to the present day. Although this is a highly personal account of the development of lighting design and technology and he admits that there are 'gaps', you'd be hard put to find anything of significance missing.

Go to www.etbooks.co.uk for full details of above titles and secure online ordering facilities. Most books also available for Kindle.